PENNSYLVANIA TRAVELER'S GUIDE

The LINCOLN HIGHWAY

PENNSYLVANIA TRAVELER'S GUIDE

The LINCOLN HIGHWAY

Brian A. Butko

STACKPOLE BOOKS

Published by
STACKPOLE BOOKS
5067 Ritter Road
Mechanicsburg, PA 17055

Printed in the United States of America

10 9 8 7 6 5 4 3 2 1

First edition

Cover design by Caroline Miller

Maps by Kevin J. Patrick

Library of Congress Cataloging–in–Publication Data

A Pennsylvania traveler's guide to the Lincoln highway / Brian A. Butko.
— 1st ed.
    p.   cm.
Includes bibliographical references (p.) and index.
ISBN 0–8117–2495–6 (pbk.)
    1. Pennsylvania—Guidebooks.   2. Lincoln Highway—Guidebooks.
3. Automobile travel—Pennsylvania—Guidebooks. I. Title.
F147.3.B88 1996
917.4804'43—dc20   95–4776
                                            CIP

*To my mother, Dorothy; my father, Andrew; and my wife, Sarah.
You've been along for every mile of the trip.*

Contents

Foreword

By the time Abraham Lincoln's life ended abruptly on April 15, 1865, his name had already been used in countless promotions and money-making schemes. Even before his election as president, a Springfield, Illinois, doctor, Franklin Blades, who was changing his profession to lawyer, asked Lincoln's permission to use his name as a reference on his business card. Lincoln replied: "I do not know whether you are Dr. Blades or not. If you are Dr. Blades you may use my name; if you are not Dr. Blades, if Dr. Blades says you can use my name, you may do so."

Two weeks after Lincoln's death, his cousin John Hanks embarked on a tour exhibiting the original Lincoln cabin and hawking canes made from Lincoln-split rails. When the cabin was set up on Boston Common, so many canes were sold that more rails were sent for from Illinois.

The commercialization of Abraham Lincoln continued at a feverish pitch throughout the centennial of his birth in 1909, so it was only natural that, four years later, the proponents of the first free highway, from coast to coast, would want to name the road after the sixteenth president. What could be more appropriate than naming a new highway that would give Americans freedom to travel the length of the country after the Great Emancipator?

Unfortunately, given today's pace of life, the way people travel has changed immeasurably since the time the Lincoln Highway was a collection of muddy roads. People once traveled for the sake of traveling—the experience en route—not just to get to the destination. Part of the adventure was the unexpected: the tourist courts where you would spend the night, the diners where you would take your meals, the attractions and gift shops you would encounter, the spectacular views of new and different landscapes, and the services along the road in case you needed assistance.

Thanks to progress, however, travel by car has come to mean fast roads with limited access, hotel and restaurant chains with their predictability and homogeneity, and AAA coming to your rescue if needed. Of course, all this has had an impact on roads like the Lincoln Highway, which are generally bypassed by today's travelers.

It's nice to know that you can still follow the old routes (not without some difficulty, though that's nothing new) and experience what's left of bygone eras. Publications such as this not only help you keep on track, but also direct your eye to interesting landmarks and reveal what no longer exists. Pennsylvania, because of its large size and its mix of urban and rural areas, has much to offer along the Lincoln Highway. If you are willing to leave the interstate, pay no attention to the clock, and open your eyes, you will be rewarded with a journey that is rich in local lore, regional food, unusual souvenirs, great photographic opportunities, and entertaining stories to tell.

For more than twenty years, in the course of my own roadside research, I have strayed from the highways on a regular basis. To my delight, I have encountered people and places as interesting and unique as those chronicled on these pages. This book is comprehensive in its listing of landmarks, past and present, and will open many doors for those who want to know more. It scratches the surface and encourages the traveler to do more digging. So take the time and plan a journey along the Lincoln Highway. Just make sure you leave enough time unplanned to take advantage of whatever the Lincoln Highway has to offer you.

—Richard J. S. Gutman
author of American Diner: Then and Now

Preface

I grew up near Pittsburgh. Every summer my family would drive to Aunt Em's in Ohio. My mom, brother, sister, and I all piled in for adventure, and we got it! My dad never went the same way twice; he just had to see what else was out there, and as we flashed past the tiny towns with gas stations and cafés, railroad tracks and pop machines, white-framed billboards and twinkling dairy bars and motels with neon signs that buzzed in the night, my destiny was forever cast.

This book, however, is not about nostalgia. It's about a way of thinking, of living. Many of the places you'll read about are still there for you to visit. Others are gone, but this may be the only documentation of places that were once very important to someone. Being old doesn't make a place neat, but there are still lots of neat old places left to discover. I hope you'll visit some of them . . . they're waiting for you.

Acknowledgments

This book is the product of many minds and hearts. Some of those who helped are now my best friends; others I knew only for a moment. It was a pleasure, and I'm indebted to all of you.

I would especially like to thank Kevin Patrick, whose doctorate covers the Pennsylvania route in great depth, whose broad knowledge was a great help, and whose maps grace this book; postcard collector Cy Hosmer, who can always find the old cards and the old places; and artist Chuck Biddle, traveling companion and very special friend, who took nearly all of the photos of borrowed materials.

Others lent generously of their time, knowledge, or collections: Fulton County commissioner Bob Garlock, collector Bernie Heisey, photographer and author John Margolies, historian Curtis Miner, preservation officer of Gettysburg Walt Powell, editor Paul Roberts, WQED producer Rick Sebak, and all the businesspeople along the way.

The following individuals also helped by sharing information or materials: Carol Ahlgren, Lincoln, Nebraska; John Axtell, Pittsburgh; Richard Bowker, Pittsburgh; Jay Byerly, Coatesville; Lugene Bruno, Pittsburgh; David Cole, Santa Maria, California; Larry Cultrera, Medford, Massachusetts; Dan Cupper, Harrisburg; Cindy Dunlap, Bedford; Marilyn Erwin, Pittsburgh; Gregory Franzwa, Tucson, Arizona; Clara Gardner, Bedford; Michael Groff, State College; Melinda Higgins, York; Drake Hokanson, Sheboygan, Wisconsin; William Kelly, Sewickley; Jerry Keyser, Powell, Ohio; Margaret Kilpatrick, Fort Loudon; Paul Korol, Crafton; David Leach, Harrisburg; David Lockard, York Springs; Randy and Debrean Loy, Germantown, Maryland; Anne Madarasz, Pittsburgh; Walt McGervey, Moon Township; Mary Means, Alexandria, Virginia; John Overmiller, East Prospect; Esther Oyster, Ashland, Ohio;

xiii

Carol Ann Perovshek, Alexandria, Virginia; Pete Phillips, Ector, Texas; Lyn Protteau, Sacramento; Ann Safley, Johnstown; Keith A. Sculle, Springfield, Illinois; Susan Shearer, Lancaster; Dr. James Shultz, McConnellsburg; Helen Solarz, Gap; Gregory W. Smith, Austin; Polly Stetler, York; Marge Taylor, McConnellsburg; Joe Warren, East McKeesport; Elizabeth Wein, Mt. Gretna; Neil Wood, Levittown; David Young, Schellsburg; and Joanne Zeigler, Bedford.

Thanks to Cy Hosmer, Kevin Patrick, and Rebecca Shiffer for their diligent proofreading, along with my brother, Kevin, and his wife, Lori, who also contributed greatly to the eastern chapters.

I'd also like to thank my friends at the Lincoln Highway Association; the Society for Commercial Archeology; the Historical Society of Western Pennsylvania; *The Daily News* in McKeesport; Kinko's in Oakland; my sister, Phyllis; Rick, Erin, and Ricky; Billy and Jonathan; Sally Atwater at Stackpole Books; Dr. Edmund Steytler; and Andrew Nikolas.

Special thanks to those who loaned materials that appear in the book: John Baeder, Nashville; Mark Bialek, Baltimore; Ned Booher, Greensburg; Peg Brindza, McKeesport; Goldie Eyles, Zelienople; Eleanor Foreman, Bedford; David B. Grubbs, Pittsburgh; Lynn Haines, York; W. B. "Bernie" Heisey, Mount Joy; Cyrus Hosmer, III, Irwin; Jack Kessler, Adamsburg; Donald A. Klanchar, Irwin; Rick Kriss, North Huntingdon; Kevin Kutz, Bedford; Steve Lintner, Haddonfield, New Jersey; John H. McClintock, Manassas, Virginia; Kevin J. Patrick, Lucernemines; Russell S. Rein, Ypsilanti, Michigan; Beth L. Savage, Bethesda, Maryland; Rebecca A. Shiffer, Philadelphia; Charles L. Shirley, Belleville; Jim Smith, Cleveland; John L. Smith, Schellsburg; and Abraham Yalom, Adelphi, Maryland.

Finally, thanks to the many librarians, archivists, corporate employees, and institutions who helped with illustrations, including Elwood W. Christ, Adams County Historical Society, Gettysburg; Dave Albrecht, David J. Albrecht Photography, Pittsburgh; Tom Alden, Stephen Hornick, and Lil Gagliardo, Tom Alden Custom Prints, Pittsburgh; Suana Skogstrom, ARCO Public Affairs, Los Angeles; Audrey Iacone,

Carnegie Library of Pittsburgh; David LeBeau, Chevron Library Services, San Remon, California; Cleveland Public Library, Cleveland; Gerry Juran, *The Daily News,* McKeesport; Joseph F. Catania, Delaware River Joint Toll Bridge Commission, Morrisville; John Heiser, Gettysburg National Military Park, Gettysburg; Lila Fourhman-Shaull, Historical Society of York County; Corey Seeman, Historical Society of Western Pennsylvania, Pittsburgh; Linda A. Ries, Division of Archives and Manuscripts, Pennsylvania Historical and Museum Commission, Harrisburg; Sonia K. Harris, Sun Refining and Marketing Company, Philadelphia; Katherine Hamilton-Smith, Curt Teich Postcard Archives, Wauconda, Illinois; Margaret Jerrido, Urban Archives, Temple University Libraries, Philadelphia; James C. Anderson, Photo Archives, Ekstrom Library, University of Louisville, Louisville, Kentucky; Amy Fournier, Special Collections Library, University of Michigan, Ann Arbor, Michigan; John Thompson, Archives of Industrial Society, Hillman Library, University of Pittsburgh; and Edward H. Hahn, Westmoreland County Historical Society, Greensburg.

Note: All illustrations courtesy of the author unless noted.

About the Text

This book follows a typical trip from east to west. It can be read at ease or used as you drive, though it's probably best to plan ahead if you're driving the route. The road is always assumed to be aligned east-west, so directions are given by compass points: north, south, east, and west. Some directions are given as *left* or *right* when compass points aren't as helpful. If you're driving eastward, you can start at the end of each chapter and easily follow the route going backward a paragraph at a time. For this book, consider 1915 as the earliest date for the route because by that time it was generally established.

The text is like a snapshot of our era, and things will certainly change, so certain information in this book may become out-of-date. No matter how large a volume, there will always be more to learn and discover. There were many more stories and historical illustrations available than could fit.

Be careful when exploring the road in urban areas where violent crime has become commonplace. Also, please respect private property when photographing or investigating a site. Finally, remember to drive safely and courteously.

—*Brian Butko*

About the Maps

My inspiration for the maps in this book were the delightful relief maps drawn by Erwin Raisz in George Stewart's *U.S. 40: Cross Section of the United States of America*. While trying to master the Raisz technique, I developed my own style of landscape representation that has resulted in a somewhat whimsical portrayal of Pennsylvania's Lincoln Highway. Half cartographic technique and half sketch drawings, the chapter-opening picto-maps present a landscape image of the terrain at a scale of 1:250,000. The topography is portrayed as if seen from an airplane always flying out of the southeast, with major landforms such as mountains and rivers accurately depicted, but minor landforms such as hollows and creeks generalized using a degree of artistic license.

Of the many routes followed by the Lincoln Highway through the years, the one represented by the bold line is the c. 1940 routing. This is the oldest of the through routes most of you will be driving. Remnant sections of older Lincoln Highway and newer Route 30 bypasses are delineated using thinner lines. Many bypassed sections, however, could not be represented at this scale. They exist, nonetheless, as lonely stretches of narrow pavement, forlorn tracks through the weeds, and ghost bridges invisibly perched atop abandoned abutments, all awaiting exploration by those compelled to rediscover Pennsylvania's Lincoln Highway landscape.

—Kevin J. Patrick

Introduction
A Lincoln Highway Primer

Welcome to the Lincoln Highway, the first automobile road to cross the United States! When established in 1913, the Lincoln Highway was little more than a line on a map that connected existing roads into a cross-country path. It stretched from New York to San Francisco at a time when roads outside towns were muddy wagon paths and automobiles were toys for the rich. The Lincoln became a primary force in changing both.

The Lincoln Highway was founded before the government got into the modern road-building business. The idea originated with Carl Fisher, founder of the Prest-O-Lite Company, maker of the first dependable automobile headlights. He was better known for developing the Indianapolis Speedway and then paving it with bricks, and would later gain even more fame for developing swampland in Florida into Miami Beach.

In September 1912 Fisher presented his idea to the leaders of the automobile industry, who enthusiastically adopted his idea. Their acceptance of a transcontinental route sprang not only from the chance to sell more cars and parts, but also from a sense of adventure and an honest desire to get Americans out of the mud. Other than by wagon or railroad, travel between cities was nearly impossible.

The Lincoln Highway Association was established in 1913 "to procure the establishment of a continuous improved highway from the Atlantic to the Pacific, open to lawful traffic of all description without toll charges . . . in memory of Abraham Lincoln." The plan simply linked existing roads into a 3,389-mile highway across the country, and the organizers hoped local governments would improve their own sections. Although the immediate goal was to build a cross-country highway, the

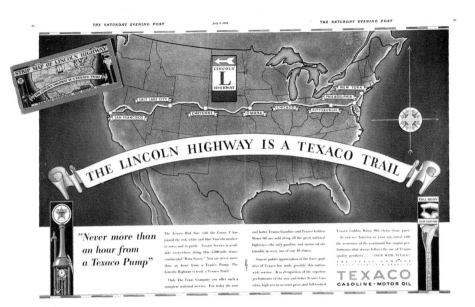

This Texaco advertisement from the July 6, 1929, issue of the Saturday Evening
Post *and small matching strip map show the staying power of the Lincoln Highway name after roads were numbered. A story about the advertising campaign's
companion map ran in the July–August 1929 issue of the* Texaco Star, *with a
similar ad on the back cover.*

Lincoln Highway Association also hoped to make the Lincoln an "object
lesson road" for the country. "Its great underlying principle," according
to the association's 1920 publication *A Picture of Progress,* "was to
stimulate the progress of highway improvement in every section of the
country and gradually bring about the establishment of an adequate
national system of connecting roads."

A system of volunteer "consuls" was devised to promote the Lincoln Highway and advance improvements. Each state that the road tra-
versed had a state consul, often the governor or some other leader in state
affairs and active in road-improvement efforts. Large states like Pennsylvania also had district consuls and, under them, county consuls. Finally,
local consuls were the association's backbone, often businessmen along
the route who had a stake in the success and improvement of the Lincoln
Highway. In Pennsylvania, men such as "Doc" Seylar on Tuscarora

The Lincoln Highway was a popular inspiration for songwriters. The "Lincoln Highway March" was even produced as a player piano roll.

Summit or Lee Hoffman in Bedford served because an improved road was good for their hotel and restaurant businesses.

People from across the country paid $5 to join the association. Many ordered souvenirs, too—"official" radiator emblems, pennants, guidebooks, and maps. Other companies also got in on the act, offering Lincoln Highway cigars, sheet music, automobile tires, and gasoline pumps. In fact, anyone with a product to sell seemed to borrow the Lincoln Highway name.

The route of the Lincoln was marked with red, white, and blue emblems, each with a large *L*. At first the colors were simply painted on telephone poles, but porcelain-enameled steel signs were soon

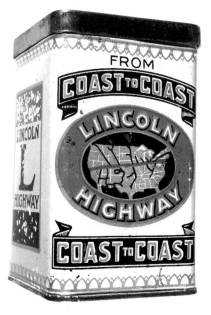

Lincoln Highway cigars came in both boxes and tins. The 25 cigars in this tin were made in Indiana, the tin by the National Can Company.

Many gasoline companies put the Lincoln Highway name on their pumps, such as this Wayne model, as illustrated in the Complete Official Road Guide of the Lincoln Highway, *third edition.*

erected. Other road groups sprang up to promote their own routes and bring business their way, adopting their own color schemes. Some of the competing routes in Pennsylvania were the Yellowstone Trail, the William Penn, the Lakes-to-Sea, the Horseshoe Trail, and the Pikes Peak Ocean-to-Ocean Highway. State maps from the early 1920s show almost 50 named highways.

Motorists became confounded by the clusters of colors or signs on poles, especially where routes converged. Sometimes more than one highway group would use the same route, which meant that a road could have as many as a dozen different names and color designations. In other cases, such as the north-south Dixie Highway, more than one road was used for the route!

In 1925 a federal numbering system was established to simplify matters. Named highways like the Lincoln were broken up, probably so that the new numbering system would take precedence. The Lincoln Highway from New York to Philadelphia was designated U.S. Route 1; from Philadelphia westward across Pennsylvania (and much of the country), U.S. Route 30. Farther west, past Wyoming, the Lincoln had numerous designations, including U.S. Routes 40 and 50. (Pennsylvania was slow to switch and referred to the entire Lincoln Highway as State Route 1 until 1930.)

Though the numbering system was now established, the Lincoln Highway was marked one last time, ostensibly to honor its namesake, Abraham Lincoln. On September 1, 1928, cement posts with bronze medallions bearing Lincoln's profile and the highway's red, white, and blue emblem were planted along the road from coast to coast, approximately one per mile. In urban areas, pole-mounted signs were still used. Pennsylvania had about 400 markers of both types, but only about 20 cement posts remain along the route today.

Although officially renumbered, the Lincoln name has endured. It never was strong in Philadelphia or Pittsburgh—those cities already had enough named roads. In smaller towns, though, you may still find Lincoln Way or Old Lincoln Highway, and you'll often see a Lincoln Motel or Lincoln Garage.

The Lincoln Highway in Pennsylvania roughly follows two very old paths: Lancaster Pike in the east and Forbes Road in the west. The Lincoln often strays far from these roads, but it follows their general corridors across the state, much like the Pennsylvania Turnpike did in the 1940s.

Forbes Road is the older of the two, carved across the Alleghenies in 1758 when the English and American colonists set out to capture Fort

This souvenir folder, from about 1925, highlights scenery, attractions, and businesses such as Jenner Pines Camp.

Duquesne (present-day Pittsburgh) from the French. When Gen. John Forbes arrived in America, he asked that certain roads be improved; a primitive path from Philadelphia west through Lancaster and York to Carlisle was deemed especially important. From Carlisle, Forbes carved his road generally following the Raystown Indian path southwest to Chambersburg and then west through Bedford to Pittsburgh. From near Chambersburg to Bedford, Forbes was able to use the Burd Road, cut in 1755 in conjunction with Braddock's expedition to Pittsburgh. From Bedford (actually the intersection of today's Routes 30 and 31 at Bonnet's Tavern), Forbes cleared an entirely new road.

The state government became active in road building in the late eighteenth century in an effort to keep commerce around York and Lancaster from going south out of state and to ease transport to Pittsburgh for Philadelphia merchants. As Plummer explained in *The Road Policy of Pennsylvania,* "The trip [from Pittsburgh] to Philadelphia was so long and arduous, and, therefore, expensive that it did not pay to send any but small and valuable articles. . . . The great difficulty of transportation was one of the causes of the so-called Whiskey Rebellion."

In 1785 Pennsylvania's first road-improvement legislation ordered a highway built from Cumberland County (Carlisle) to Pittsburgh, basically improving Forbes Road. About the same time, farmers from the rich lands around Lancaster got an improved road to take their goods to Philadelphia. The Philadelphia-Lancaster Turnpike, or Lancaster Pike, was approved and begun in 1792. Lancaster Pike became the first long-distance road in the country built of macadam, a durable and low-cost roadbed of gradually sized stones fitted into one another. (It was a recent invention by a Scotsman, John McAdam.) The design also called for a raised center to enhance drainage. The 62-mile Lancaster Pike cost $450,000 and took two years to complete and another two of final adjustments. Construction was financed by stock issued to shareholders, and dividends were paid by tolls collected from users. The revolutionary road surface, however, more than made up for the expense, and the Lancaster Pike became a huge success.

All sorts of traffic took to the route, but none are as well remembered or as mythologized as Conestoga wagons. The wagons, made in Lancaster County's Conestoga Valley, were fitted with outward-sloping sides so that freight hauled over the bumpy mountains would settle toward the center. They were colorful in a typically Pennsylvania Dutch way—the bodies a brilliant light blue, the wheels and running gear vermilion, and the tops white. They also sported bells to alert taverns and towns that a wagon was arriving, but if you got stuck and an equal-sized wagon pulled you free, you had to relinquish your bells—so to arrive safely was to "be there with bells on." The drivers' favorite cigars were "stogies," their name derived from Conestoga.

Following the success of the Lancaster Pike, the Harrisburg and Pittsburgh Turnpike Road Company was incorporated in 1806 as an even longer toll road, but its length proved unmanageable and no work was done. In 1814 an amendment to the earlier act was passed approving a line of five turnpikes from Harrisburg to Pittsburgh, roughly following Forbes Road but incorporating lesser grades and a straighter course (going through Stoystown, for example, instead of Somerset). These turnpikes proved more feasible, and four of them were later adopted as part of the route of the Lincoln Highway: Chambersburg to Bedford, Bedford to Stoystown, Stoystown to Greensburg, and Greensburg to Pittsburgh.

A string of 10 turnpikes between Philadelphia and Pittsburgh (through Harrisburg) was complete by 1820 and collectively known as the Pennsylvania Road (or sometimes the State Road, Great Road, or Philadelphia-Pittsburgh Turnpike). They prospered at first, but profits were always small, and the newly developing railroads and canals began taking away business in the mid-nineteenth century. Turnpike traffic waned, and the roads fell into disrepair.

By the twentieth century a new contraption was showing up on the roads, but in Pennsylvania, the Farmers' Anti-Automobile Association would have none of it. They published these rules for drivers, extracted here from *The National Road:*

1. Automobiles traveling on country roads at night must send up a rocket every mile, then wait ten minutes for the road to clear. The driver may then proceed, with caution, blowing his horn and shooting off Roman candles, as before.

2. If the driver of an automobile sees a team of horses approaching he is to stop, pulling over to one side of the road, and cover his machine with a blanket or dust cover which is painted or colored to blend into the scenery, and thus render the machine less noticeable.

Various guides were available to help travelers on the Lincoln Highway in Pennsylvania; the Gulf map is from 1920, the Lincoln Highway Association book from 1915, and the Mohawk-Hobbs guide from 1927.

3. In case a horse is unwilling to pass an automobile on the road, the driver of the car must take the machine apart as rapidly as possible, and conceal the parts in the bushes.

The arrival of the automobile and cries for better roads from bicyclists helped revive the old turnpikes. When Pennsylvania established its State Highway Department in 1903, it was reported that 1,100 miles of toll roads were in use. The 1903 legislative act and a follow-up in 1905 provided for state assistance in reconstructing township roads, but it wasn't until the Sproul Act of 1911 that a system of roads to be constructed and maintained at the sole expense of the state was established. Pennsylvania also held its first statewide Good Roads Day on May 26, 1915, in which tens of thousands pitched in to improve hundreds of miles of dirt paths. In 1916 the federal government instituted grants to the states for highway construction, and in 1919 Pennsylvania began the gradual reconstruction of the Lincoln in all concrete pavement.

The Lincoln Highway Association chose a path across southern Pennsylvania as part of its cross-country route but used a shortened version of the Pennsylvania Road; instead of angling north from Lancaster through Harrisburg and Carlisle, the Lincoln followed established (but less-traveled) turnpikes from Lancaster through York and Gettysburg to Chambersburg. The Lincoln Highway Association worked to abolish all tolls along its route, and local municipalities bought the roads from toll companies one by one. The last toll section (not counting bridges) on the whole cross-country route was near Lancaster. Tolls were abolished September 5, 1918, with joyous ceremonies.

Hundreds of different tourist court directories helped midcentury travelers decide where to stay.

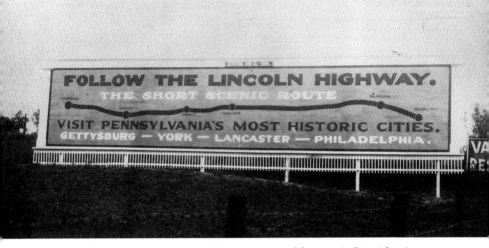

A billboard near York advertised the eastern part of the route in Pennsylvania.
Vandera's Restaurant was in Chambersburg. COURTESY GETTYSBURG NATIONAL
MILITARY PARK

Since the Lincoln Highway was the main, and at first the only, way
to span the continent by auto, it saw a tremendous amount of activity.
Pennsylvania probably saw more traffic than any other state along the
Lincoln, as wealthy and curious easterners headed west for adventure.
Pennsylvania was still mostly rural, so the 360 miles of highway left a
great physical and commercial imprint. Businesses sprang up to serve
the traveler at each bend and on every mountaintop.

The Alleghenies were the mountains to cross, and they were a for-
midable barrier. Early automobiles usually overheated on the way up, so
enterprising businessmen put rest stops at each summit to offer free
water. They hoped travelers would stay for a soda or sandwich, and to
make sure, most every mountaintop stop sprouted a lookout tower with
telescopes.

Motorists were often heading to particular tourist destinations in the
state—Philadelphia, Gettysburg, Lancaster, Pittsburgh. Along the way,
towns like York, Chambersburg, Bedford, and Ligonier also offered a
range of historic and natural attractions. One of the surprises awaiting
travelers were the funny-shaped buildings—competition for business
produced giant coffeepots and shoes and ships, restaurants in airplanes

and blimps, and an assortment of gas stations and tourist cabins with attention-grabbing gimmicks or catchy names.

The road's path was constantly being straightened, and after the mid-1920s, road cuts shortened much of the circuitous route in Pennsylvania. Twenty years after its establishment, almost 300 miles had been cut from the Lincoln's cross-country length.

Today we're lucky to have a dynamic mixture of old and new. Modern Route 30 has bypassed many sections of the original Lincoln Highway, where a slower pace and many of the old roadside businesses can still be found. And modern road improvements, like the bypasses or the ever-near Pennsylvania Turnpike, make getting to a particular section of the old Lincoln fairly easy for those wanting just a taste of the old.

I hope you'll give the Lincoln Highway a try. Visit the nonchain businesses. Buy a local newspaper. Skip the bypasses for the routes through towns. You'll find it can be just as much fun as a trip to the "regular" tourist sites, and maybe more. You'll certainly get a better feel for the region than you would out on the interstate. So let's get on the road and see what's out there!

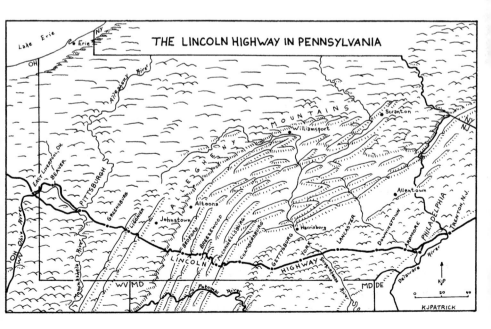

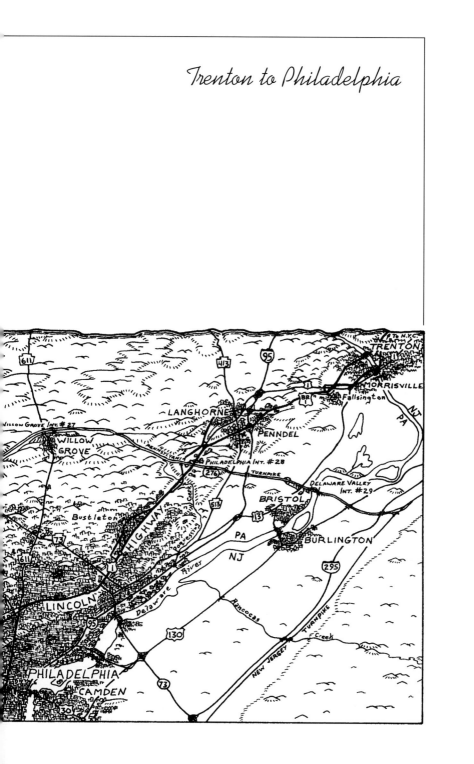

In 1681 William Penn was granted land in America as payment for a debt owed his father by the English crown. Penn, who had recently converted to the "radical" Society of Friends (Quakers), wanted a place where men of all faiths could live in harmony; the king wanted to rid England of religious dissenters. That land grant became "Penn's woods," the commonwealth of Pennsylvania. William Penn eventually settled near what is now Morrisville, Pennsylvania; his reconstructed estate, Pennsbury Manor, is 5 miles south of town.

Just before Penn's arrival, the King's Highway was cleared from present-day New York to New Castle, Delaware, passing through Morrisville and Philadelphia. It was the first major road in Pennsylvania, and a well-traveled corridor. The Lincoln Highway followed its general course 230 years later, and by that time it was lined with businesses.

The route of the Lincoln Highway itself changed somewhat over the years; today we can take any of three routes over the Delaware River from Trenton and say it's the Lincoln. This situation of parallel routes arises constantly when following the Lincoln Highway because of bypasses and route changes through the years. It's especially vexing from Trenton to Philadelphia, where heavy traffic forced the route to be realigned and reconfigured many times.

The extension of Roosevelt Boulevard northeast from Philadelphia is the main factor in the realignments here. Improvement of Roosevelt (also called Northeast Boulevard or just the Boulevard) began at Philadelphia's Broad Street in 1913. The first leg stopped at Rhawn Street just short of Pennypack Circle. It was extended a couple miles to Welsh Street in 1920, and in 1923 the road pushed over the city line, where it became "Lincoln Highway" and was rerouted through Penndel to Langhorne Gardens.

In this chapter, as in some others, the Lincoln is divided into sections where there's more than one important route to be followed. That way, you can either explore all the parallel routes in a section or choose an era (say 1915, or the present) and stick with that across sections. This chapter is divided into seven sections, with breaks at Fallsington, Janney Station, Trevose, Haldeman Avenue, Rhawn Street, Broad Street, and ending at Philadelphia's City Hall.

SECTION I. TRENTON TO FALLSINGTON

On Christmas night of 1776, George Washington and the Continental Army crossed the Delaware River in a snowstorm, surprised the

Calhoun Street Bridge, Lincoln Highway, Trenton, N. J.

The Calhoun Street Bridge, built in 1884, still carries travelers across the Delaware River into Pennsylvania. COURTESY JOHN H. McCLINTOCK

sleeping British (actually, their Hessian mercenaries), and captured Trenton. The crossing is recalled in the well-known painting of Washington standing in a boat as he and his men cross the icy water. The location is now marked by a town called Washington Crossing, just north of Morrisville, Pennsylvania.

At Trenton, three bridges carry traffic across the Delaware River into Morrisville: the Calhoun Street Bridge, the Lower Trenton "Free" Bridge, and the Route 1 bridge. We'll explore the first two routes, but not modern Route 1, an expressway that opened about 1950.

1915–1920 Route. Morrisville sits directly across the Delaware River from Trenton. Originally called Falls of the Delaware, the town was renamed Morrisville for merchant Robert Morris, the "financier of the American Revolution," who had a mansion here. The first bridge used by the Lincoln Highway was the Calhoun Street Bridge, a narrow bridge with an open grate deck. It's named for the street in New Jersey that it leads up to, and it pours traffic onto Trenton Avenue in Morrisville.

Those tracing the old Lincoln Highway begin their trip through Pennsylvania with a pleasant surprise: a 75-year-old iron marker sits at the end of the Calhoun Street Bridge. Emblazoned with the Lincoln Highway logo, it shows the directions to New Jersey and Pennsylvania and the route's ends, New York and San Francisco. It also reads "Leb-Iron Permanent Guide Board, The Lincoln Highway Official Guide Post Adopted A.D. 1917, Cast by the Lebanon Machine Co., Lebanon N.H., Patent Applied For." If you want to stop and see the marker, make two lefts and park immediately south of the bridge. Before taking pictures, though, check with the guard in the adjacent booth; you may have to get

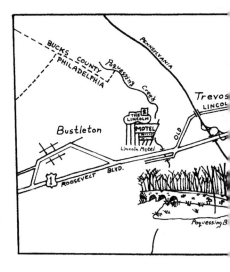

permission from the bridge's owner, the Delaware River Joint Toll Bridge Commission, located a few blocks south in Morrisville, near the end of its other bridge.

Leaving the Calhoun Street Bridge, we begin climbing up Trenton Avenue. To the south is Pizza Rama, with a big neon sign on its roof; to the north is American Fabricare, housed in an old drive-in restaurant. A bit farther, we pass a little mall to the south with a Dunham's store that looks like an old theater, but folks there say it was always a retail store. Barely .5 mile from the bridge, we're into a suburban residential area, and we pass the Lincoln

At the end of the Calhoun Street Bridge stands this directional sign for the Lincoln. It's pictured in the Lincoln Highway's 1921 road guide as an example of markers placed at each state line. (PHOTO 1994)

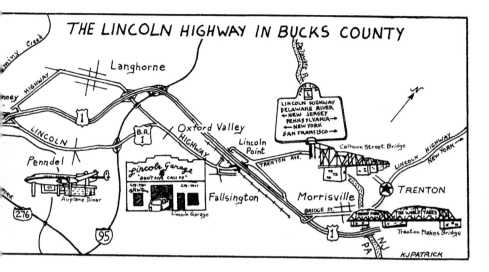

Arms Apartments to the south. About 1 mile from the bridge, the Morrisville Drive-In Theater once sat to the north, but it's now gone.

After traveling 1.5 miles from the Calhoun Street Bridge, we reach the intersection of Pine Grove Road and Routes 13 and 113. We continue southwest on West Trenton Avenue, passing Lincoln Point business park, crossing a small bridge from the 1930s, and begin climbing a small hill. Just 2.5 miles from the Calhoun Street Bridge, we meet the 1920–c. 1950 Lincoln Highway route out of Morrisville at Lincoln Point, once home to Lincoln Point Filling Station. We'll further explore Lincoln Point in the next segment.

The route we're following originally continued straight (in a southwest direction) and crossed a bridge over the railroad tracks to where Trenton and Yardley Avenues meet in Fallsington. Going straight today still takes us over the tracks, but on a four-lane bridge built in the 1950s (and bypassing Trenton and Yardley Avenues). It meets the 1920–c. 1950 route at the traffic light south of the Fallsington underpass. In Section II, we'll look for the original bridge across the tracks.

1920–c. 1950 Route. The route across the Calhoun Street Bridge was used only from 1915 to 1920. Since it was a toll bridge, and the Lincoln Highway Association wanted a tollfree route, a bridge to the south

Lincoln Point Filling Station, looking northeast, July 1934. The Lincoln Point Restaurant, lined with windows behind it, is advertised in a later postcard as the Interstate Glass House Restaurant. The intersection of Trenton Avenue (to the left) and Bridge Street (to the right) is now the site of Clover Shopping Center and has changed so drastically that the location is unrecognizable. COURTESY PA STATE ARCHIVES, RG-12 DEPT. OF HIGHWAYS

was offered as an alternative, becoming the "official" route in 1920. A new bridge replaced it in 1929 and still stands today, famous for a currently nonfunctioning neon sign along its length: "Trenton Makes The World Takes."

At the end of this Lower Trenton "Free" Bridge is a plaque to the south giving a short history of the bridges. To the north are a few small businesses, some with old "ghost" signs such as one for Wrigley's gum.

We start along Bridge Street, also Route 32 south, and as we head west through the first intersection, there's H-L's Bait and Tackle Shop to the north in a c. 1940 metal diner that appears to be factory-built by the Silk City Company. Dan, who bought it in 1979 when it was a lawn mower shop, says it was called the Transit Diner when brought here in 1946. He adds that the metal structure makes repairs difficult, and says, "I'd tear it down if I had the money." Next to it is Howell's Hardware in an old car dealership, now an equally old store. On the southeast corner at Pennsylvania Avenue is Pryor's Drugs, with a nice neon sign. About 1 mile from the bridge, we pass numerous old garages on both sides. Pennsylvania's 1940 WPA guide says Morrisville "has much charm, but along the main route this aspect is hidden by gasoline stations, garages, repair shops, and lunch wagons, which provide 24-hour service for the ceaseless flow of motor traffic between Philadelphia and New York." Most traffic now stays on the Route 1 bypass.

We cross into Falls Township but see no businesses except the Morrisville Golf Farm with miniature golf to the north. Route 1 is to our south. Bridge Street would have continued slightly south, "crossing" Route 1, but the new road has erased it. Instead, we merge with current Route 1. We're on an expressway but stay to the right and angle off toward Fairless Hills following Business Route 1.

Looking southwest to the Yankee Clipper Diner, across from Lincoln Point Filling Station, July 1934. This may later have been the Triangle Diner, advertised in Tail-Gate *truckers magazine in 1950 as lying 1 mile outside of Morrisville on Route 1 and "Owned by an x Truckie who knows the wants of Truckies. All our cooking done at the place." The road heading to the horizon is Bridge Street on its way to the Fallsington underpass.* COURTESY PA STATE ARCHIVES, RG-12 DEPT. OF HIGHWAYS

We continue straight, now on Woolston Drive (or Lincoln Highway), and Route 1 is again parallel to our south; the old path of Bridge Street is south of Route 1. We continue to follow signs for Fairless Hills, and near the Country House Motel to the north, there's a turnaround loop for those going east—you can no longer go east into Morrisville on this old alignment.

At 2.5 miles from the Lower Trenton "Free" Bridge, we meet West Trenton Avenue (the road we took on the 1915–1920 route). The 1928 Mohawk-Hobbs guide lists Lincoln Point at 2.4 miles from the "Free" Bridge, so this area is surely its location. Our alignment continues west on Woolston Drive (or Lincoln Highway), but we pause to examine this area.

Lincoln Point was originally a three-way intersection where Trenton Avenue and Bridge Street (now Woolston Drive) met. From there, Trenton Avenue continued toward the railroad tracks and turned left over a bridge, probably following Makefield Road (or Yardley Avenue) across the tracks. Eventually, Bridge Street was extended west from Lincoln Point to the Fallsington underpass, avoiding the bridge. We continue that way now.

We head west on Woolston Drive (or Bridge Street or Lincoln Highway), though the original alignment was probably where Route 1 is today. We follow the signs for Route 1 north and Tiburn Road and turn left .5 mile from Lincoln Point. We stay in the left lane; the right lane turns to Route 1 north, the expressway. At the traffic light at Stony Hill Road, we look straight ahead to the Fallsington underpass. This route is followed in the 1925 AAA Eastern Tours, which says that .5 mile from the three-corner (Lincoln Point) intersection, travelers should go "L. thru R.R. underpass and R. beyond."

The accompanying illustration of the Fallsington underpass in 1934 shows Stony Hill Road and two roads and small bridges closer to the tunnel than the road we just traveled. The road in the foreground was the Lincoln Highway, today lost in a field of weeds (an old abutment, perhaps from the right-hand edge of that road, can be found along the stream). To the left, another road across the stream appears blocked in the photo. Perhaps it was an even earlier road from Lincoln Point to the underpass.

We continue straight from the traffic light and go under the railroad. At the next traffic light, we have Business Route 1 north to our left, Busi-

North of the Fallsington underpass, looking west, July 1934. The road next to the Essolene sign is Stony Hill Road, and it looks like it once continued to the extreme left, across a bridge that's been blocked. The Lincoln Highway alignment in the foreground is also gone, moved north and parallel to Route 1.
COURTESY PA STATE ARCHIVES, RG-12 DEPT. OF HIGHWAYS

ness Route 1 south to our right, and an old Lincoln Highway alignment (Main Street) through trees ahead and to the left.

SECTION II. FALLSINGTON TO JANNEY STATION

We'll begin this section by looking for the 1915–1920 alignment that passed over the railroad tracks to Fallsington. At the previous underpass traffic light, we proceed south and make the first left onto Trenton Road. At the first intersection, we meet the original route of the Lincoln—to the left, the short piece of Main Street heads back to (but no longer meets) Business Route 1 at the Fallsington underpass. Main Street would have been used until sometime after the Fallsington underpass was built for Stony Hill Road in 1917.

Straight ahead is Trenton Road, also the original Lincoln; it continues until a sharp right bend onto Yardley Avenue. At that bend, the original Lincoln instead turned left over the railroad tracks. If you park and look

The Lincoln Garage west of Fallsington. (PHOTO 1994)

around, you'll see that the tracks are below grade level. Although no longer there, the bridge is mentioned in the 1914 *Blue Book.*

A clue to the left turn onto the bridge is an old iron "State Highway" sign warning of a "sharp curve ahead" on Trenton Road. Of course, there's still the sharp right turn onto Yardley Avenue, but the sign is old enough to have indicated the sharp left onto the bridge. The street names are another clue: Trenton Street is obviously an extension of Trenton Avenue from north of the tracks; Yardley Avenue would have crossed and met Makefield Road (its alignment north of here has since been moved), which heads north and merges into Yardley-Morrisville Road outside Yardley.

Back at the traffic light south of the Fallsington underpass, we head west on Business Route 1 south. (Route 1, an expressway, parallels us to the north.) The road narrows from three lanes to two, and after .2 mile is the Lincoln Garage to the south. Hidden by trees, it's easy to miss, but if you look you're sure to see the huge silhouette of Lincoln's head on the facade and the motto, "Don't Cuss—Call Us."

We pass the Lincoln Crossing Office Campus to the south, and just after that, the former U.S. 1 North Drive-In Theater. It's across from an old stone house and behind an apartment complex, but little remains of it. We also pass the Ace and the Falls Motels, and an old trailer park to the south. About 2.5 miles from the Fallsington underpass is Lincoln Motors to the north, across from Oxford Point Shopping Center.

Just south of here is Levittown, famed for being the country's second large-scale housing development. The houses were mass-produced, each going up in less than one day, and the whole area was preplanned to include schools, playgrounds, and shopping centers. It was built between 1951 and 1955 by Levitt & Sons, Inc., who modeled it after their earlier success, Levittown, New York. The name, of course, became symbolic of postwar suburbia.

We cross Oxford Valley Road and pass Lincoln Plaza to the north along with Sesame Place, a children's amusement park with a Sesame Street theme. This area is known as Oxford Valley, where the Checker Inn Camp once had gasoline, a general store, free camping, and rooms in a house. To the south, the old Roosevelt Drive-In Theater showed X-rated movies in recent years, but little remains except a sprawling asphalt parking lot. The Roosevelt was owned at one time by the Budco chain, which had a number of drive-ins along the Lincoln Highway in eastern Pennsylvania, including the Exton, the Columbia, the Stoneybrook, and the Lincoln. Continuing straight, the Lincoln brings us into Langhorne Gardens.

The road divides, and two different Lincoln Highway routes head toward Philadelphia: the original route through Langhorne and a later one through Penndel. Modern Route 1 is also still north of us. Following are the two routes from this point to where they meet at Janney Station, named for a long-gone train depot.

1915–1923 Route. We get in the right lane and follow State Route 213 south to Langhorne. We see car dealers to the south, including Reedman's, perhaps the world's largest car dealership. Reedman's covers more than 150 acres and has 20 showrooms. There's even an overpass leading to the dealership's test track to the north. We continue downhill, crossing over I-95, then under Route 1, 1.5 miles from where the route split.

Now we drive along shade-lined Maple Avenue into Langhorne. The town is named for Jeremiah Langhorne, chief justice of the province from 1739 to 1743. We cross Route 413 and pass through the center of

*10/16/50. Dear Kip, Your dad had dinner here tonite. You would have enjoyed
this diner for there are lots of stools and booths—lots of lights and many things
to explore. Take good care of mother and I'll be home soon—Dad." The Golden
Arrow was built by Comac, a relatively obscure maker of diners in Irvington,
New Jersey.*

Langhorne, a small town with many historic buildings, including the Town Hall, built in 1910. We see the Langhorne Hotel, Tavern, and Restaurant and to the south a large Italianate house that looks to be apartments now. We also pass numerous old stone buildings, such as a Friends meetinghouse.

Just shy of 3 miles from our road split, we leave Maple Avenue, turning south at a traffic light onto a road marked Old Lincoln Highway. It sometimes also appears on maps as Old Oakford Road, and it runs through rural suburbia. The road is very straight as it passes Our Lady of Grace Cemetery and Neshaminy School. At 1.5 miles from where we turned onto Old Lincoln Highway, we reach a fork and bear right to follow the old road. (Bearing left would take us to Route 1.)

The road narrows, tops a hill, then starts down and dead-ends. Trees and a load of dirt block the road, though we can see its continuation in the distance. Although the road may have gone straight a century ago, the

Poplar's Inn in Langhorne Gardens, "Home of Good Eats." Cabins can be seen to the left and right. A pavilion sits behind the restaurant and store in the middle. The 1927 Mohawk-Hobbs guide indicates that camping cost 50 cents and the inn's "seven good cottages" ran $2. COURTESY BERNIE HEISEY

1915 Lincoln bent left and crossed the railroad tracks. The old stone bridge abutments are visible where the Lincoln crossed at Janney Station; they're overgrown, but we can see some asphalt brought up by the roots of a tree. We can also see the four-lane Route 1 bridge to the south.

To continue west, we must backtrack to the fork for Route 1 and turn right. We merge onto Route 1, an expressway here. As we cross a bridge over the railroad tracks, the old abutments are to the north, near a large billboard and electrical wires. A half mile later, we take the Neshaminy exit, which bears off to the right. We're now near Janney Station, and it's here that our next route briefly joins us.

1923–c. 1970 Route. At Oxford Valley, we pass the Blue Fountain Diner Restaurant, an early 1960s Fodero. Perhaps it's the former location of the Tail-Gate Diner, which advertised in *Tail-Gate* magazine as being at Oxford Valley, "On the spot where Mom & Pops Use to be." Immediately after the traffic light at Woodbourne Road, we pass an empty used-car lot to the north. The sales office appears to be the old Poplar's Inn store and restaurant; its dozen or so cabins are long gone. The *Shell Tourist Accommodation Directory and Trailer Space* for 1940 showed Poplar's still there (but by then only three cottages) and "This 'L' Do Tourist Cabins" .5 mile north of South Langhorne.

We now pass Reedman's to our north; the old Langhorne Raceway used to be to the south. We're at the Glenlake area listed in old tourbooks. There's a Friendly Ice Cream Shop to the north, more car dealers, and various malls to the south. A mile from the split, we go over I-95. The road becomes a four-lane, with few businesses.

About 2 miles from where the roads split, the road bends to the left, and on the right there's a big sign for Skyline Car Wash and Diner. The diner is a 1950 Paramount brand, now covered in red brick. Across the street, to the south, is the Airplane Family Restaurant & Diner, with a huge silver 1954 Lockheed Super G Constellation propeller airplane, moved here in 1967 after serving around the globe. The plane is elevated, overlooking the road. The airplane was being rented for parties, but it's closed for now because of water leaks, although the restaurant beneath is still open.

About 1 mile ahead is Toppin's Ice Cream to the south. It has an old diner sign out front, though it's really just a remodeled ice cream stand. We continue downhill into a tree-filled valley, over a tiny 1936 bridge,

The Airplane Diner in Penndel features a 1954 Lockheed Constellation above the restaurant. (PHOTO 1991)

and back uphill. A gathering of houses to the south may be an old remnant of the Lincoln Highway. The railroad tracks are now to our north, and after another mile, our four lanes split. A sign alerts us: "Old Lincoln Highway next right."

This 1923 routing joins with the expressway ahead; that's why the opposite lanes split off. Our westbound lanes go under Route 1, and we can see the billboard to the right where the early bridge abutments were found. At this point, the 1915–1923 and 1923–c. 1970 routes converge, and there's a little pulloff where we can catch our breath. Behind us we can see Route 1 and the Janney Station-area bridge abutments. Ahead, the road splits: to the left is Route 1; to the right, the old Lincoln Highway. There are also two other roads to the right parallel to the Lincoln, one a grass-covered ramp, the other an access road to a reservoir. It's possible that both served as the road at one time. We're at Janney Station now, but before continuing west, let's look at that part of Route 1 that is behind us.

1970–Present Route. While on the 1915–1923 route, we passed under Route 1 just after Reedman's. From there south to Oakford was a novel experiment in highway building. This stretch was built in 1938 to avoid the congestion of the Penndel route, which itself had been built just

*An aerial view of the Janney Station interchange looking northeast, May 1939.
The original route is to the upper left, the 1923 bypass is to the upper right, and
the 1938 four-lane superhighway is in the middle. Oddly, the approach to the
bridge across the tracks on the original route has been retouched on this photo,
above and right of "Reading R.R."* COURTESY PA STATE ARCHIVES, RG-12 DEPT.
OF HIGHWAYS

15 years earlier to relieve the Langhorne route. Drivers heading northeast after 1938, though, had to exit onto Bellevue Avenue in Langhorne Gardens to continue toward Trenton; the superhighway ended, and that's why the road through Penndel continued to be marked as Route 1 until recent decades. The route from Bellevue Avenue northeast to I-95 was opened about 1972 and from there to Fallsington wasn't complete until the 1980s. Today's Route 1 drivers stay on the freeway built in pieces from near Oakford all the way to New Jersey.

SECTION III. JANNEY STATION TO TREVOSE

From Janney Station, the Lincoln Highway followed two routes to Philadelphia. Old photos show a sign here giving equal status to both ways but distinguishing them as the two-lane and the four-lane routes.

1915–1923 Route. We stay to the right for the two-lane route and cross the concrete Neshaminy Creek Bridge, built in 1921 to replace a covered bridge. (Neshaminy is an American Indian name meaning "double stream.") At the end of the one-way bridge, we cross Bristol Road and continue straight; the town of Oakford is just north. To the south is the Mall Motel, an older place now named to attract customers from the nearby Neshaminy Mall. The next intersection offers the chance to get to the mall or to Route 1 and the Pennsylvania Turnpike.

Continuing southwest, to our right is Penn Valley Mobile Home Park, once the location of Penn Valley Park. Its listing in the 1927 Mohawk-Hobbs guide tells of free amusements, an enticement to stay for the 50-cent camping. Cabins were to be built later (the following year's guide lists two).

Continuing west, the Turnpike passes overhead at Street Road; this area is listed in period guidebooks as LaTrappe. Farther ahead, what looks like an old garage is now Roosevelt Memorial Park Maintenance Building No. 1, across from Roosevelt Cemetery. The area to the north is known as Linconia, a likely derivation of the Lincoln Highway name. Ahead is an intersection with Route 1; to our right was once the Ridge Farm Tourist Camp, later called Liberty Bell Deluxe Cottages. They're listed in the *American Motel Association Motel Guide and Trip Diary* for 1941 as the "most modern and up-to-date tourist court in Philadelphia." There were also rooms available in the main house owned by Leonard Ridge, who later expanded the complex into a trailer park.

There were many other tourist homes along this stretch of the

Penn Valley Park was 1 mile north of the Philadelphia city line in the vicinity of Eastern State Hospital. The "Largest Free Amusement Park in the World" also offered a restaurant and tourist camp. Another park postcard, postmarked June 1933 and signed by a Geo. Walsh, asked, "Dear friend: Why not have a picnic at our park? One they will always remember. Swimming for all ages and other amusements." Walsh Avenue is nearby. COURTESY BERNIE HEISEY

Ridge Farm Tourist Camp was an "Official A.A.A. Camp" located on "Lincoln Highway at Roosevelt Boulevard, 17 miles north of City Hall" and offering a "Modern and Homelike place to stay," according to this postcard.

Ridge Farm Tourist Camp evolved into Liberty Bell Deluxe Cottages and then Liberty Bell Trailer Village. The farmhouse is to the right in each view. The "open air theater" to the left is the Lincoln Drive-In. An office park has since erased everything.

Lincoln, such as the Stagecoach, a colonial home 1 mile south of the city line. There were also a number of motels just north of here according to the 1940 Shell guide: back 1 mile were Dill's Tourist Camp and the Shell Camp (with 23 cabins), and near the traffic light were Sunnyside Tourist Cabins and Blue Light Cabins.

At the light is a former Krispy Kreme donut shop, now a green-roofed Suds beer takeout. As we cross Route 1, the road is blocked by a dirt mound where the route continued, and we'll explore it on foot in Section IV.

1923–Present Route. There's very little of note on this wide stretch of Route 1. There are a number of large motels, many dating from the 1950s and '60s, but some are closed and abandoned. The sprawling George Washington Inn to the south is scheduled for demolition. We pass an operating Penn Motel, Howard Johnson's, and American Motel. The Clover Motel, built in the late fifties, had a tall neon sign when it was here, and the Trailblazer Diner advertised in *Tail-Gate* magazine in 1950, "Truckies Always Welcome" and "Hot meals at all

The Trailblazer Diner was on Route 1 in Trevose, 1 mile north of the Phila-delphia city line. Diners were common in eastern Pennsylvania because of the proximity to the many diner manufacturers in New Jersey.

hours." These places lost much of their business after I-95 superseded Route 1, and many are now gone. We arrive at the traffic light where the former Krispy Kreme is now a beer distributor, the old Lincoln crossing from left to right.

SECTION IV. TREVOSE TO HALDEMAN AVENUE

1915–1923 Route. We cross Route 1 to follow the original Lincoln Highway, and our road quickly dead-ends at a mound of dirt and a "Bridge Closed" sign behind the Lincoln Motel. We can, however, park and climb the dirt to find a wonderful stretch of old road beyond. This was part of the Byberry and Bensalem Turnpike, and it served as the Lincoln until 1923, when Roosevelt Boulevard (Route 1) was extended through here. Part of an old stone arch bridge remains over Poquessing Creek. It's very picturesque, though it seems to be a local late-night gathering spot, as beer bottles and shopping carts fill the area. The creek has also washed out large parts of the roadbed, making a geological survey of the roadbed convenient. This section shrinks to a footpath but goes for a while through a wooded area. It ends at Burling Road, which can be reached from the other side, though Burling is marked a private road.

1923–Present Route. As we drive west on Route 1, the Lincoln Motel is to the south and the abandoned Poquessing Creek Bridge and road are behind it. To the north is the Interplex office park, the former site of the Lincoln Drive-In Theater. Going over Poquessing Creek, we cross Philadelphia's city limits. The road becomes six-lane each way, and we stay to the right to avoid the inner express lanes—there's nowhere to pull over on them, but if you're just passing through and not interested in stopping, they make your drive easier. We soon pass Burling Road, the access road to the old stretch of Lincoln Highway to the south, but you must turn around and head east if you're interested in seeing that route.

Roosevelt Boulevard, built both to handle large volumes of traffic and to offer a leisurely "parkway" atmosphere, today does a poor job of both. The road from here to Philadelphia is congested and offers little in the way of roadside attractions. The few bypassed sections have reverted to a slower pace through suburbia.

To the south is a store with five huge letters, "BASCO," covered

The deserted Poquessing Creek Bridge, behind the Lincoln Motel, was part of the Byberry and Bensalem Turnpike. (PHOTO 1991)

with the word "BEST" in tiny print. The store was designed by Venturi and Rauch; each letter is 34 feet high. A Nabisco plant is to the north, and we can smell the cookies baking. The Ritz of Philadelphia at Bennett Road is a modern mirror and glass diner with connected cocktail lounge and bakery.

SECTION V. HALDEMAN AVENUE TO RHAWN STREET

1915–1923 Route. Shortly after passing the turn to Route 63 south, we make a right on Haldeman Avenue. This was the route until 1923, when Roosevelt Boulevard was extended. At the time, Haldeman, and the road east of it, was still called the Byberry and Bensalem Turnpike. Today, Haldeman is wide and suburban. After .5 mile, we cross Red Lion Road, and Haldeman becomes four-lane but remains suburban. We're now in Bustleton, and at 1.3 miles from the turn, we bear left onto Bustleton Avenue.

This part of Haldeman and Bustleton was used from 1915 until the adjacent section of Roosevelt was completed in 1923; it's now mostly strip development. A mile later we meet Welsh Road; the 1915 route continued west on Bustleton, but when Roosevelt was completed through Pennypack Circle in 1920, westbound drivers could turn south onto Welsh to meet the new highway.

We continue west on Bustleton, which is four-lane but divided. This road, with its suburban houses, was developed long after the Lincoln Highway left this route. We cross Pennypack Creek, and the houses start giving way to shopping centers. Just over 2.8 miles from bearing onto Haldemen, we turn left onto Rhawn Street and quickly meet Roosevelt Boulevard.

1920–Present Route. Roosevelt Boulevard opened through this area in 1923. As we continue on the six-lane Roosevelt, we pass Haldeman Avenue. A half mile from Haldeman is the Red Lion Diner to the north, a converted stagecoach tavern redone in Tudor style. It has a c. 1960 sign that announces, "Famous for Roast Beef. Over 125,000 lbs. sold yearly!"

When we cross Welsh Road, this section of Roosevelt dates from 1920. Traffic would have used Welsh from 1920 to 1923 while Roosevelt was being extended northeast. Welsh was once the location of

An underpass on Roosevelt Boulevard south of Bustleton, 1924. COURTESY
UNIVERSITY OF MICHIGAN, SPECIAL COLLECTIONS LIBRARY

Evergreen Farms, listed in a 1925 National Motorists Association guidebook as offering "Family Dinners, Supper Dances, and Saddle Horses at
City Rates," attesting to the gentility of the area at the time.

We pass the Mediterranean-style Tiffany Diner (advertising "Cock-
tails"), then cross a bridge over Pennypack Creek and Pennypack Park.
We go under Pennypack Circle and soon meet Rhawn Street, with a
miniature golf course at the intersection. William Rhawn was a bank
president who lived in this area a century ago.

SECTION VI. RHAWN STREET TO BROAD STREET

Roosevelt Boulevard was completed from Rhawn Street southwest
to Broad Street by 1913. It has served as the Lincoln Highway and Route
1 ever since. We pass the Hub Motel to the south, and signs for Cottman
Avenue and I-95. Ben and May Vorsanger's Guest House Tourist and
Trailer Park used to be at Cottman Avenue, as advertised in the *Trailer
Tour Map of the United States.* In fact, the Guest House has the only ad
in that map, which advertises its adjacent trailer sales business. As we
continue, both sides of the road have 1940s red brick row houses. A bit
farther, some are made of stone.

We pass under Oxford Circle; the other lanes would take us through the circle. It's hard to recognize as a traffic circle because of the underpass, and the crossing roads have been reshaped to look like any other intersection. Still heading west, we round a bend; to our north once lay the old Sears warehouse and store, a brick structure with looming clock tower and lots of blue art deco detailing, demolished in October 1994. We pass a Chinese restaurant with a big neon sign on the roof; to the south is Regan's bar.

Regan's is worth a stop to photograph its nice neon, including an arrow and sign indicating the "Ladies Entrance." Of course, ladies can use the main entrance today. The green neon-lit bar is a comfortable place where you can ask about the old places along the road. Locals may tell you about the Blue Light Cabins that sat across from the Lincoln Drive-In in Trevose (where the Lincoln Motel is). They say the cabins were a favorite stop for those leaving the movies—$4.50 for 4 hours back when.

Regan's on the Boulevard has had a "Ladies Entrance" since 1944, but today only the sign remains, not the restriction. (PHOTO 1994)

Back on the road, we head west again. A lot of roads angle off, and every little triangular sliver of land seems to have an old gas station on it. Signs for Hunting Park Avenue (Route 13 south) appear, and 2 miles from Regan's we're faced with three ways through Philadelphia.

SECTION VII. BROAD STREET TO CITY HALL

Like most urban areas, Philadelphia had no real need for the Lincoln Highway; the city already had its share of paved streets and cars to fill them. Urban routings were sometimes arbitrary, left to local officials, and mapmakers also created their own routings.

In Philadelphia, alternative routes through and around town were always offered. Although the Lincoln could be said to "officially" head south on Broad Street to Center City, a course on Hunting Park and City Line Avenues was popular enough to have had the Lincoln Highway markers erected in 1928. We'll explore both the Broad Street and the later Hunting Park and City Line courses. Route 1 now cuts parallel to Hunting Park Avenue, but we'll ignore that modern bypass.

1915–c. 1920 Route. The intersection of Broad Street and Roosevelt Boulevard has changed greatly over the years. In a way, they no longer intersect; Roosevelt becomes Route 1 and goes underneath Broad, although just north of that (at Broad's street level) is The Roosevelt Boulevard, probably an original incarnation of that road. (*Note:* If you're heading northeast on Roosevelt toward New Jersey, it starts as a three-lane, but watch for parked cars in the outer lane.)

Starting south on Broad, we pass an old neon Buick dealership sign at Gordon Buick to the east and cross Hunting Park Avenue. Some streets occasionally cross Broad at an angle; one such is Germantown Avenue, which comes in from the northwest at Erie. There we find a Checkers, one of a growing fast-food chain, resembling an old drive-in restaurant. We pass through a nice little commercial section on both sides of the road and see an old "ghost" sign at the northeast corner of Sedgley Avenue advertising "Auto Radios Repaired." After Rising Sun Avenue, we approach a large railroad overpass. Next to it is North Philadelphia Station, a reference point in early Lincoln Highway road guides but now shuttered, painted over, and covered with graffiti.

The southwest corner of Broad and Lehigh Avenue, just past the station, was once the site of the Baker Bowl. Officially named National

This grand Atlantic station was at the intersection of Northeast (later Roosevelt) Boulevard and Hunting Park Avenue, serving those going in or out of Philadelphia on Broad Street. National Petroleum News *reported in 1918 that "Fifteen attendants are on duty here till 11 P.M., when the shift changes and during the early hours a single watchman suffices also as attendant." Note the backlit terra cotta signboard and colonnade. A similar station, with a completely circular "temple," was on the other end of town at Walnut and 40th Streets. Stations like these were meant to silence critics who opposed traditional gasoline outlets.* COURTESY ARCO

League Park, the baseball field was the home of the Phillies from 1887 to 1938. After the original burned in 1894, the ballpark was rebuilt, the first in the United States to incorporate a cantilever design to eliminate many of the view-obstructing columns. When the Phillies moved five blocks west to Shibe Park in 1938, Baker Bowl struggled on with events such as midget auto racing. It was demolished in 1950, and today, no evidence remains of its baseball days.

We pass an old gas station at Cumberland Street, cross Susquehanna Avenue, and to the right see the Uptown Theater, still nice looking, but now with a sign saying, "Come Worship With Us." We pass Temple University, which occupies both sides of the road for a few blocks, and cross Montgomery Avenue; here the little sidewalk vendor carts start appearing. We pass Betty's Auto Glass in an old gas station that also served as Bassett's Auto Tags, and at Poplar Street we pass a White Castle and another old gas station. At Girard Avenue was once the Majestic Hotel, with 500 rooms and a garage connected, now the site of a McDonald's.

Ridge Avenue crosses diagonally, and there we see the old Lorraine Hotel, well known to early travelers and still operating as the Divine Lorraine Hotel. Broad was also known for its many car dealerships, and just south of Potts Street on the left side is the 1916 Roman Building, with a flying spoked wheel in relief on the facade. More art deco dealerships appear, and we cross Spring Garden Street. At Noble Street to the left is the Steak and Bagel Train, an old railcar on tracks. It's adjacent to the North American Building; an auto ramp goes up its side.

The Philadelphia Inquirer building on the west side was built in 1924

Paving of the 800 block of North Broad Street with Belgian block, October 1938. Those traveling through Philadelphia were alerted in the Lincoln Highway Association guidebooks to sound their horns at all street intersections. COURTESY PA STATE ARCHIVES, RG-12 DEPT. OF HIGHWAYS

of white limestone and terra cotta. We cross Callowhill Street; to the left is the Packard Building, designed by Albert Kahn, a leading designer of industrial buildings, including many Ford Motor Company factories; by 1938, 19 percent of all architect-designed buildings in the United States were Kahn's work. The 1910 Packard factory on Philadelphia's "automobile row" was one of the earliest uses of reinforced concrete; it now houses luxury apartments. Also in this row was the Seiberling Rubber Company, founded by longtime Lincoln Highway Association president Frank Seiberling in 1921 after he was forced from Goodyear, which he had also founded. Finally, we reach John F. Kennedy Boulevard, the northern border of Penn Square, which circumnavigates City Hall. A few blocks to the east is the Liberty Bell and Independence Hall, where the Declaration of Independence was signed in 1776.

c. 1920–c. 1960 Route. We cross over Broad Street on Hunting Park Avenue, where we see an old White Tower restaurant that's now a check-cashing business. Within a few blocks the area looks dreadful—buildings are boarded up, trash lies everywhere. We cross railroad tracks and soon pass under more tracks. We pass an old Pure Oil station, now painted brown with a dark brown roof.

The Eastern Casket Company may once have housed a Lincoln Garage at 2245 Hunting Park Avenue. We pass the beautiful Budd Company building and the Tastykake bakery with a little clock on its rooftop billboard. The rest of the five-story buff-colored building has funky blue and aluminum trim. We cross Allegheny Avenue, where there was once a 1928 Lincoln Highway marker. At the Pep Boys factory, service center, and parts store, there are life-size statues of the "Pep Boys," Manny, Moe, and Jack.

We enter another run-down section, and at Ridge Avenue, we turn right and go under railroad tracks. The route in the 1924 LHA road guide uses the shortcut of Allegheny to Ridge. Either way is fine. To the right is the former Dobson Mills, now called Chelsea and converted to apartments. All of the buildings in this complex are reportedly constructed of Wissahickon shist, a local rock outcropping. We pass under the big twin bridges of Route 1, and a post office tells us we're at East Falls Station in Philadelphia.

The road curves some to the right at Indian Queen Lane and passes through a small business district. The old Falls Bridge is to the left, and signs direct us to I-76, Route 1, City Avenue, and Lincoln Drive. We turn left and stay left for City Avenue. We cross over a road with a strip of restaurants, and loop onto the bridge over the Schuylkill River. Signs alert us for I-76 east and west, but we go straight ahead on Route 1 south, or City Avenue, which is three lanes wide, crossing over the Schuylkill Expressway.

We cross Presidential Boulevard in an area known as the Golden Mile for all the office and retail buildings located here. We cross Bala Avenue and Old Lancaster Road. Going uphill, we pass St. Josephs University and cross a decorative bridge over the Main Line railroad tracks. We cross 63rd Street, and just 7 miles but many minutes from the Broad Street intersection, we reach Lancaster Avenue in Overbrook. Lancaster Avenue is Route 30 and once again the original Lincoln Highway.

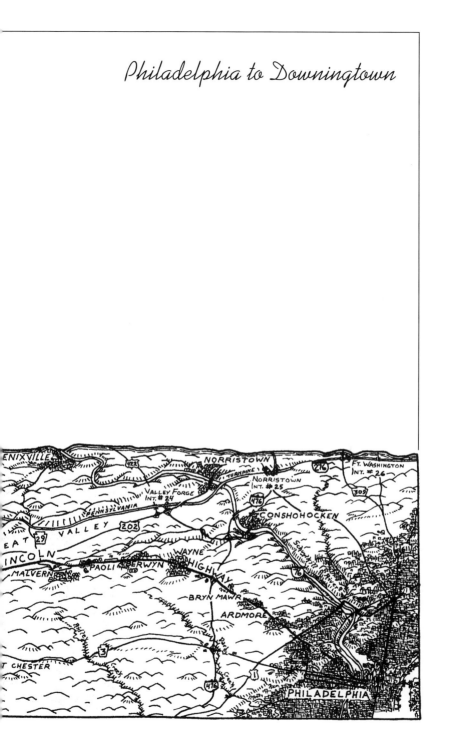

Most people associate Philadelphia with our country's founding fathers, and for good reason: Many important events took place here, including the signing of the Declaration of Independence on July 4, 1776, and the adoption of the U.S. Constitution in 1787. Philadelphia also served as the nation's capital from 1790 to 1800. The city has an even earlier history, however.

Swedes, Dutch, and Finns were already living at the site overlooking the Schuylkill and Delaware Rivers when William Penn received his land grant. Penn envisioned a city like his colony, tolerating all religions; the name Philadelphia is Greek for "city of brotherly love." Penn wanted an orderly city laid out on a grid pattern, but when he arrived in 1682, he found some already established streets. Penn gave the north-south streets numbers and named intersecting streets for local trees and flowers, such as Walnut and Chestnut.

Early Lincoln Highway travelers heading west from Philadelphia were faced with a variety of alternate routes. The most direct, with the longest tradition, headed west from City Hall on Market Street and then angled northwest onto Lancaster Avenue (Lancaster Pike). A popular alternative was a pair of one-way streets south of Market: Walnut and Chestnut. Travelers could also go north through Fairmount Park, which became easier with the opening of the Benjamin Franklin Parkway in 1920. Maps from the 1950s even show Route 30 using both the Schuylkill Expressway and a route that crossed the river on Girard Avenue.

The Lincoln Highway was often rerouted to keep the through traffic away from congested areas and commercial districts. A 1928 report by the U.S. Bureau of Public Roads stated, "On the 88 miles of the Lincoln Highway from Chambersburg to Jennerstown the average daily density of traffic was 800 cars per day, whereas it was 3,940 per day on the 35 miles from Philadelphia to Coatesville." Most business owners, though, wanted the recognition of being on the Lincoln Highway; the 1917 *Chester City Directory* even contains an ad for a Lincoln Highway Garage at 10th Avenue and Morton Street in Chester, 15 miles off the Lincoln Highway! The operator was probably hoping that the highway might branch south to Washington, D.C.

In the first section, we'll look at the two most popular routes. They converge at Lancaster Avenue and 63rd Street in Overbrook.

Looking west in the 1500 block of Market Street, March 1941. Note the Horn and Hardart Automat to the south, one of dozens of those eateries in Philadelphia and New York. COURTESY INQUIRER COLLECTION, URBAN ARCHIVES CENTER, TEMPLE UNIVERSITY LIBRARIES

SECTION I. CITY HALL TO OVERBROOK

Market Street and Lancaster Avenue Route. From City Hall, we head west on John F. Kennedy Boulevard (originally Pennsylvania Boulevard). The original route via Market Street is one-way eastbound from City Hall to 20th Street, so we have to take JFK to 20th. At JFK and 16th is the Philadelphia Visitors Center, which can provide maps and brochures. At 20th Street we drop down to Market and proceed west. Crossing the Schuylkill River, we see Amtrak's 30th Street Station to the north and the post office to the south. Skirting Drexel University to the south for a couple blocks, we turn north on 36th Street to get to Lancaster Avenue (34th comes south from Lancaster).

Lancaster Avenue is an interesting drive, full of many buildings and businesses, most of which have seen better days. Still, a building on the southeast corner of 39th Street proclaims Lancaster Avenue as "The Rodeo Drive of West Philadelphia." We pass a variety of theaters, gas stations, old signs, and storefronts, in particular Clearview Dry Cleaners at the corner of Haverford Avenue and Sun Ray Drugs just west of 40th Street. One of many neon signs is for Platt's Candy Novelty Shop, advertising "Fresh Roasted Peanuts." An old Pure Oil station on the corner of Westminster Avenue sits battered.

A Lincoln Highway Garage was located at 4854 Lancaster, perhaps where a white horse sign now hangs next to the Union Tabernacle Baptist Church. Trolleys roll past as we spy Colonial Iron Craftsmen to the north, with most of the neon gone from its porcelain sign. Unfortunately, lots of trash and graffiti line the street here. We pass a couple more old gas stations, and the trolley leaves us at Lansdowne Avenue.

We pass the Ace Diner to the north, with one of the oddest diner remodeling jobs ever—a worn but still intact Silk City from about 1940 is now hidden behind a sidewalk-to-sky mansard roof. Railroad tracks run behind the diner, and to the west, in an old gas station, we spot the Georgia Boy BBQ. The Lincoln Highway once passed under the railroad, perhaps at 56th, and stayed north of it for a couple blocks. Today that underpass is mostly filled in. The road would have emerged on Malvern Avenue. Continuing west, we pass another old diner, now almost com-

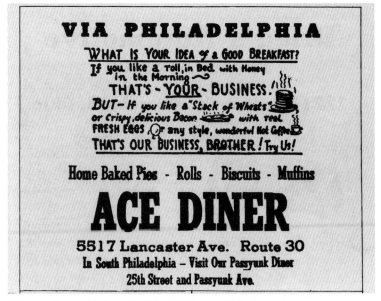

This Ace Diner ad is from the July 1950 issue of Tail-Gate, *a truckers magazine.*

pletely remodeled as Anna's Pizza, just east of the former Green Hill Theater, now the Church of God. Finally, we cross 63rd Street.

Walnut Street or Chestnut Street Route. Walnut Street is three blocks south of City Hall and can be reached when circling Penn Square (around City Hall) by continuing south on 15th Street, the western leg of the square. In town, Walnut is tight with congestion and old storefronts. As we head west on Walnut and cross the river, it's a bit of a freeway, so we make sure to stay in the center. We see some lunch wagons, mostly pretzel vendors, on the corners as we pass the University of Pennsylvania from about 30th to 40th Streets.

Atlantic built one of its elaborate "Greek temple" gas stations at the corner of Walnut and 40th in 1918. It was only Atlantic's tenth station in the area. A contemporary article in *National Petroleum News* tells that the round temple, "copied from an ancient Hellenic design, contains the salesroom and cashier's office. . . . The interior is finished in mahogany and bronze, while the dome and sides are in the white tile . . . flanked by an imposing Ionic colonnade to the rear." Both were illuminated with concealed lighting to "obtain the custom of the night passenger car trade" and to overcome "the erroneous, yet persistent, notion of many persons that lights near gasoline, even if encased in a glass globe, are dangerous." The station had 15 pumps in white pedestals along the colonnade, with an attendant for each one! When leaving, customers were "given a vest pocket road map . . . a lead pencil and booklets on lubricants as souvenirs."

After 40th Street, the area becomes a mix of row houses and small businesses, such as a 1950s Thriftway, with a parabola-shaped roof, at 43rd Street. About 4 miles from Center City, after crossing 62nd Street, we turn right, or north, onto Cobbs Creek Parkway, which soon becomes 63rd Street.

We head north on 63rd and go under SEPTA's Market-Frankford elevated line (the "El") at the 63rd Street Station. As we head uphill through residential neighborhoods, it's best to stay in the center lane. After .5 mile, we cross Callowhill Street; to the east, on the right side, is VIP Cleaners at 413-17 63rd Street. This brick building, with a roofline that rises to a point in the center of the facade, was once the location of a Lincoln Highway Garage. We cross Girard Avenue and follow trolley tracks, keeping alert for trolleys making a right turn from the middle

The Lincoln Highway brought gas stations to otherwise residential neighborhoods such as Walnut and 54th Streets, August 1922. COURTESY INQUIRER COLLECTION, URBAN ARCHIVES CENTER, TEMPLE UNIVERSITY LIBRARIES

lane. Less than 1 mile from Walnut, we arrive at Lancaster Avenue and turn left, or west, on the original Lincoln Highway.

Note: If you are traveling west to east, you take Chestnut into town rather than Walnut (both are one-way). You'll pass lots of row houses and some business sections, such as around 52nd, where sidewalk vendors offer fruit, vegetables, and videotapes. Set back from the road at 42nd Street is the American Diner, a late-1940s Paramount-brand diner remodeled by Swingle. It's open 24 hours on the weekends. From there you'll pass through the university area and cross the river into town.

SECTION II. OVERBROOK TO DOWNINGTOWN

Heading west on Lancaster Avenue from 63rd Street, we cross Drexel Road and see the Lincoln Court Apartments on the northwest corner of Overbrook Avenue. They include a Lincoln Court Dining Room, and "Lincoln Court" is carved in cement above the doors. We reach City Line Avenue (also called just City Avenue), with the Overbrook Presbyterian Church on the northeast corner. The northwest corner once had a tollhouse for Lancaster Pike.

The Pennsylvania Railroad, which offered commuter service on its parallel Main Line, purchased Lancaster Pike from 52nd Street west to Paoli for $20,000 in 1876 to prevent the extension of competing streetcar lines into the suburbs. Tolls were collected on the pike until 1917, when the state highway department acquired the toll road for $165,000.

Now that we've crossed the city line into Montgomery County, the road becomes tree-lined, wide, and suburban. We quickly come upon a Lancaster Pike marker to the north in front of St. Charles Seminary; it's marked "5 M to P," indicating the distance to Philadelphia. We pass some old stone homes, and 1 mile later is the "6 M to P" marker to the north just before Clover Hill Road.

We cross Wynnewood Road. Some of the approaching suburbs, such as Haverford and Bryn Mawr, have Welsh names derived from those who settled just before William Penn arrived in 1682. Ardmore, Irish for "high ground," was originally named Athensville, but the Pennsylvania Railroad chose to rename its station (and therefore the town) in 1873 to sound more distinguished.

Suburbia now gives way to businesses. One that we pass to the south in Ardmore is the Chung Sing Chinese Restaurant, formerly Dean's Diner, now with a green pagoda-style roof. It was built by the Fodero company in the 1950s. Another tollhouse once sat at Church Road, and on the southwest corner is the former Viking Inn, which was

Looking east on Lancaster Avenue in 1919, with City Line Avenue to the left.

QUAKER LODGE MOTOR HOTEL, ARDMORE, PA.

N. Darwyn Gallup, owner of the Quaker Lodge, wrote to the Tourist Court
Journal *in October 1940, "We have five cabins at present all with running hot
and cold water, and we expect to install three more before spring. We have 22
rooms in our lodge house . . . and accommodations for 100 trailers with electric-
ity and running water to each." The lodge advertised, "Small enough to know
you. Large enough to serve you. A good night means a good morning." The site
of such hospitality is now a shopping center.*

famous for its revolving smorgasbord and identifiable by its Tudor exterior. Established in 1931, the Viking claimed to be "the only Scandina-
vian restaurant in Philadelphia and vicinity."

The Lower Merion Township Building on the north side has the 7-
mile Lancaster Pike marker at the edge of its parking lot. We continue
through Ardmore's business section and come upon the Ardmore Theater to the south; to the north, a building called 63 West is long and buff-
colored, with deco trim, and houses various businesses. To the south, we
pass an IHOP (International House of Pancakes), with its big blue roof.

When the Lincoln Highway was established in the teens, Ardmore's
main industry was truck manufacturing at the Autocar plant. Founded in
Pittsburgh, the company moved to Ardmore in 1900 to take advantage of
the railroad and the turnpike, and their proximity to Philadelphia. The
Autocar was one of the leading makes of American cars at the time and

was reportedly well made, advertised as the vehicle that "cannot blow up or burn up!" The company offered the first multicylinder car with shaft drive, as opposed to chain drive as on bicycles. Trucks were added to the line in 1907 (with an 18-horsepower engine beneath the driver's seat) and proved so popular that trucks became the company's sole product after 1911. A new brick Autocar plant was built on the north side of the Lincoln Highway in 1915.

In 1920, Autocar donated two specially painted trucks and paid their operating costs for the marking of the Lincoln Highway. This was arranged by David S. Ludlum, president of Autocar and a founder of the Lincoln Highway Association. That initiative resulted in enameled steel markers from New York to Omaha (as shown in an illustration in the Ligonier to Pittsburgh chapter). Autocar peaked at about 2,300 employees during World War II; the company was acquired by White Motor Corporation in 1953, which moved manufacturing to nearby Exton. The Ardmore factory burned in 1956 and is now the site of the West Ardmore shopping center. Autocar trucks are still produced under the White-GMC banner.

Today Ardmore is perhaps best known for Suburban Square, one of the country's first department-store-anchored shopping centers when it opened in 1928. The idea was to have one-stop shopping for offices, retail, and grocery needs. The limestone buildings are a restrained art deco but have been remodeled in recent decades. Suburban Square can be reached by crossing under or over the Main Line railroad tracks to the north, and following the signs for the shopping center. Early motorists could have stopped at the Red Lion Inn and general store at the corner of Greenfield Avenue, built in the 1850s on the site of an earlier tavern of the same name, or at a nearby municipal tourist camp in the 1920s.

Sunoco built its first service station in Ardmore in 1920. Old photos of the station show the cross street as Lehigh Avenue, but no Lehigh exists today; perhaps it was an earlier name for Woodside Road, where locals believe the station to have been. By 1928, Sunoco had 500 stations in the northeast; by 1940, some 9,000 outlets. Sunoco's specialty was a premium gasoline called Sunoco Blue, which was tinted blue for the early glass "visible" pumps. The station in Ardmore was probably a result of Sunoco's first refinery and ship-building subsidiary on the Delaware River at nearby Chester.

The first Sunoco gas station opened in Ardmore in 1920 on the Lincoln Highway. The street signs say "Lancaster Pike" and "Lehigh Avenue," but no Lehigh can be found today; locals say the station was at Woodside Road, where a Sunoco still sits. Note the Sun Oil tanker cars behind the white tanks. COURTESY SUN REFINING AND MARKETING COMPANY

Ahead to the north is Robert Swartz's camera store, which can easily be spotted by the big camera-shaped sign hanging out front. Bob opened his store in 1950 and designed the sign in 1951. He is a local historian and has a number of old photos displayed at his shop, where he sells copies of the Lower Merion Township history book. He's also researched the Lancaster Pike markers and says that Major Price was awarded the contract to furnish and place the milestones in 1795. Price was the proprietor of the William Penn Inn on the pike just east of Wynnewood Road.

Robert Swartz has lots of old photos inside his camera store in Ardmore. (PHOTO 1994)

The stones were cut locally, and distances were measured from the Market Street Bridge in Philadelphia.

To the south, the Whitehall apartments are interestingly decorated with a large tile border and tile pictures. There's another pike marker at Llanalew Road, "8 M to P," that lies low in the hedges on the northeast corner. In this vicinity, Lincoln Highway travelers would have stopped at a tollgate. According to the 1914 *Blue Book,* a ticket for up to 60 cents got toll payers to Paoli; they were given coupons to leave at four tollgates along the way.

We pass through Haverford, almost unnoticeable except for Haverford College, founded by the Society of Friends in 1833. As we reach Bryn Mawr's business section, we pass a neon sign for Marita's Cantina, a Mexican restaurant, to the south and the Bryn Mawr Theater to the north.

Like Ardmore, Bryn Mawr was also renamed by the Pennsylvania Railroad, and in fact, the whole lay of the town was redone in 1869, when the railroad chose to straighten its alignment. And like Ardmore, the new name meant "high ground," but this time in Welsh. Bryn Mawr had a car-manufacturing plant too—the Pennsylvania Auto Motor Company, which began production in 1906 but was bankrupt by 1911.

Lancaster Pike and Route 30 don't always follow the same path, even though some pike markers show up on Route 30. As proof, Old Lancaster Road comes in from the northeast, then branches off to the south (becoming Conestoga Road in Delaware County), and doesn't rejoin Route 30 until past Wayne. There's another Lancaster Pike marker to the south in front of Ludington Library, just before Bryn Mawr Avenue. To the north, we see the former Bryn Mawr Garage, which still has its name and a winged wheel on the facade of brick with inlaid blue tiles.

We head downhill through Rosemont's business district. The McDonald's we pass to the north was the site of Jim & Bill's Mari-Nay Diner, named for the branches of the armed forces its owners served in, the Marines and the Navy. Their first diner was a c. 1940 Kullman brand with glass-block corners and red fluting below the stainless steel; the second was a much larger 1955 Kullman that survived into the late 1980s. Rosemont didn't have an auto factory like Ardmore or Bryn Mawr, but Derham Body Works built automobile bodies in the first half of the century. We continue west past Norwood Avenue, past a large stone municipal marker, and climb a hill with dense trees to our north. We level off and soon pass Villanova University, established 1843.

As we cross Route 320, there's another large municipal marker on the southeast corner. We pass the Villanova Diner to the north, in a former Howard Johnson's. We pass under I-476, and soon pass a giant turnpike marker reproduction, "12 M to P." We pass through Radnor and St. Davids and into the Wayne business section; to the north is the China Buddha, a Mountain View brand diner now painted cream color, and next door the stately Wayne Hotel. A block away, after crossing Wayne Avenue, we find the striking Anthony Wayne Theater, also to the north, and .5 mile past that, Minella's Main Line Diner, a 1960s Fodero brand diner to the south.

About 5 miles north of this area is Valley Forge National Historic Park, site of the Continental Army's encampment during the winter of 1777–78. Here, Washington's army of twelve thousand kept the British

The Anthony Wayne Theater in Wayne. (PHOTO 1994)

Army bottled in Philadelphia. Though some two thousand troops died, the Continental Army emerged a more organized force.

The branch of Conestoga Road (Old Lancaster Road) that was south of us now rejoins but will soon branch off to the north. At Sugartown Road, the large "14 M to P" pike marker sits on the southeast corner. Just past the intersection, the Milepost Inn is closed, but around the back is a drawing of the "14 M to P" marker. To the south we pass a Marriott Courtyard, the former site of the Main Line Drive-In Theater. The drive-in operated year-round from the 1950s until the end of the 1975 season.

To the north, Old Lancaster Road branches off under the Main Line. This was part of the original Lincoln Highway, and it returns to Route 30 just over 1 mile later after passing through Devon. If we turn right through the underpass (at the cottage-style gas station) to follow it, we see vacant ground uphill on the north side. This was the site of the Pennsylvania Fireworks Display Company from about 1920 until 1930. According to Bob Goshorn in "When the Fireworks Factory in Devon Blew Up," published in the *Tredyffrin Easttown History Club Quarterly,* the plant exploded on April 3, 1930, resulting in 10 deaths and numerous injuries. Noise from the blast was reportedly heard as far as 50 miles away in Trenton, and cars on Old Lancaster were pushed off the road! All 14 buildings were destroyed, leaving "great holes, like shell craters, in the black, pock-marked earth." The Bentner Box Company, a quarter mile away on the Lincoln Highway at Valley Forge Road, had 1,700 panes of glass and their steel sashes blown out. "Cars passing on the Lincoln Highway were commandeered to take some of the more seriously injured to the Bryn Mawr Hospital . . . to the east the area of damage extended for five miles."

If we're following Old Lancaster Road, at Valley Forge Road is a yellow house to the north that was once Lamb's Tavern, established in 1812, now a private home (its roof and chimney were torn off during the fireworks explosion). We pass the "15 M to P" pike marker to the north, embedded in a low stone wall below hedges, about three houses before Devon State Road. At the corner of Devon State Road, a repair garage is attached to an old log house, probably once Ye Olde Log Cabin Tea Room, in a 1732 inn. Old Lancaster then turns left through an underpass and rejoins Route 30.

If we skip Old Lancaster Road and stay on Route 30, we pass the little cottage-style gas station to the north, and ahead, to the south, is the Devon County Fairgrounds. The street signs here read Lincoln Highway. Less than .5 mile west of here once sat the Lincoln Inn hotel and dining room. We cross Lakeside Avenue, and Old Lancaster Road comes back under the railroad tracks to meet Route 30.

Just to its east we passed the Berwyn train station to the north, and just west of the station is a pike marker behind the guardrail, "16 M to P." Old Lancaster again turns to the north, heading over the tracks. At the west end of this stretch, near the Daylesford train station, is the former Blue Ball Tavern to the north, established in 1794, now a private home.

Back on Route 30, we pass through an older business section. We rise a bit above the Main Line tracks to the north; to the south, we pass the site of the former Twaddell's Diner (west of Del Chevrolet). Beginning in 1948, brothers Hi and Hib Twaddell operated a diner on Route 30 in Paoli, upgrading to a Swingle-brand diner in 1958. The new diner came in seven sections. It was later remodeled and operated most recently as Orleans Restaurant, but the whole thing was bulldozed in October 1994.

We enter Paoli, where a welcome sign tells us the town was founded in 1755 and was named for the Corsican patriot Pasquale Paoli, who led Europe's most democratic constitution at the time. Paoli has entered the

Opened in 1958, Twaddell's was the first Swingle-brand diner ever built. The Paoli-area diner was bulldozed in 1994. COURTESY CLEVELAND PUBLIC LIBRARY

language for the "Paoli Massacre," in which the British surprised the Continental Army under Gen. "Mad" Anthony Wayne in 1777. We cross Route 252 and soon pass Paoli's train station to the north.

To the south is Matthews Ford, the oldest Ford dealer in the state, according to James G. Matthews, who recalls: "It's been a Ford dealer since 1921. My uncle, Walter T. Matthews, owned the dealership then. I was born in a house right next to the road in the heart of Paoli in July 1912, so I have seen a lot of changes in this area. I remember the Lincoln Highway when it was a two-lane stone road. They put oil on the roadbed in the summertime to keep the dust under control."

Jim was born above his family's grocery store at the corner of Lancaster Pike and Spring Street in Paoli. When the grocery was sold in 1916, his uncle Walter went into the automobile business, selling Chevrolets, Maxwells, and Overlands. In 1921 he received his own Ford franchise, and in 1923 a new showroom was started that's still used today. Walter also sold Ford's Fordson tractors and in 1927 was the country's top-selling Fordson dealer. That brought a surprise in 1928: he received the first Model A sold to a dealer in the whole country. After that, the dealership's cars were made at a Ford assembly plant in Chester until about 1953 (a similar plant in Pittsburgh along the Lincoln still stands). Jim still remembers every detail of his first sale, a Ford V-8 for $565 in 1933.

One mile after entering Paoli, we arrive at the intersection of King Road, where the Cottman Transmission to the north was once a diner. The original route went south to Malvern here, so we bear left on King Road, following the Main Line tracks. After .5 mile, we pass a stone house with a mansard roof to the south. Across the street, a wooden fence fronting the Rusticraft fence company lies where the road once passed under the railroad tracks at Green Tree Station. Green Tree Camp offered supplies and camping here for 50 cents a night, according to the 1927 Mohawk-Hobbs guide. Because that road no longer exists, we proceed west into Malvern and turn north on Bridge Street, which crosses over the tracks; on the other side, it meets Old Lincoln Highway.

We turn right and backtrack briefly to the east on Old Lincoln Highway and soon come across a cement Lincoln Highway marker to the south, or our right. It points to the right, indicating where the tunnel used to come through. Absolutely nothing remains of that underpass. There's

Looking southwest along the Lincoln Highway (King Road) to the Malvern underpass, December 1931. The stone house on King (at Arlington Avenue) remains, but Jones' Service Station, the Green Tree train station, and the underpass (out of sight to the right) do not. On the right, between the station and the pole, note the Rusticraft fence company, which remains but has expanded its facility to the foreground. Also note the Lincoln Highway sign below the gas pumps and the tiny sign above it pointing left to a tourist camp, likely the Green Tree Camp. COURTESY PA STATE ARCHIVES, RG-12 DEPT. OF HIGHWAYS

now a driveway there, but according to a nearby resident, the station sat where the house is now, and the road ran about 10 yards west of the driveway; you can see traces of pavement at the nearby fence. The road we're on becomes Central Avenue and continues to Route 30, but since it's not the Lincoln, we turn around here and head west again on Old Lincoln Highway.

To our north, we pass the Villa Maria Academy, and at the intersection with Bridge Street, Herzak & Herzak Auto Repair has an old air pump and a green neon-ringed clock in its window. We continue downhill, and near the bottom there's a sign for Old Lancaster Avenue to the left, which we follow. This old section of the Lincoln leads to the General Warren Inn, opened in 1745 as the Admiral Vernon after English Admiral Edward Vernon. It was renamed the Admiral Warren in honor of

Peter Warren and his naval victories during the French and Indian War; after the Revolution, it was finally renamed the General Warren for American patriot Joseph Warren, who died at the Battle of Bunker Hill.

Just before the inn, the road curves north and dead-ends. The Lincoln originally went through a stone underpass here, and though it's still visible, it's completely filled in. We must turn around and backtrack to Old Lincoln Highway. There, we turn left and go downhill to Route 30 (also called Lancaster Pike on the street sign).

Turning left, or west, on Route 30, we pass under railroad tracks and arrive at the Route 29 intersection. The Warren Inn underpass would have emerged to the south, across from the intersection. Just past Route 29 to the north is a tiny motel for sale.

At the intersection of Conestoga Road (Route 401), a McDonald's to the south was once the location of the Candlewyck Diner, replaced by Delite's fast food, itself later replaced. Tourist cabins lie nearby to the south, possibly Brackbill's Motel, which was 2 miles west of Paoli. Its

Approaching the General Warren Inn, looking west, December 1931. The 1928 cement Lincoln Highway marker indicates a right turn to an underpass, which today is filled in but still visible. COURTESY PA STATE ARCHIVES, RG-12 DEPT. OF HIGHWAYS

postcard shows cabins and a "colonial homestead," and it advertised "Christian Standards."

As we head west, the road begins a long straightaway, and we soon come to the Frazer Diner, a c. 1940 O'Mahony-made diner. Frank Cavalati, owner and former operator who lives behind the diner, says it was originally the Paoli Diner. Inside, operator Tony Pilotti has kept intact the six tables, 18 stools, tile floor, wood trim, and marble counter. Back on the road, Swayne's Camp is listed in this vicinity by the 1927 Mohawk-Hobbs guide, 2 miles past Green Tree Camp. The 1940 Shell guide shows Swayne's Tourist Camp offering 12 cabins.

We pass Lincoln Court Shopping Center and soon come to the Quaker Motel to the north, operated since 1948 by Mr. and Mrs. Henry Eyden. It retains the charm of a midcentury motel—no telephones, but beautiful knotty pine walls and furniture, plus reading lamps with deer-hoof bases. Out front is a large, round, blue sign with neon. Farther up the hill, Lisa Marie Psychic Readings is in one of the old Hillcrest Cabins to the north. We cross Route 352 south.

Trucks parked along Route 30, somewhere between Paoli and Philadelphia, April 1946. COURTESY STANDARD OIL (NJ) COMPANY COLLECTION, PHOTO-GRAPHIC ARCHIVES, UNIVERSITY OF LOUISVILLE

The Quaker Motel is a time capsule surrounded by change. When guests arrive, necessities are laid out on the beds, including large maps of Pennsylvania featuring stylized illustrations of c. 1960 tourist spots. (PHOTO 1993)

    The Malvern Meeting House Restaurant to the south was the Frazer Restaurant and Tourist Camp. The back cabins, which face each other, are now painted dark green to match the eatery. To the west, Frazer Lanes has a big plastic bowling pin by the road. We pass Planebrook Road and Barry's Sports Car Service, and next door is a roadhouse with cabins behind. Across from it is Eastwood Automotive, which sells auto-theme gifts, including a Corgi-brand Mack truck decorated as one of the Goodyear Wingfoot Express trucks with "Coast to Coast Lincoln Highway" emblems.

    At the top of the next hill in Glenloch is the Sheraton Great Valley hotel built around an eight-bay wide stone house. Across the street, hidden by trees, is a Swiss Gothic mansion originally known as Glen Loch ("lake of the glen" in Scottish). The house, with peaked roofs, gables, and a four-story corner tower, was built in 1867 for a quarter million dollars by William Lockwood, who made his fortune manufacturing paper shirt collars. The surrounding estate included three separate farms, tenant houses, and four railroad stations. One station, Glen Loch, was the last

FRASER TOURIST CAMP
20 Modern Cabins — Single and Double.
Clean, Sanitary and Roomy. Some with
showers, baths, toilet and hot and cold
water.
High Elevation, picturesque scenery. Location Route Lincoln Highway, 22 miles
west of Phila., Pa., at Fraser, Pa.

6829

The Fraser Tourist Camp offered "20 Modern Cabins." Many of those cabins remain. PRIVATE COLLECTION

Main Line station of the Pennsylvania Railroad. The railroad adopted the name without asking permission, however, so angering Lockwood that he changed his estate's name to Loch Aerie.

Lockwood also gave the railroad permission to use water from the estate's springs to power its steam locomotives, but the railroad took too much and left the estate without water. Although Lockwood won most of the ensuing legal battles, it left him broke. Today only the house and 26 acres remain from the original estate.

Lockwood's daughters lived here until 1967, when the property was bought by Daniel Tabas, owner of the Tabas Hotel in Downingtown. It was abandoned and gained notoriety for a shootout there between rival motorcycle gangs. Tony Alden bought the house in 1980 and has since lovingly restored it to its original grandeur.

We cross the intersection for Route 202, where a recently completed Route 30 bypass goes west to the current bypass around Downingtown. Beyond, we see white stucco buildings on each side for the Church Farm School, a prep school for boys. The 1914 *Blue Book* alerts drivers in this area to "blow horn at each cross-road or fork for next three miles," a primitive form of traffic control.

We go over Ship Road, past the Ship Inn to the north, a 1796 tavern that has the "25 M to P" Lancaster Pike marker inside. A sign says we've entered Exton, and to the north is the former William's Deluxe Cabins, built in 1937 as separate cabins. Founder Leon H. Williams added more cabins through the years but sold them in 1964, when they were renamed the Tudor Motor Inn. Most are now linked under one roof and used as weekly or monthly apartments. There were two adjacent gas stations: what is now Ichabod's News, in a Tudor-style building with a steeply pitched gable roof, was an Esso, and a tiny auto tag service was a Texaco. The whole complex was listed on the National Register for Historic Places in 1988.

Crossing more tracks, within .2 mile we're at the former Guernsey Cow restaurant, originally called the Dairy Grill. A 1960 postcard tells us that it was under the same management since 1931. The "World's Largest Cow" was across the road but has been taken down. The restaurant is scheduled for demolition, and it looks like a five-bay stone house next to it may go too, replaced by an expansion of Exton Square Mall.

William's Deluxe Cabins in Exton were built in 1937 by Leon Williams, who ran the affair until 1964. This postcard is by the Albertype company, known for making nicely tinted but not very detailed cards.

The Guernsey Cow in Exton was well known for its huge cow across the street. The restaurant is closed and scheduled for demolition.

An early 1920s view of Clyde Reese's Valley Creek Coffee House, which sat across from the Guernsey Cow restaurant just east of Route 100, about where Mario's restaurant is today. There is a Lincoln Highway sign on the pole.
COURTESY BERNIE HEISEY

Across the street is Mario's Eastside Italian restaurant, the approximate location of the former Valley Creek Coffee House. Earl Reese, owner of the Ingleside Diner west of Downingtown, recalls that his parents operated the coffeehouse from 1921 to 1945. The local post office was also in their restaurant, and his mother "did all the cooking and was also the postmistress."

We reach the junction of Route 100. A dozen miles south of here is Kennett Square, home to Longwood Gardens, with its botanical displays, and Phillips' Mushroom Museum, which bills itself as "the only museum that fully explains the history, lore and mystique of mushrooms" and honors the "World's Mushroom Capital."

West of Route 100 is Whiteland Towne Center, site of the former Exton Drive-In Theater, which closed in the late 1980s after resorting to X-rated movies. We cross Whitford Road; a store selling reproduction hardware is in the former Whitford White House, an old inn. Now we head into farmland sprinkled with nineteenth-century houses and open

At Reese's the pace of change in just the last several decades becomes apparent. The gas pumps have clock faces, and on the White Flash pole a sign reads, "Atlantic Credit Cards honored." The Reeses owned the coffeehouse until 1945.
COURTESY LINDA MAHAN

fields. As we pass from West Whiteland Township to East Caln Township, the Route 30 bypass crosses overhead. We continue straight on the original Lincoln Highway, now Business Route 30, and pass Mickey Rooney's Tabas Hotel to the north; the deserted Downingtown Inn across the street recently fell to a Hechinger's store.

To the north, we quickly come upon the Downingtown Market Place, an old mall with individual outdoor entrances for each store in addition to an inner mall. It opened in 1952 and now thrives by being like the marketplaces of old; in addition to selling tools, food, and other essentials, the mall is like a flea market with a little bit of everything. It's not very fancy, but how many other malls offer a golf driving range and the state's largest remote-control race-car track? In the past year, gun, dog, cat, and horse shows, as well as wrestling tournaments, were also featured.

Across the street is Jim's Service Center with a little Mobil Pegasus on it. We pass more stone buildings, including a Friends meetinghouse to the south .5 mile later. Route 113 meets us from the north, and in the next block, we see older houses of all varieties, including the former Downingtown Tea House to the north, today a

THE TEA HOUSE
Lincoln Highway (U. S. Route 30)
Downingtown, Penna.

Tel. Downingtown 440

Will re-open for its Thirtieth Season
on Thursday, April 2, 1942

Luncheons   Afternoon Tea   Suppers

PARKING FACILITIES

LILLIAN C. MOORE   MARION L. ANDERSON

BLANCHE P. IRVINE
American Antiques
Furniture · Glass · China · Silver

Teahouses, such as this one in Downingtown, were common early in the twentieth century. The 1947 edition of Duncan Hines's Adventures in Good Eating *states of this one: "It is unusual to be seated at such a well-appointed table. Linen and Wedgewood [sic] add distinction to the very good meal." The house was built by Thomas Downing in 1729.*

BRIDGE ACROSS BRANDYWINE CREEK ON LINCOLN HIGHWAY, DOWNINGTON, PA.

This 1801 stone bridge still carries traffic across the Brandywine in Downing-town. COURTESY JOHN H. McCLINTOCK

CPA's office. Now we enter the Downingtown business district. At the main intersection are State Route 282 west to our north and Route 322 east to our south. Here, early motorists could have stopped at the Swan Hotel, which claimed to be "the Lincoln Highway's greatest eating place." To the north at Kerr Park is the c. 1700 Downingtown Log House, the oldest documented extant structure in Chester County. We cross the east branch of Brandywine Creek on an 1801 stone bridge, and continue straight as the right lane angles off to Route 322 west.

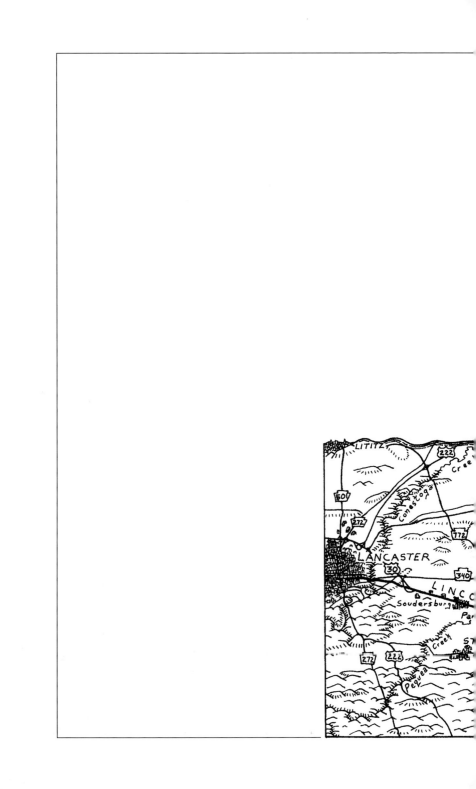

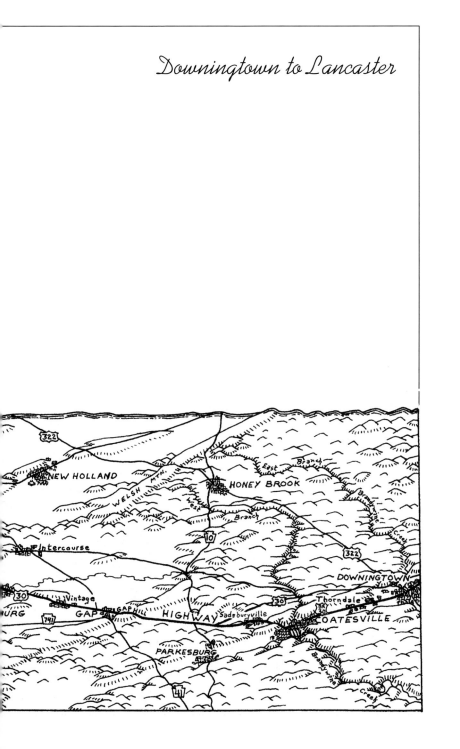

Downingtown to Lancaster

Downingtown was settled in 1710 by emigrants from Birmingham, England. It once had many paper and textile mills and was originally named Milltown, but it was later renamed for local mill owner Thomas Downing. The town was a major supply depot during the Revolutionary War (as was Lancaster).

We follow the Business Route 30 west signs heading out of Downingtown and pass more businesses, including the Downingtown Diner, recently renamed the Cadillac Diner. The original Downingtown Diner was known to millions for being smothered with slime in the 1957 movie *The Blob*. It was demolished and replaced in the early 1960s, but it's still in the same location, is the same make of diner (Silk City), and had the same name until recently, when new owners renamed it. One of

A truck is stalled between Paoli and Coatesville, April 1946. COURTESY STANDARD OIL (NJ) COMPANY COLLECTION, PHOTOGRAPHIC ARCHIVES, UNIVERSITY OF LOUISVILLE

Zinn's Diner opened in 1957 at Mr. and Mrs. Christian Zinn's Ingleside Farms, Thorndale. Now the Ingleside Diner, it has been owned and operated by Edna and Earl Reese since 1973. A Zinn's Diner still operates near Denver, Pennsylvania.

the owners is Howard Twaddell, son of the Twaddells who ran Twaddell's Diner in Paoli. This diner had been remodeled and sat empty for years but is now restored with a fifties theme.

Heading west from the diner, we pass Modern Cleaners to the north; it looks as though it could have been a theater at one time, with a pointed overhang and neat neon sign, but the cleaner has been there for many years. One mile from the diner, we pass Ciarlone's Dairy Bar drive-in, selling cakes, pies, and novelties. Railroad tracks are to our south, and 1 mile from Ciarlone's, we pass Ice Cream Junction to the south.

We're surrounded by strip businesses and malls as we pass a turn for Route 340 west to our right. This was originally the Great Conestoga Road, which went west to Lancaster; from 1733 to 1741 it was improved and renamed the Philadelphia Road, one of the early King's Highways. It was later superseded by Lancaster Pike. Heading into Thorndale, we pass a Kmart, the approximate location of the small White Orchard Camp, listed in the Mohawk-Hobbs guide as 2.6 miles west of Downingtown in 1927.

We arrive at the Ingleside Diner, originally called Zinn's, opened Christmas Eve 1956 by Mr. and Mrs. Christian Zinn, their third diner in the area. (Their first was in Coatesville 10 years earlier, perhaps the Town Diner.) Built by the Fodero company, the L-shaped diner arrived in seven prebuilt sections. The Zinns sold it in 1966 to the Scott brothers, who renamed it the Ingleside. The current owners are Edna and Earl Reese (son of Clyde Reese of the Valley Creek Coffee House in Exton). They bought it in 1973 and have retained the feel of the old diner—even the rooftop sign is still in the same pink neon script as the original, as is a matching bakery sign. A miniature golf course was also added out back in recent years.

The Coatesville Drive-In Theater was also in this vicinity years ago on the north side of the road. Surprisingly, newspaper ads from the summer of 1955 indicate the theater was showing family fare on weekends but X-rated movies during the rest of the week.

To the west .5 mile is the "34 M to P" Lancaster Pike marker, in the deep grass to the south. It's near a speed limit sign, across from Barley Station strip mall. A little over 1 mile from the diner is Jim's Steaks, a drive-in restaurant to the south.

We cross the Caln Bridge over railroad tracks. The 1930 iron bridge used to zigzag over the tracks, but it was rebuilt from 1992 through 1994. The folks at the Crestmont Two Diner, located right at the west end of the bridge, can tell you all about that. Manager Susan Michnuk says the diner

The Gizmo, just east of Coatesville, called itself the "Home of Chicken in the Basket." "Good" and "Food" alternated on the neon sign.

cut its payroll by two-thirds during the bridge closure. The shiny stainless-steel diner is a 1948 Paramount, and its silk-screened manufacturer's tag can still be found inside among the train decorations. The diner was formerly the Madison, then Anthony's, but when Susan's parents took over, they named it after Crestmont Farms, where they live. Susan adds that her parents bought it in 1978. "They used to come here when they were kids, and now they own it."

As we head into Coatesville, we pass through a residential section, then into a small business district where the street signs say East Lincoln Highway. Looking for the Town Diner at 823 East Lincoln Highway, we find it's gone, as is the Lincoln Highway Inn at 349 Main Street, replaced by Coatesville Towers apartments. Another landmark destroyed by urban renewal was the Coach and Four Inn; the hotel's name represented the number of horses accompanying a stagecoach. Ahead in the main business district, there's a big "Hot Bagels" sign to the south; Lipkin's, with a 1950s green glass and stainless-steel facade, to the north; and a little city park on the southwest corner at First Street.

Coatesville was named by its first postmaster, Moses Coates, though it's unclear whether he named it for himself or his grandfather of

The Town Diner was in Coatesville at 823 East Lincoln Highway, opposite the high school and not too far from today's Crestmont Two Diner.

LINCOLN HIGHWAY INN, ON LINCOLN HIGHWAY, COATESVILLE, PA.

The Lincoln Highway Inn was in downtown Coatesville at 349 Main Street. Advertisements in the LHA Road Guides and the 1927 Mohawk-Hobbs guide said, "30 modern rooms . . . meals 45 cents–$1."

the same name, an Irish Quaker who settled in Pennsylvania in 1717. Steel and textiles were long the town's major industries. The 1924 Lincoln Highway Association guidebook warns that the local speed limit was "15 miles per hour, enforced."

Continuing west, we cross over railroad tracks and a stone bridge and are surrounded by the mills of Lukens Steel, the world's largest steel

A sliver of bypassed road sits at the end of this 1930 iron bridge on the west end of Coatesville. (PHOTO 1991)

plate rolling mill when built. The Lincoln Diner once sat between Church Street and the Brandywine Creek, now a fenced parking lot for Lukens. The diner was a reconditioned O'Mahony purchased in 1935 and operated by Stan Viguers Sr. The diner stayed open 24 hours to accommodate shift workers from the mill. Viguers opened the LeMoyne Diner near Harrisburg in 1941 but closed this one in 1943, anticipating that he would be drafted for World War II. He also later operated the Harrisburg East Diner.

We start uphill, past the Route 82 turnoff, past turn-of-the-century row houses, and across a short iron bridge. Known locally as the "checkered bridge," after its old paint scheme, the 1930 bridge is so rusty that its demolition is imminent. At the end, a short piece of the old Lincoln

Breakfast at the Coatesville Valley Diner, 1.5 miles west of town, April 1946.
COURTESY STANDARD OIL (NJ) COMPANY COLLECTION, PHOTOGRAPHIC
ARCHIVES, UNIVERSITY OF LOUISVILLE

breaks off to the south. Business Route 30 heads through a rock cut, further evidence of a bypass. As we level, there's farmland to the north with some stone houses. The Valley View Diner, "Your Headquarters for Fine Food," was in this vicinity; a 1943 notepad from the diner placed it 1.5 miles west of Coatesville. It's probably the same diner later known as the Coatesville Valley Diner.

As the fields pass by, we come to Sadsburyville about 4 miles from downtown Coatesville. A 1799 eight-bay inn with two front gables, formerly the Sadsburyville Hotel or just The Tavern, is now Harry's restaurant, open daily. It's been run since 1973 by Harry and Athena Lymberis, and they're now assisted by their son John and their son-in-law. John researched the tavern for his architectural thesis, which aided in a recent restoration of the building. Both the inside and outside needed extensive work, and John says the dining room is now especially cozy with its exposed wooden beams.

Downhill, we pass Lincoln Crest Mobile Homes Park, the Sadsbury House to the south in a dip, and then to our north the remains of Drake's Spanish Court. The motel's west side is still intact, including the word "Office" above the corner door, but the name and the rest of the white paint is peeling badly. A later office and store that was built in the center

Sadsburyville was home to Conner's service station, restaurant, and tourist rooms. COURTESY D. B. GRUBBS

DRAKE'S SPANISH COURT
4 Miles W. of Coatesville, Pa.—Route 30
Sadsburyville, Pa.

YEAR 'ROUND CABINS
Steam Heated — Rooms with Bath
Individual Garages

OFFICE

"This is where I am sleeping tonite." Much remains of Drake's Spanish Court, 4 miles west of Coatesville, but you can no longer stay overnight. COURTESY BERNIE HEISEY

also remains, but it's now a house. The 1940 *Shell Tourist Accommodation Directory* lists 29 rooms starting at $1.50 a night. The 1945 AAA directory, which gave terse descriptions of each accommodation, describes Drake's 24 rooms as "inviting." Behind the motel is a new housing development called Lincoln Manor.

We pass more farms, and just before we rejoin the Route 30 bypass are a few cabins surrounded by pine trees to the north, the former Dunroaminn Camp. Today, an old iron sign says "Hilltop." The stretch of Route 30 after the bypass is full of trucks heading in and out of Lancaster, so be careful if you stop to take pictures.

At the top of the hill to the north is a stone house with a little stone marker, "43 M to P, 19 to L." A barn-shaped chiropractic office in the dip is the former Walnut Grove Farm, which had a 50-acre nut grove and made and sold Walnut Grove Candies. We soon pass the Keystone Motel to the south, which old postcards show with a gas station and snack bar out front and "Rooms as you like it," then we pass the former Olga's Restaurant and Atlantic gas, now just a home hidden behind trees. After passing a house advertising "Fresh Brown Eggs," we top a big hill and cross into Lancaster County. A farm to the south with a low stone

Dunroaminn Tourist Camp

LINCOLN HIGHWAY (R. 30) 5 MILES WEST OF COATESVILLE
20 MILES EAST OF LANCASTER, PA.
Cabins - Showers - Rooms - Bath - Trailer Parking

PKSBG. 12-R
Telephones: 126J-2

MAILING ADDRESS
PARKESBURG, PA.

The Dunroaminn Tourist Camp had an inviting name. Note the 1928 cement Lincoln Highway marker in the middle, next to the pole.

A Lancaster Pike marker sits in front of this typical eastern Pennsylvania stone house, just left of the telephone pole, indicating the mileage to Philadelphia and Lancaster: "43 M to P, 19 to L." Truck traffic west of the Coatesville bypass is always heavy. (PHOTO 1991)

wall was the Mt. Vernon Farm, best remembered for an old postcard advertising it for sale. Across the street is Mt. Vernon Auto Sales, and the adjacent building is likely the old Mt. Vernon Hotel.

We approach the top of a hill, and Dan's restaurant is to the north, though it never opened for business. Next door is the Antiques & Oddities store, which still has two tourist cabins nestled in the high grass. Owner Sam Cosella has been selling a little bit of everything out of a former restaurant for 25 years. Just ahead, the road branching to the north is called Old Highway; the main road is marked Lincoln Highway. The bypassed part lasts less than .5 mile and looks like a residential street now. It quickly crosses over to the south, serving as an access road to some houses, and then runs through a hilly, scenic farmstead. (*Note:* If you're traveling west, it's very hard to pull out from this road.)

The 1927 Mohawk-Hobbs guide lists the Queen Oak Camp with a store, camping, and eight furnished cottages 9 miles west of Coatesville. The 1940 Shell guide lists the Coach Light Camp with six cabins 9 miles west of Coatesville. Perhaps these two and the Edgewood were the same.

The Edgewood, 9 miles west of Coatesville, offered the use of a pool to patrons and displayed a sign stating, "no beer sold here." COURTESY BERNIE HEISEY

We continue downhill, overlooking farmland. In the front yard of a farmhouse is a well-cared-for marker that says, "47 M to P, 15 to L." We pass turns to State Route 897, then 41. The Route 41 intersection is very busy and includes the Gap Diner on the southwest corner. The diner has a neat vertical backlit sign and a banner on top announcing "Local-Dutch-Amer.-Cooking." Gap is immediately south on 41 and is so named because of a gap in the mountain ridge. William Penn visited here in 1700; legend has it that Penn Rock, just south on 41, is where he plotted his land holdings.

After passing a couple of old garages, we come to the intersection of Route 772, which has a historic house on every corner. Actually, 772 no longer cuts straight across—the road to the north has been slightly rerouted to the west, though the old alignment is still obvious. The four houses, named the Kennedy Houses for their builder, were the first houses in the village of Gap (then called Rising Sun).

Taking pictures in this area can be a frightening venture, and in fact, PennDOT wants to widen the road from Route 41 to Route 896, but houses such as these would be threatened. The corridor averages 20,000 vehicles per day, 20 percent more during tourist season, plus horse-drawn carriages. A complete bypass has been ruled out, but not a one-directional bypass, which would leave the road here one-way also. The numerous historic resources have led to the designation of this stretch of highway as one of the "10 Most Endangered Scenic Byways" by Scenic America, a Washington-based national conservation group.

We pass the small Oh! Shaw Motel to the south, named for the original owners. It has changed little over the years and still has a great sign with "Motel" in neon and an arrow made of little incandescent bulbs. It also has a sign indicating "American owned and operated." Just ahead is the Stage Coach Motel, opened in 1960 by the Martin family next to a 1794 stagecoach stop known as the Sign of John Adams and across from a large stone barn. Jennings' tourist camp was also near here in the 1920s.

We head uphill, past a sign for Groff Tourist Home farm home lodging, and we come around a bend to find Lengacher's Swiss Cheese House. This is one of the few old-style roadside businesses left, and it's a must stop. You'll find a selection of Pennsylvania Dutch foods, candies, apple butter, pretzels, lots of cheeses, and really good fresh sandwiches. Art and Martha Lengacher, and now their daughter Edith, have run the

The Oh! Shaw Motel in Gap still has its catchy name.

Lengacher's Swiss Cheese House, in Kinzers, has remodeled some over the years, but it's one of the few vintage lunch stops left in the area. This postcard states: "Arthur and Martha Lengacher make their own delicious and nutritious Swiss Cheese. The Lengachers came to Lancaster County from Switzerland a number of years ago." COURTESY CY HOSMER

place since 1957, and even before that they had a little road stand where they sold gas and cheese. They made their own cheese until recently, when state regulations made it too difficult. Oh well, you can still see the big spotless copper kettles through the glass windows. The whole place is beautiful, and you can even have your lunch at an outdoor picnic table.

Frank Graham of Gap motoring on the Lincoln Highway in 1926. COURTESY
UNIVERSITY OF MICHIGAN, SPECIAL COLLECTIONS LIBRARY

Having eaten enough, we head west again, past the Paradise Hills
Motel and the Kinmo Motel to the south. Across from them is the Rough
& Tumble Engineers Historical Museum, displaying antique farm equipment. We pass through the tiny town of Kinzers, and a sign alerts us,
"Next light, turn left for Red Caboose Motel." The novelty of this motel,
located just south of our route, is that each room is an actual train
caboose, and the TVs are in pot-bellied stoves. As we enter Vintage, we
see the Vintage general store, and the Vintage Sales Stable has a life-size
cow statue out front.

This route was part of Lancaster Pike, and when the 1918 *Red Road
Book* was published, there were still a number of tollgates along the
route. West of Kinzer, there were four: at 2, 4, 7.5, and 10.5 miles distant, the last at the Witmer Bridge into Lancaster.

Farther west, the Dutch Town and Country Inn to the north is a
modern restaurant, not the older one portrayed in postcards, and ahead, a
"51 M to P, 11 to L" stone marker sits in a front yard on the north side.
Descending a hill, we pass Basketville to the north and the huge Den-
linger lumberyard to the south, former site of Rosey's Auto Graveyard.
Paradise Motor Lodge is hidden to the south, and we find a cement Lincoln Highway marker behind the guardrail to the south just before crossing over railroad tracks. The little village on the west side is in old
guidebooks as Leaman Place.

In 1919 Rosey's Auto Graveyard was a big enough attraction to warrant a post-card, but it's gone, and so is its treasure trove of old cars.

Mr. and Mrs. John Kellenberger operated this restaurant from 1937 to 1945 in Paradise. Originating as the Sign of the Buck tavern, it later served as a residence and then, in the 1920s, as Aunt Sue's Kitchen and Paradise Lodge. COURTESY BERNIE HEISEY

We quickly pass into Paradise, settled about 1800 by Dunkards and Mennonites, German Anabaptists. A mile after the bridge is an Exxon Quick Mart, which used to be Milley's Service Station.

Old houses line the road, and as we cross another bridge, the 1740 Revere Tavern, now a Best Western, is to the north; to the south, Will Char Gifts sells hex signs, local handicrafts, and lawn ornaments. We pass Fisher Motors, an old canopied garage, then, to the south, the Paradise Village Shops, offering more crafts and collectibles. The center of it all is Jacob and Jane Zook's house, now home to Jacob Zook's Hex Shop. In 1942, Zook bought three hex signs from a paint salesman, spawning a lifetime love affair with the art form. Today, Zook's hexes are sold worldwide. Zook is now assisted by his daughter Jane Witmer (a twelfth-generation Pennsylvania Dutch), who creates new hex designs, and Ivan Hoyt, who carries on the tradition of hand-screening the designs. The colorful hex signs are said to ward off evil and bring good luck. They are often found on barns, but not those of the Amish, Mennonite, or other plain sects.

Milley's sold tires, sporting goods, clothing, and appliances. "Sunday August 22, 1948. I thought it would be interesting to get some cards from here to see what Paradise really looked like, but this is all I could get—probably because it was Sunday—nothing much open. Still, if you were out of gas, or had a flat, this would probably look like Paradise to you." The building survives as a gas station and minimart. COURTESY BERNIE HEISEY

*Professor Johnny Ott, hexologist, and Jacob Zook, the "Hex Man of Paradise,"
offered signs for every situation, from "sore feet" to "farmer with unhappy
pigs" to "mother-in-law troubles." Zook is still the first name in hex signs.*

Down the road, to the north, is Almost Paradise, which offers more
lawn ornaments; on the south side, across from the E.U.B. Church, is
the former Strine's Motel, a brick building with a canopy. Less than .5
mile later is a rambling building that was once Boyer's Restaurant and
Swiss cheese plant.

Going downhill, we come to Mr 3 Ls, a big paper collectibles store.
You'll find a little bit of everything here, though with minimal organization. (Who has time with so much stuff?) Look for the yellow sign to the
north. Ahead is a small Red Carpet Inn with about 15 rooms.

Finally, we come to another of those increasingly rare mid-twentieth-
century roadside attractions, Dutch Haven, easily identifiable by its tall
windmill. According to owner Paul Stahl, the first business here was
called Franklin's Windmill Inn, which sold ice cream and gasoline. Dutch
Haven was constructed around that building and opened in 1946 by Roy
and Alice Weaver to offer Pennsylvania Dutch cooking and a gift shop
loaded with all sorts of souvenirs. The complex grew to include other
buildings and attractions, such as Animal Haven and Chief Yellow Hands
Indian Trading Post, but the nonhistoric buildings were sold after Stahl
bought the business in 1991; they now comprise the adjacent Village of
Dutch Delights, which includes a barbecue restaurant and antiques store.

Dutch Haven has been slightly remodeled and now offers crafts in its
windmill-topped building along with its famous shoo-fly pie, a traditional

Two miles west of Paradise c. 1930. Note the interurban tracks to the right.
COURTESY PA STATE ARCHIVES, RG-12 DEPT. OF HIGHWAYS

Boyer's, 7 miles east of Lancaster, advertised its Swiss cheese factory, restaurant, gift shop, and tourist accommodations. It later became Brown's and consisted only of a restaurant and gift shop. COURTESY NED BOOHER

Pennsylvania Dutch dessert made with white flour, brown sugar, cinnamon, refiners syrup, and other ingredients that make for a gooey pie. Stahl says he still uses the same recipe Alice Weaver brought here a half century ago, and he offers free samples in case you want to try it first. You can also pick up some great old Dutch Haven souvenirs such as postcards or place mats.

The Netherlands-style windmill plays to the local use of the word "Dutch," but the eighteenth-century settlers here were not actually Dutch, but Germans. The Amish, Brethren, Lutherans, Mennonites, Moravians, and others who settled locally were German religious refugees from the Rhine Valley, not from Holland or the Netherlands. In their own language, they were *Deutsche,* and this word was corrupted to "Dutch." The misconception that the Pennsylvania Dutch were actually Dutch was further reinforced because most of the German settlers sailed to America from Rotterdam, Holland, a major port at the end of the Rhine River, which flows through Germany.

Just a couple doors down is Miller's Smorgasbord, famous for its wide spread of food. Unfortunately, some of these big buffet places can be pretty expensive, but Miller's continues to draw huge crowds. A gift

Once called "Ye Dutch Haven" and "Dutch Haven Amish Stuff, Inc.," the windmill-topped building still thrives as "Dutch Haven" by selling shoo-fly pies. In this 1950s-era view, it even attracts some locals.

Miller's Restaurant and Frozen Custard Shop

Miller's has grown into the most popular Pennsylvania Dutch smorgasbord in the area. It has always featured the traditional Dutch "seven sweets and seven sours" with each meal. COURTESY BERNIE HEISEY

shop was recently installed, but it offers mostly crafts and glassware. For roadside souvenirs, we'll have to wait a few miles.

At the traffic light, we can go north to Ronks or south to Mill Bridge Village. There you'll find the only remaining two-span covered bridge in Lancaster County, which, with 28 covered bridges, plus two on the border, has more than any other county in the state. The 1844 bridge also has a side entrance, apparently built to serve an adjoining road.

At the intersection we find Ronks Road Auto Sales in an old gas station; Ronks Motor Inn sits to the north. We continue through farmland dotted with homes and businesses, and to the north is the Wayside Inn bar and motel, its cabins replaced by a line of motel rooms. We also pass the Nomad Motel, which had a beautiful neon sign in the shape of a big curving arrow until 1993, when a plastic sign replaced it. It's good to see that the Lancaster Motel across the road still has its neon sign.

To the south we see an Amoco Sico-Serve Plaza, once the site of Hart's U.S. 30 Diner. It was bought by an actor from the "Dallas" TV show and moved to California in the mid-1980s. Taking its place across the street is Jennie's Diner, a mid-1950s Silk City-built diner with a period "Air Conditioned" sign above the door.

Meiers' Wayside Inn, 5 miles east of Lancaster, boasted camping, heated cabins, and "quick lunch." The cabins are gone, but the Wayside Inn remains. COURTESY BERNIE HEISEY

A souvenir ashtray from Hart's U.S. 30 Diner.

The U.S. 30 Diner is now the site of an Amoco gas station and minimart.

The Route 896 intersection was a quiet place just a few years ago, but the Rockvale Square outlet mall has changed that. On the southeast corner, the Robert Fulton Steamboat Inn is a full-size replica of a steamboat. Built in the tradition of Bedford's Ship Hotel, it offers all of today's amenities. Some 20 miles to the south on Route 222, the Robert Fulton Highway, is the birthplace of Robert Fulton, whose *Clermont* was the first commercially successful American steamboat.

A farm show arena with a large cow out front once sat on the northwest corner, but it's been replaced by stores. To the northeast is one old holdover, however: the Dutch Pines Motel. On the southwest corner is Rockvale Square. Behind the mall lies a lone tourist cabin from the Whispering Pines camp, which was likely displaced by the outlet mall. You'll find the pale yellow cabin in a yard on Rockvale Road.

Just past Rockvale, to the north, is the Willows Restaurant and Motel. Starting in 1931, it was a landmark in this then mostly rural area. Judging by the number of postcards they produced, the restaurant and motel prospered over the years. There are still 33 motel rooms in tree-lined surroundings, and the restaurant is now part of the Glass Kitchen

Whispering Pines Camp, 5 miles east of Lancaster, was likely where Rockvale Square now sprawls. "Where we stayed August 1938. . . . Fine cottages and fine meals." COURTESY CY HOSMER

THE "WILLOWS". LINCOLN HIGHWAY EAST - ROUTE 30 - LANCASTER PA. R.D. 4

This aerial view of the Willows shows the cabins behind the restaurant, just to the left of a large greenhouse.

chain, but the Willows name is also used by a more widely advertised area resort, and another outlet mall has opened across the road.

On the west side of the Willows is the Willow Hill Bridge, a covered bridge that you can still drive through. It's a restoration of a historic covered bridge, completed in 1962 using many parts from another bridge; a nearby plaque tells the whole story. On the other side of the bridge is the Amish Farm & House, which offers tours of an 1805 home and operating farm, including a springhouse, lime kiln, and lots of animals. To the south is the Canadiana Motor Inn.

Now we get into a mostly modern strip of restaurants and motels, though they're geared to the local tourists. We pass the Family Style restaurant and shops, the older Congress Inn and the Classic Motel to the south, and the Garden Spot Motel to north.

We approach Wonderland Cinema, the Wax Museum of Lancaster County, and finally, our souvenir mecca, Dutch Wonderland. It's an early-1960s amusement park, heavy on Pennsylvania Dutch themes but with a huge castle for a facade. Inside, the gift shop has crafts and all kinds of good stuff with the Dutch Wonderland name on them, including

Dutch Wonderland peeks from behind the Running Pump Inn, which it displaced about 1960. The 1799 inn was moved across the street to the east of Joe Myers' Restaurant, now Lapp's Restaurant. The inn is now a private home.

rulers, shirts, keychains, magnets, ashtrays, baby bibs . . . you name it. It's worth a stop just to see the gift shop.

Across the road, the former Running Pump Inn overlooks Lapp's Restaurant; the Dutch "Horn of Plenty" Restaurant used to be here (itself in an old Howard Johnson's). Also to the south are the Mill Stream Factory Shops, site of the old Sky-Vue Drive-In Theater. Ahead is Lincoln Beverage and Lincoln Properties to the north. The Lancaster Mennonite Historical Society, with bookshop, museum, and library, is just south on Millstream Road. Here, you can learn about the differences between the Amish and the Mennonites and get assistance in locating Mennonite tourist homes and good Pennsylvania Dutch food. There is also a full-size reproduction of the Hebrew Tabernacle.

Going uphill, the Dutch View Motel (on the north) and the Dutch Village Motel (on the south) were both recently converted to an Econolodge. At the top of the hill we reach the Route 30 bypass, where the old Lincoln Highway becomes Route 462 and remains so through Lancaster and York. It would be nice to see the road renamed Old Lincoln Highway, or at least Business Route 30, for there's no indication that 462 is the old Lincoln. Now on 462, we dip under the bypass, and to the south is the Amish Homestead, like the Amish Farm and House but now closed. Across from it to the north is a deserted building that used to be the Garden Spot China Company. Starting in 1935, its products—pottery, gardenware, glassware, and Pennsylvania Dutch gifts—were displayed in front of the long building, but the store has relocated. At the top of the hill to the south is the Donut Tree, with a wavy tree sign, the former site of the Hyway Diner, operated by the Savage family.

Beth Savage recalls: "The Hyway Diner was owned and operated by my grandfather, Roy Arnold Savage, who was always known as Arnold. My grandfather also leased and ran the Mobil gas station next door. The diner was bought and moved from some unknown location in Philadelphia in 1937 because he wanted to own his own business after the Depression. (He had worked previously as a plasterer.) My father, Robert Arnold Savage, worked in the diner on and off from high school

A colorfully decorated outlet mall now occupies the site of the Sky-Vue Drive-In Theater, shown here in 1981, its last season. COURTESY REBECCA SHIFFER

*Inside the Hyway Diner, just east of Lancaster, about 1940. Behind the counter,
Roy Arnold Savage is at far right and his son Robert is third from right. Savage
also operated an adjacent Mobil station.* COURTESY BETH L. SAVAGE

in 1938 until 1943, when he went to the Army, and he ran the diner for a
year before going to college in 1949."

After Arnold died in 1951, his widow, Elva Thomas Savage, owned
and ran the diner until about 1956, when she sold it. "The guy who
bought it from her went out of business in about six months. My mom
and dad were married in 1950, and they owned and operated another
restaurant on the Lincoln Highway in the mid-1950s, known as the Window Box. It was located at the corner of Washington Road, a quarter
mile west of the Coatesville Airport, in a nineteenth-century house right
on the road. When Lukens Steel had a major shutdown, the economy
went downhill considerably, and they sold out and moved. The building
burned to the ground some years later."

To the north is the Lincoln Haus Inn, which bills itself as an Amish
bed and breakfast. The *American Motel Association Motel Guide and
Trip Diary* for 1941 listed another tourist home on the east end of town:

the Blue Spuce, a "beautiful stucco home with green shutters" and a "green neon sign," run by Mrs. Lawrence. Approaching Lancaster, at Bridgeport we meet up with the Old Philadelphia Pike, Route 340, which has been to our north. The Mari-Bob Diner, which once sat at this intersection, had a sign advertising "Nothing fancy, just good ole shirt sleeve eatin'."

We continue downhill into Conestoga Woods, crossing the Conestoga River over a long cement bridge (site of the 1880 Witmer Bridge), past the 1742 Conestoga Bar and Restaurant and an old brick garage to the north, and start back uphill. The original route through Lancaster went straight on King Street, but that's now one-way going east, so we get in the right lane and turn right onto North Broad Street, still following Route 462. A couple blocks later, we turn left onto East Walnut Street, which is also one-way.

The streets are lined with row houses as we head into the downtown area. We can stop at the Visitors Center by turning south on North Duke Street and following the signs. Penn Square is one block south of us, at Queen and King Streets.

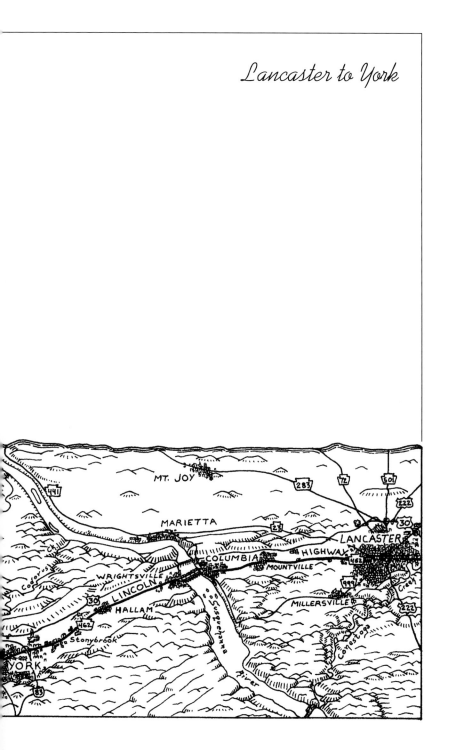

Lancaster was a major city during the Revolutionary War and served as capital of the nation for one day, September 27, 1777, as Congress fled Philadelphia from the British. It was also the state capital from 1799 to 1812. The region is a rich agricultural area, the reason Lancaster Pike was built between the city and Philadelphia. Mention of Lancaster also brings to mind images of Amish buggies and farms; not only have roadside businesses capitalized on this, but they also have perhaps perpetuated the image. Today, Lancaster is the nation's fifth most popular travel destination. People's fascination with the "plain people," as the Amish and Mennonites are called, has led to an overwhelming wave of curiosity and tourism surrounding these people who shun publicity.

Heading west from Lancaster's Queen Street, we cross North Prince Street (at 146 North Prince is the Book Haven, a store selling used books) and a block later is the Outback Bird and Reptile Shop, in an old gas station. Just after North West End Avenue, we get in the left lane to follow Route 462 west, and turn left onto Race Avenue. There are directional signs for Wheatland, the home of President James Buchanan, the state's only native-born president. The estate is named for the nearby wheatfields. To follow the old Lincoln west, stay in the right lane and turn right on Columbia Avenue, Route 462.

We'll briefly double back, however, and head east following King Street, the original route of the Lincoln. We pass some row houses, and very soon we have to stay to the right at a fork in the road. We follow Route 462 east here, and we reach South Prince Street after just 1 mile. As we approach Penn Square, it's no longer a traffic circle, so we stay in one of the two right lanes to continue straight. The Central Market on the square is open Tuesday, Friday, and Saturday, offering a wide variety of food. It's been in operation since the 1730s. Almost as old is Demuth's, 114 East King Street. It's the oldest tobacco shop in the United States.

Past the square .5 mile, we see the King Theater Apartments, an interesting adaptive reuse of an old deco theater; the neon sign has even been preserved. Then we pass the Lancaster County Prison, which looks like a big castle, not unlike Dutch Wonderland. After just 2 miles, the road converges with the oncoming lanes of 462.

Back at Race Avenue, we head west on Route 462, passing the Toll House Inn to the north and then a stone mill with "Maple Grove" painted on it to the south. Behind it there's a small bridge that led to the Maple

Grove swimming pool; the pool was recently filled in, however. To the southwest is the Maple Grove Diner, which looks like a mid-1970s chain restaurant; a similar place, Dempsey's Diner, sits to the north. Just past all of these is an old McDonald's sign with a single big golden arch, a pair of McDonald's (or someone's!) family coats of arms on the sign. Across from that is an old Arby's, now a Vietnamese restaurant. Columbia Avenue, a parallel road to the south here for a short distance, is an old highway segment.

According to the 1914 *Blue Book,* early Lincoln Highway travelers would have stopped at a tollgate in this vicinity and bought a ticket for 25 cents, then left coupons at three more stops between here and Columbia. After crossing the Susquehanna, another 18 cents would get travelers to York and 30 cents more to New Oxford, all the time using the coupon system.

We pass Route 741 and then 2208 Columbia Avenue, pictured in Hokanson's Lincoln Highway book; it looks like the road has been widened into Mrs. DeHart's front yard, and the "Tourists" sign is gone.

The Old Mill Hotel, built in 1777 and probably named for the Maple Grove Mill, advertised chicken and waffle dinners, as well as rooms: $1 for running water, $2 for those with a private bath. A porte cochere for autos was between the last two pillars, leading to the back of the house. COURTESY BERNIE HEISEY

Large swimming pools like the Maple Grove were once quite common but are a rare find today. Maple Grove pool, 1 mile west of Lancaster, held 1.5 million gallons of water before it closed and was filled in.

In the next block is Burnside Donuts in an old drive-in restaurant-style building, "Established 1946." There are some old gas stations, then the Lincoln Park plan of homes to the north and Leisure Lanes bowling to the south, and the small Mid-Way Hotel tavern back on the north side.

The Cozee Court lies 5 miles from downtown Lancaster. Owner Gerri Bomberger says that it used to be called National Cabins, run by a man named Schaffer. The cabins are now modernized and linked under one roof, and Gerri rents her rooms by the day or week. They look well cared for. The 1940 *Shell Tourist Accommodation Directory* lists Bower's Cabins as 5 miles west of Lancaster, which would put them right about here. This is also about where Brader's Drive-In and Miniature Golf Course was located in the 1950s.

We pass the Mountville Diner to the south, a plain-looking café with a short counter, and we cross a bridge to enter Mountville. Beyond town, we head into farmland and pass the 4 Seasons Motel, the former Lichty's, to the south. It's listed in the 1945 AAA directory as open April through December (before it stayed open all four seasons!) and as "best accommodations" for this area.

Owner J. O. Brader stated on his postcard, "We serve tasty sandwiches and Bar-B-Ques and Refreshments at our cool and delightful Snack Bar." Today Brader's is gone. COURTESY BERNIE HEISEY

Lichty's offered steam-heated cabins and free garages from April through December. It's now called the 4 Seasons Motel.

Route 30, meanwhile, remains north of us; we can see it at times, and some side roads offer access to it. The Pleasant View Motel is to the south at the Prospect Road intersection ("6 modern furnished units with tile baths," according to its 40-year-old postcards). A local motel listed in the *American Motel Association Motel Guide and Trip Diary* for 1947 is Bransby's Tourist Village, 1.5 miles east of Columbia, featuring brick cottages, "real Dutch cooking," and "circulating ice water," apparently an early form of air conditioning. A double room was $4.

An old road section branches off to the north, but it's blocked by a fence. It emerges behind the Prospect Diner, a 1954 Kullman-brand diner with an overhanging roof, a new feature of Kullmans at the time. At our last visit, everyone sang along when "Blueberry Hill" came on the jukebox! The old road rejoins 462, and we quickly come upon a neat vertical sign for the West Motel, its 12 rooms (with ceramic tile showers) set back from the road. On the north side is a stone turnpike marker "71P, 8L, 2C," indicating mileage to Philadelphia, Lancaster, and Columbia.

We head downhill past the Columbia Drive-In Theater, seeing cows lazily graze behind it in the summer. Now uphill, we pass a closed Jamesway and see a "Welcome to Columbia" sign telling us that the

Columbia Drive-In Theater was revived in recent years but is reportedly slated for development as a shopping center. (PHOTO 1992)

20 FAR EAST KENNELS ON LINCOLN HIGHWAY, COLUMBIA, PA.

A postcard of the Far East Kennels in Columbia, about 1928. A highway depart-
ment photograph refers to it as the "chow dog kennels," perhaps a clue to the
oriental pagoda theme. It's now the site of a factory. COURTESY CY HOSMER

town was founded in 1788. Just after that, the pagoda-style Far East
Kennels used to sit where the Grinnell factory at Malleable Road to the
north is now located. We go downhill past the Cycle Den in an old
garage, over railroad tracks, and back uphill, and then ease down past a
Napa auto parts store.

The parking lot adjacent to the Napa store is where Bob's Diner once
sat. Bob Weisser came back from World War II and heard that diners
were a good business—probably from his dad, who owned the land
where an older diner operated. The Napa, in fact, was Weisser's American garage, which Bob's dad built about 1922 to offer "Day and Night
Service," with a couple of pumps out front. In 1947 Bob and his mom
went to various diner factories and found that "Mountain View was the
best, very accommodating." They bought a diner with no previous experience, but they must have learned quickly—they stayed there 44 years.

The diner stayed open 24 hours until the Route 30 bypass was built
in the 1960s. Inside, the diner had lots of blue trim, including vinyl seats,
checkered curtains, part of the ceiling, and the door. Bob says that there
used to be jukeboxes in the booths, too, until the town put an amusement
tax through. Some of the sandwiches they were selling when they closed

Bob's Diner, at 134 Lancaster Avenue, has been replaced by a parking lot.

were the "Twister," the "Shifter," and the "Texas Doggie." The diner closed in October 1990 and was carted away in April 1991, with plans for restoration and resale. "I made a lot of friends in that diner," Bob says.

As we enter downtown Columbia on Route 462 (Lancaster Avenue), we pass 6th Street, where there was once a Lincoln Highway Garage. Ahead is the Rising Sun Hotel at Cherry Street. We then come to a five-way intersection. To the left is Locust Street, which you can follow to visit the Columbia Market House and Dungeon, part of which served as the local jail. The arch-roofed 1869 market building on South 3rd Street just south of Locust offers self-guided tours of the jail Monday through Saturday except in winter.

To follow the Lincoln, we bear right onto 5th Street, and in a couple blocks we must turn left on Chestnut Street to follow 462. Another interesting detour, straight ahead on 5th, is the National Watch and Clock Museum, featuring thousands of historic timepieces, including towering musical clocks. A tourist information center is a few blocks past that, near the Route 30 bypass.

On Chestnut, we head west and can see the art deco Veterans Bridge spanning the Susquehanna River. The town was originally called

Wright's Ferry but was renamed when being considered as the site for the nation's capital. The port was long an important shipping point for lumber and tobacco. The ferry was replaced by a bridge in 1812, which itself was replaced in 1834. This bridge lasted until it was burned down to halt the advance of the Confederate Army in 1863 during the Gettysburg Campaign. The next bridge was damaged by wind, and a steel one was built in 1897. Lincoln Highway motorists had to share this bridge with trains! The two could not share the toll bridge at the same time, however, leading to traffic jams when faulty signals would allow a car or horse-drawn wagon to proceed onto the bridge as a train approached. The bridge was demolished in 1964, but the stone piers remain.

The current Veterans Memorial Bridge was dedicated on Armistice Day 1930 and still serves Route 462, the Lincoln Highway; the Route 30 bypass to our north uses the Wright's Ferry Bridge, opened in 1970. The Veterans (or Columbia-Wrightsville or Lancaster-York Intercounty) Bridge is more than a mile long and crosses from Lancaster County into York County. According to the 1940 Pennsylvania WPA guide, red

Columbia-Wrightsville Bridge
Between York, Pa. and Columbia, Pa.
The Largest Bridge Spanning the
Susquehanna River

11009

Looking east to the ornamental Columbia-Wrightsville Bridge, opened in 1930. Its 48 arches made it the longest multiple arch concrete bridge in the world. It was a toll bridge until 1943. The old railroad and automobile bridge is to its left in this view, but only its piers remain today.

roses have traditionally been grown near the bridge's eastern (Lancaster) approach, white roses on the western (York) approach; this was derived from the English royal houses of Lancaster and York and their families' badges. A white rose symbolized the Yorks, a red the Lancasters (hence the fifteenth-century "War of the Roses"). You'll often see references to the White Rose or Red Rose city or county.

As we reach Wrightsville, we curve to the right, then left, and proceed uphill on Hellam Street, still Route 462 west. The original Lincoln Highway crossed the river from this street. At the top to the south is Schopf's Motel, recently the Silver Screen but originally known as Fogelsanger's. Back in the 1940s, its postcards showed teeter-totters and advertised "Cabins—Eats—Showers—Running Water—Innerspring Mattresses." Guests also had the use of a community kitchen. Today we still see some of the brick and frame cabins. Along with Fogelsanger's, the 1940 *Shell Tourist Accommodation Directory* lists Rainbow Place as also being 10 miles east of York, while a 1926 AAA camping guide lists Wake's camp 9 miles from York, accommodating 300 cars.

To the north, the Lincoln Lodge (also recently called the Yellow Shutter Motel) advertises mirrored waterbeds. Across from it is Dietz's roadside stand, selling a wide range of fruits and vegetables. There's little traffic on this stretch as we enjoy farmland on both sides. We pass Snyder's Motel to the south, with "Reasonable Rates, Weekly, Monthly," and about 8 rooms. Across from it is East Lincoln Bowling Lanes and Jim Mack's ice cream, miniature golf, arcade, and mini zoo. Through a dip, we come back up and pass the Alpine Motel (formerly Becker's) to the north. At the top, there's a big Wise-brand owl in front of an old building that looks like a general store, and some worn cabins behind it. This was likely Able's Cabins (and later Wagner's and Myers'), listed in the 1940 *Shell Tourist Accommodation Directory* as 7 miles east of York with 11 cabins and, like Fogelsanger's, a community kitchen.

Next door is the Hellam Township building, and across the street is a 1928 Lincoln Highway marker in front of a field of corn. A red brick gas station sits to the north, and then we enter the borough of Hallam less than 4 miles from the bridge. (The borough is spelled Hallam, the township Hellam.) The street is lined with houses, little garages, and other businesses, including a number of antiques stores, and to the south is a yellow 1730s inn known briefly as the Chicken Pie Place. Hallam also used to have a Lincoln Highway Garage.

In the center of town is Running Brook Antique Shop. Inside, Guy Keemer can be counted on to discern local history questions. He remembers Stewarts' Cabins, which sat right across the street from his shop. By the 1930s they were called Sellers', but by World War II they were gone, though an adjacent garage remained.

Within 1 mile we head out of town, passing a couple of nice baseball fields to the south, and the Frosty Freeze Drive-In with its nice neon sign. At the intersection of Eriesville Road, Route 30 is accessible to the north. On the northwest corner is the Tourist Inn, with a bar and restaurant and some rooms; to the south a bar was once part of Kreutz Kreek Manor, listed in the 1940 *Shell Tourist Accommodation Directory* for its 13 cabins with community showers and toilets but private kitchens. This undoubtedly began as Manor Camp, listed in the 1927 Mohawk-Hobbs guide for 25-cent camping and six cabins. Ahead, Second Time Around antiques to the north looks like it may also have been a motel.

About 1 mile from the Eriesville intersection is Shoe House Road to the north, which leads to the famous Haines Shoe House. Mahlon "The Shoe Wizard" Haines built a shoe sales empire in central Pennsylvania and northern Maryland that included more than 40 stores. Haines had a flair for outlandish advertising, calling himself "Colonel" Haines and

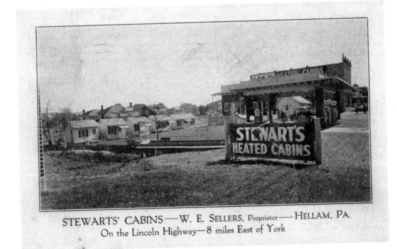

STEWARTS' CABINS——W. E. SELLERS, Proprietor——HELLAM, PA.
On the Lincoln Highway—8 miles East of York

Stewarts' (later Sellers') Cabins were at Prospect Street, now the site of a motorcycle dealer. The disgruntled sender of this postcard commented, "Cabins in this part of the country is punk like most everything else."

The Haines Shoe House was built as a promotional gimmick overlooking the Lincoln Highway. The Route 30 bypass now rumbles past its door just to the north. In 1995, Ruth Miller, 69, bought it. She plans an antiques shop with a food truck out front.

Fans of the Shoe House will find souvenir fans especially common, but there are many other collectibles. The signboard has nail holes, as if it had been on a post.

offering money to smokers if they promised to quit and to those in a crowd who could identify him. The Shoe House was his ultimate gimmick. Built in 1948 (when Haines was 73) of stucco over a wood and wire framework, there are seven rooms but really only enough space for a small family. The shoe motif is everywhere, including a stained glass window with an image of Haines in it. Haines offered the house free to elderly couples, who could live for a weekend like "kings and queens" at Haines's expense. After 1950 it was also offered to honeymooners who had a Haines Shoe Store in their town. After his death, it served as an ice cream parlor but deteriorated until it was bought at auction by Haines's granddaughter Annie Keller. She restored and briefly operated it as a tourist attraction, but a new owner has plans for an antiques shop.

Many postcards survive of Dr. Crandall's Health School, 5 miles east of York. It was an osteopathic sanitorium in a turn-of-the-century Georgian mansion on landscaped grounds. The 1924 Department of Highways guide lists the grounds as a spot for free camping, but the complex burned in 1949.

We see more businesses as we near York. The Chateau Motel to the north has wood framing around each section of doors. To the south is Mom's Diner in a block building; it began as a gas station in 1928 and has also been called Harvey's, Daisy's, and Myers' Diner through the years. Across the road is the Olde York Valley Inn, a big motel from the 1960s. We cross a bridge over railroad tracks—a quarter mile past it was Big Hand Camp, which, according to the 1927 Mohawk-Hobbs guide, had a general store and camping for 50 cents. At a curve (with Locust Grove Road to the south) is a historic marker for Camp Security, a stockade just south of here that held British prisoners during the Revolution.

We're now in Stonybrook, with the Stonybrook Drive-In Theater to the south. It has a beautiful curved entryway that looks almost like the back of a screen tower, but it's just a marquee with the theater's name. The drive-in closed in the 1980s, while an indoor cinema rose next door, but the sign, projection booth, snack bar, and screen still stand; only the ticket booths have gone recently.

The Spheel Grund Motel used to be next to the cinema, but it's gone. Nearby is the Flamingo Motel to the south, at the sign of the pink flamingo. To the north is a 1960s-style Maple Donuts with a neon sign. To the south are a couple of places named for the road: Lincoln Way Grooming Shop and Lincoln Way Flower Shop.

This ad for the Stony-brook Drive-In The-ater east of York touts the advantages of the drive-in over the indoor theater: "Smoke your head off if you like" and "No ups and downs to let the trampers and knee-knockers by." COURTESY MARK BIALEK

At the intersection of Route 24 is the Modernaire Motel, run by Deb and Robert Straw. Deb's parents bought the place in 1966, and the Straws have run it alone since 1985. They do good business, despite having lost their AAA rating several years ago when their 21 rooms were considered too small and their neon sign too garish! Deb says they get a lot of tourists and traveling businessmen, and they'd expand the motel if they could. When you enter, you'll be greeted by their rottweiler dogs, as the lobby serves as the family's living room.

Farther west is Barnhart's Motel, another family-run place, and to the south across from the York Mall is the former site of Playland, a complex that included a roller rink, miniature golf, amusement rides, and a giant above-ground pool. The 80-by-120-foot pool opened Memorial Day 1948 and was dedicated to local soldier Charles Sternbaugh, killed

The Modernaire Motel has changed little over the years except for the entrance, which was moved from the curved corner to the side.

during World War II. Advertisements said the pool was filled from fresh water springs and that it had "picture windows," where one could wave to friends from two below-water windows in the lobby. In the 1960s, the pool was incorporated into the Playland Motel, which was built around the pool and advertised itself as having the "world's largest motel pool." Eventually, the complex was sold off and the motel was bulldozed in 1992; the land now sits vacant and for sale.

Across the street sat Ye Olde Valley Inn, a 1738 tavern that was threatened when the shopping center was being built by the McCrory Corporation and the road was being widened in the early 1960s. The original structure was saved—the front portion of the western end—and moved to Susquehanna Memorial Gardens, a cemetery to the southeast, where today it serves as offices.

To the north is a Coca-Cola bottling plant, with the famous script name carved in relief and "1942" below that. Fat Daddy's to the south is in the old Lincoln Woods restaurant, now painted green and purple. The York Market Place (formerly the York County Shopping Center) to the north has just been outfitted in what we'll call the "art-techo" style, a conglomeration of peaks and triangles along the facade.

We approach the Haines Road–Memory Lane intersection, a Taco Bell sitting where the beautiful Bowman GMC dealership was built in

The Playland complex included a roller rink, miniature golf, kiddie rides, and "the world's largest pool." The Playland Motel would later be built around the pool, with 30 of its 53 rooms opening onto the deck. Ye Olde Valley Inn sat across the street, where the enlarged sign on this postcard is. COURTESY BERNIE HEISEY

Ye Olde Valley Inn in Stonybrook was moved to a nearby cemetery in 1962. Note the York County Traction Company interurban tracks on the south side of the road; when the road was widened in 1933, they were abandoned. COURTESY UNIVERSITY OF MICHIGAN, SPECIAL COLLECTIONS LIBRARY

1948. The dealership closed after a merger in 1987, and the curved-front showroom was demolished in 1993. The Hess gas station next door was supposedly one of the sites of the York Diner. Its address was listed as 2333 East Market Street in 1960, but it moved to 2985 in 1962. The diner was reportedly operated by the family that owned Playland, and the York Diner name was later used for their restaurant, which was in a house adjacent to Playland. Hap Miller's restaurant sat nearby. On the northwest corner is Plaza 2331, a small shopping center decorated in red and green plaid; this was originally Mary Macintosh dry cleaners, where passersby could watch the garments go past the large second-floor windows.

Ahead, we pass under I-83 and head into the residential outskirts of town. On Market at Ogontz Street, there's a 1928 Lincoln Highway marker in a front yard on the northeast corner.

As in Lancaster, the route through York is now composed of two one-way streets. At Harrison Street, Market becomes one-way going east, so we must turn right on North Harrison; from the intersection we can see the Lincoln Highway Garage and Family Restaurant to our southwest. The garage opened in 1921 and was touted as the first drive-in gas station along the Lincoln between Pittsburgh and Philadelphia. Founder Stewart Lehman also operated a Rickenbacker car dealership

The York Diner was originally at 37 North George Street, downtown York. A period matchbook emphasized that its home-cooked food was "prepared by a woman chef."

Hap Miller's Truck Town Restaurant, 1 mile east of York, advertised that it was open 24 hours and "Scientifically Air-Conditioned." It became Archie's Restaurant.

there, along with selling fishing and hunting supplies.

Through the years, the Lincoln Highway Garage was known for its many gas pumps with a wide variety of brands—at its peak, it had 13! Amoco and Atlantic were sold from the time the station opened, and Standard Oil (later Esso, then Exxon) from 1928. The garage even formulated a couple of its own brands, including Sportsman's Special in 1957.

The station is now run by Lehman's grandson Lynn Haines. Lynn says he was born right across the street and began his career with the station's fishing department by digging for worms in his parents' yard. His biggest challenge came in 1990, when federal regulations forced him to buy new underground tanks. Their size precluded him from carrying more than one brand of gasoline, so he doubled his order from his Exxon distributor. Haines tried to negotiate a better deal for his bigger order, but failing, he switched to another local distributor. Exxon, however, considers any station that switches dealers as a "new" station that must abide by its current standards, which meant bulldozing the station and erecting self-serve pumps and a minimart! So after more than 60 years, Haines switched to Texaco, which merely made him repaint to its color scheme. Much of the station's charm is intact, as is a room dedicated to the history of the garage and the Lincoln Highway. Haines even keeps a Rickenbacker there!

The Lincoln Highway Garage, shown here in April 1921, began as this small building, still part of today's block-long structure. COURTESY LYNN HAINES

A crowd waits to gas up at the Lincoln Highway Garage, c. 1961. COURTESY LYNN HAINES

Following the signs for Route 462, we turn left onto East Philadelphia Street. We pass blocks of brick row houses and cross North Duke Street 1.5 miles later. We're now at George Street, and the central square is one block south.

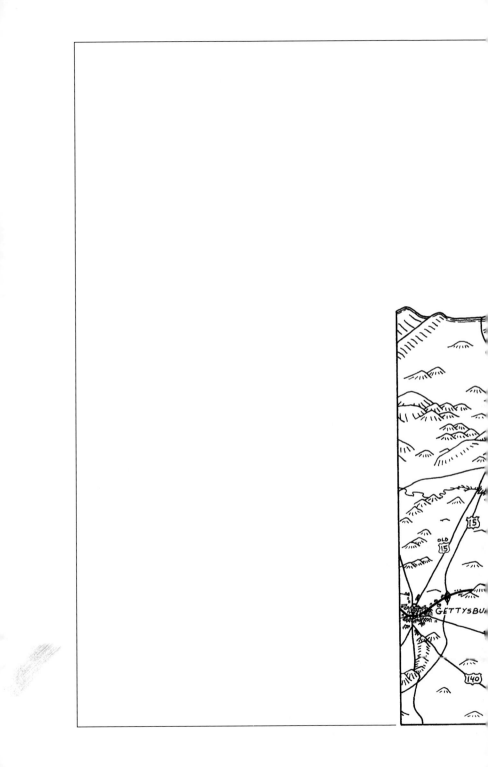

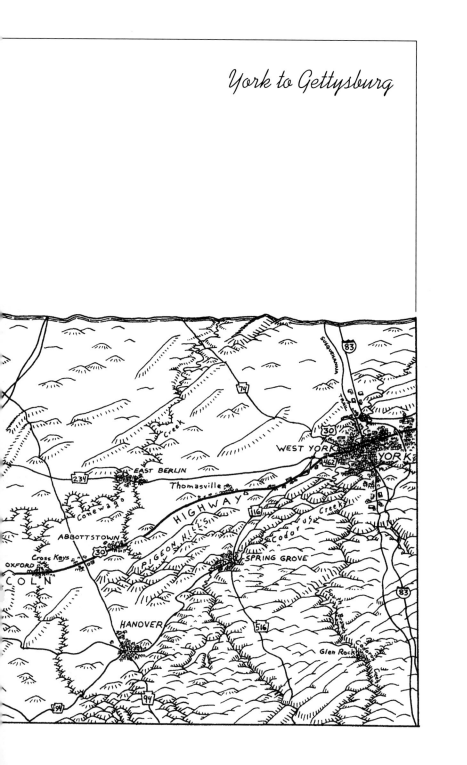

York to Gettysburg

York was the first town founded west of the Susquehanna River, in 1741. While the British occupied Philadelphia, York served as the nation's capital from September 1777 to June 1778. An agricultural center, York County once led the United States in cigar production. Although still an important agricultural area, York became a manufacturing center, and in the early years of the twentieth-century, at least seven makes of automobiles were manufactured locally, including the Pullman from 1903 to 1917. Local attractions today include the Harley Davidson Motorcycle Factory and Museum and the York Barbell Weightlifting and Strongman Halls of Fame.

A York man was greatly responsible for the fund-raising efforts of the Lincoln Highway Association. William Hart, Chicago manager for the tony *Town and Country* magazine in 1915, was a friend of LHA vice president Roy Chapin. In a 1951 *York Dispatch* article, Hart recalled that the project was "moving at a snail's pace" so "I suggested that Chapin write an article about the highway for the magazine." Hart then "obtained 3,500 copies of the article, encased them in leather binders with a solicitation note from Chapin, and mailed them to 'the wealthiest families in America.'" Hart said there were two more steps to his plan: contacting every newspaper in the country and enlisting door-to-door, merchant-to-merchant canvassers for funds. Because the official 1935 LHA history omitted his story, Hart donated his materials to the University of Michigan, calling them a "missing link" in the Lincoln Highway story.

Heading west from George Street, we immediately pass the Central Market House to the south, the traditional gathering spot for merchants and farmers to sell their wares. Today you can buy a wide range of foods and goods in this 1888 Romanesque Revival hall on Tuesday, Thursday, and Saturday mornings.

It's only a couple of blocks till we reach Pershing Avenue and cross Codorus Creek. We continue past row houses and finally intersect with Carlisle Avenue (Route 74), which comes from the northwest. Signs for Route 462 tell us to turn left, and after two short blocks, we make a sharp right onto Market Street. In the triangle of land formed by the intersection of Carlisle and Market Streets is the Fire Museum of York County, and beyond it the York County Fairgrounds.

For those traveling east or wanting to drive the original route through town, follow Market Street east from here, where it becomes obvious

Codorus Creek flooded its banks in August 1933. This view looks west on Market Street from Pershing Avenue in downtown York. The creek's name is an Indian term meaning "rapid water." COURTESY PA STATE ARCHIVES, RG-12 DEPT. OF HIGHWAYS

that Market was the original two-way route of the Lincoln—it's more commercial than Philadelphia Street. Among the highlights are the Farmers' Market building at Penn Street, selling local meats and produce, and once you cross the bridge over Codorus Creek, the Colonial Courthouse to the north, a detailed replica of the building where in 1777 the Continental Congress adopted the Articles of Confederation, the document the United States operated under before the Constitution.

"Continental Square" at George Street is only a few blocks away, and then the historic district begins. Among some of the more recent buildings are the restored Yorktowne Hotel, which served Lincoln Highway travelers, and the Rose Motor Club with its AAA emblem on a steel-encased, rotating sign in purple neon. Also here is the York County Museum, housing a Conestoga wagon and some examples of locally made automobiles, and the Agricultural and Industrial Museum. Heading east, we pass a number of row houses. The brick-front building at 747 East Market was the location of the Lincoln Highway Cigar Store in the teens, now barely recognizable. We eventually arrive at the Lincoln Highway Garage.

The Lincoln Highway Cigar Store, c. 1916. The 1915 York City Directory lists Harry E. Melhorn's store at 747 East Market Street. The building survives, remodeled. The front of the postcard says, "I work day and night here. there is all my lofers," and on the back, "I am going to work on the ice wagon and in the after noons I am going to learn to fix auto tire and it is good pay . . . Good By. Jesse" (postmarked April 1916). COURTESY BERNIE HEISEY

Now we head west out of town on Market Street (Route 462). Just west of Pearl Street is a fire station with a cement Lincoln Highway marker on its front lawn. The 1936 and 1941 Federal Hi-Way Homes guides list Eyster's Tourist Home at 1615 West Market, and the 1941 *Blue Book List* offered Landis' Easy Rest Tourist Home at 2211 West Market.

At a fork, we stay left past Bill Boring's Car Lot, which has a neon sign and arrows. At the 2600 block is Lincolnway Bowling Alley to the north, with its own nice neon bowling sign. There's also a Lincolnway Fire Company and Lincolnway School nearby—the Lincolnway name remains very popular in York.

On the outskirts now, we pass a music store to our north with a large keyboard on its sign; this was once Pottery Hill. The Pfaltzgraff company began making pottery in the York area in the nineteenth century. George W. Pfaltzgraff helped the company grow beyond its regional bounds, but in 1935, after serving as president for 17 years, he sold the company. The next year he constructed a home and retail store called Pottery Hill, where he sold assorted ceramics and gifts. George also had an Atlantic station adjacent (the building remains to the west), and he operated the store until his death in 1956. The Pfaltzgraff company bought the location in 1960, and it became its first retail outlet. Pfaltzgraff now has factory outlets across the country, but its headquarters remains in downtown York on East Market Street—the Lincoln Highway. Its old art pottery and kitchenware can be found in flea markets and antiques shops across the country.

The Route 30 bypass meets us from the northeast, and Route 462 ends. We quickly come upon the modern West York Diner to the north; across the street was the Lincoln Way Office of the Dauphin Deposit Bank (closed in 1994). Two brick tourist cabins lie behind it, each a double unit. Just west of the bank is Lee's Diner. The June 1952 issue of *Diner & Restaurant* magazine announced that Elmer and Grace Paxton had bought their red and blue Lee's Diner new from the Mountain View company. After various owners, it's now run by a partnership that

Tollgate number one on the York-Gettysburg Turnpike, West Manchester Township, York County, looking west, October 1917. Lincoln Highway motorists had to pay tolls on this turnpike until 1918, when the state and county governments jointly purchased the 16-mile road for $96,000. COURTESY PA STATE ARCHIVES, RG-12 DEPT. OF HIGHWAYS

includes the son of a former owner. On the morning of our visit, they've already used 540 eggs before noon! Behind the diner is Lincolnway Pool, and across from it is Smith's Motel (originally Myers), now advertising its 14 rooms for sale.

At the intersection of Hanover Road (Route 116) is a Rutter's minimart, and 1 mile later to the south is the beautiful screen tower to the Lincoln Drive-In Theater. It's painted bright aqua green and reddish orange, but it's been closed for years and is rapidly deteriorating. The aqua-green center is the original tower, and the orange wings were apparently added for Cinemascope pictures.

A half mile later we enter Thomasville, really just some houses strung along the road. West of town is the Thomasville Inn (formerly San Remo Inn) bar and restaurant, with a big windmill out front, and the Lincoln Fire Company. Beyond, to the south is the White Horse Diner, a small older place, and to the north is Lincoln Way Chiropractic Center.

West of York, June 1933. The road would soon be cemented and widened.
Today a Rutter's minimart stands in the fork at Route 116, but the stone house to
the right remains relatively unchanged. COURTESY PA STATE ARCHIVES, RG-12
DEPT. OF HIGHWAYS

There's a cement Lincoln Highway marker on the southwest corner of Grant Road, in tall hedges. Across the highway is Martin's Potato Chip factory. Katy in the gift shop tells us, "You just wouldn't believe what goes into a potato chip until you see the tour!" It's Martin's only factory, and the company makes only chips, although it distributes other products. The tour ends in a little store that sells chips, shirts, hats, and seconds (the ones that mix when a line converts over from flat to ridgy chips or plain to barbecue). Other local snack companies offering tours include Snyder's of Hanover and Herr's.

We continue through farmland past a small airstrip to our south, and 1 mile later the Jefferson Motel proclaims "American owned" on a homemade sign. The U.S. 30 Auto Mart is past that, and then Route 30 Seafood, offering steamed crabs. Another seafood restaurant is the Rambler Inn, an older place with a neon arrow pointing to its parking lot. Then to the south is a tiny section of old road.

The *Shell Tourist Accommodation Directory* for 1940 lists a pair of cabin camps in this area: Rambler's Rest (7 cabins) and Eyster's Camp (6 unheated cabins), both 9 miles west of York; Rambler's Rest was likely at today's Rambler's Inn. We pass through the tiny settlements of LaBott and Farmers, then a string of about eight cabins from the old Pine Motel lies perpendicular to the road, across from an old gas station. A half mile later is the Pine Ridge Inn, which also offers seafood and has a roof outlined in red neon.

This area is still rural, and we pass many large, attractive barns. To the north is O'Brien's Restaurant with a lounge and motel. This is the former Lincoln View Motel. Today the rooms look in disrepair, some of them refaced in stone, others untouched and deteriorated. The 81 Diner 1 mile later has a large triangular sign that flashes. It's a small place with good food, as well as bumper stickers and orange hunting caps with the diner's name. Just west of the diner is a Road of Remembrance marker to the south. This marker and another in Wrightsville were erected in 1922 as part of a memorial to local sons and daughters who fought in World War I. The most visible part of the program was a tree-planting effort across the county dedicated to fallen soldiers and part of a wider nationwide movement. The Woman's Club of the United States undertook the planting of trees along the full length of the Lincoln Highway. For $2.50, local participants could choose a tree of their liking—elms,

An aerial view of the Lincoln View Motel. "Dear folks—Made about 200 miles today. Staying here tonight and it is lovely. Love to all, Elsie and Hubert" (postmarked August 6, 1950).

Dedicating the Road of Remembrance near York, Memorial Day 1922. Trees were planted from Wrightsville to Abbottstown in honor of World War I soldiers. COURTESY PA STATE ARCHIVES, RG-12 DEPT. OF HIGHWAYS

oaks, and maples were the most popular. Each tree had a metal tag shaped like a federal highway shield, with information about the soldier.

The family of one soldier wrote to the York organizers: "As a family, we have decided to take a tree in honor of our son, Albert D. Bell, Chaplain, who died in action in France, Oct. 13, 1918, and lies buried in a cemetery near Toul. If we may choose the place of planting we would prefer for several reasons that it be between York and Gettysburg, as York was his home and ours, and Gettysburg the home of his wife." Unfortunately, the more than 1,500 trees planted did not last; disease, car accidents, and road widenings took their toll, and 30 years later their number had been reduced to a few hundred. Today some undoubtedly stand tall, but no pattern is discernible.

As we enter Abbottstown, many nineteenth-century houses line the road. Once a major center for cigar making, the town was known as Berwick until 1911. Except for the addition of a minimart, the center square at the junction of Route 194 has changed little over the years. On

Looking west to the circle in Abbottstown, March 1936. The Hotel Altland west of the square is advertising all-you-can-eat chicken and waffles for 75 cents.
COURTESY PA STATE ARCHIVES, RG-12 DEPT. OF HIGHWAYS

the southwest corner is the Altland House (sometimes called the Hotel Altland), an old inn that received its present facade in 1911, perhaps to celebrate the town's new name. The Haugh family has run the hotel since 1954; five rooms are still available, along with two restaurants. Just west of the square is the Hofbrauhaus, serving sauerbraten and schnitzel a little below street level. The road west of here has a middle turning lane, and we spot a sign for Lincoln Speedway.

To the north is a giant auction barn, this one alone in a field. It used to be the location of Hubcap City, with hubcaps spread everywhere, but that moved 4 miles west. We pass more farms and various antiques stores, and an old pike marker to the north in front of a wooden fence reads "P 102, Y 16, G 12." We pass the Cross Keys Motel and the Keystone Diner .5 mile later, then Shakerbox Antiques and A Touch of Antiquity, two antiques stores.

We reach the junction of Route 94, known as Cross Keys. Just a couple of miles south toward Hanover is Crabb's Tropical Treat drive-in ice cream stand, which still has pull-up speaker service and a great neon sign on the roof: a twist cone with a palm tree and an arrow. At the inter-

Looking west to the Cross Keys intersection, May 1935. Note the Cross Keys Inn to the south and its gas station to the north. There's a turnpike marker at the northeast corner, immediately left of the Route 94 sign.

Proprietor John E. George stated on the back of his Cross Keys Diner postcards, "Seating Capacity of 70. 24 Hour Service. Est. 1937." COURTESY CY HOSMER

The 4-Square filling station, east of New Oxford. COURTESY ADAMS COUNTY HISTORICAL SOCIETY

section of Routes 30 and 94 is the Cross Keys Family Restaurant to the northeast, once the site of the Cross Keys Diner. The small Country Junction Café is to the northwest in an old garage. To the southwest are the Brethren Home and the Cross Keys Village personal care complex, which says, "Visit our gift shop!" This was the location of the Cross Keys Inn, which was replaced by a more modern hotel in the mid-1930s that featured a Hammond electric organ for nightly entertainment.

A half mile later, Steamers (the former Bar 30 Crab House) is on the south, and homes are appearing in the clearing to the north. Now Hollywood Estates, this was the site of the Cross Keys Drive-In Theater. In its heyday, the drive-in had country-western bands play before the movies. When the theater closed in the 1980s, it began to be demolished bit by bit. The marquee was offered free to a good home; unfortunately, however, most homes thought it too big or too new, despite its age and craftsmanship. After trying countless institutions, the State Museum in Harrisburg arranged for its removal and storage; it awaits restoration and display.

Down the road, we pass Colonial Auto Sales, which has an awning and bright green soda pop sign, apparently from a restaurant at the site. Then to the north is a Getty station, a rounded red brick building with "Aero Oil Company" inscribed at the top and a pointy 1960s-era roof.

We arrive at the New Oxford square and fountain; on the north lawn of the square is a cement Lincoln Highway marker. Many eighteenth- and nineteenth-century buildings fan out from the square. On the southwest corner is the Hotel Oxford and a number of antiques shops. Heading west from town, there are more antiques stores and malls, and a

The Cross Keys Drive-In Theater was replaced by housing, but the sign may have a new life at the State Museum in Harrisburg. (PHOTO 1989)

Abraham Lincoln, on a 1928 cement marker, keeps an eye on some golf carts west of New Oxford. (PHOTO 1993)

couple of blocks west and to the north are a pair of huge malls, though the signs on Route 30 are hard to spot. Paul's Model Railroad Shop is west of town to the south in two old passenger rail cars.

The road here is marked Lincoln Way. We pass the new Hubcap City and, just west of it, a place selling numerous ceramic lawn ornaments. A cement Lincoln Highway marker lies low to the south, near a row of golf carts for sale at Plant Mill Road. Just past it is Black Shutter Antiques, also to the south. The Lincoln Highway Tea Room was once in this area.

The 1940 Shell guide lists Martin's 10 units around here, 6 miles east of Gettysburg, and as we head toward Gettysburg, we pass a couple of cabins to the south. Farther west is the former Edgewood Motel, once cabins in a wooded setting. Today mobile homes are sold from the run-down remains of the motel. Along with Edgewood Glen (as the seven cabins were originally called), the 1940 Shell guide also lists Rocky Haven Cabins in this vicinity.

Soon we're at Sunken Gardens, where each tourist cabin is painted a different color of the rainbow. It's listed in the 1947 *American Motel Association Motel Guide and Trip Diary* as open from March to December, rates starting at $2.50, and owned by Mr. and Mrs. Black. Glenn and

Tollgate number four on the York-Gettysburg Turnpike, Hamilton Township, Adams County, looking west, October 1917. In between this and the number one tollgate were number two in Jackson Township and number three in Paradise Township. COURTESY PA STATE ARCHIVES, RG-12 DEPT. OF HIGHWAYS

Irene Toot now own the motel, which they bought about 1964. Unfortunately, it has been closed for a few years, and one cabin was recently torn down. In its prime, though, the 19-cottage motel offered shuffleboard, horseshoes, a croquet court, and a Hammond organ concert every night, just like the Cross Keys Hotel. According to Mrs. Toot, Sunken Gardens was named before the road was filled in. "There used to be a big dip out front." In fact, most of the Lincoln Highway followed an undulating course in its early days. The Toots recall that it was built in 1936 by the Herrick brothers, and it had two central outhouses. Eventually the Herrick brothers parted ways, and one built the Holland Motel next door. The Holland Motel is still in business and advertising low rates (in the $20 range) for its cabins.

Across from the motels is Lincoln Logs restaurant, advertising "Crab Feed Tonite." It's a sight to see, both for the rustic decor of the log building and for the way customers go mad for the crabs. Tables are covered with newspaper, and waitresses continually dump big baskets of crabs in front of hungry hammer-toting diners.

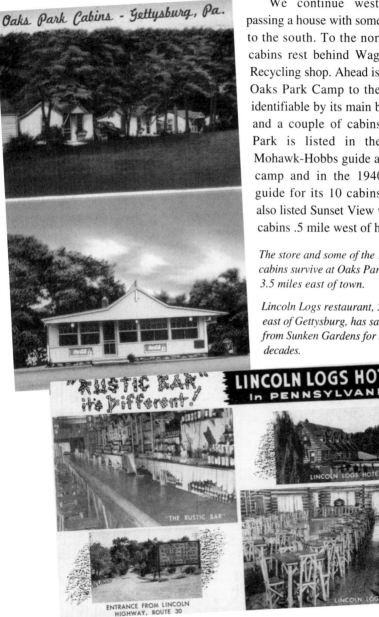

We continue west, soon passing a house with some cabins to the south. To the north, two cabins rest behind Wagaman's Recycling shop. Ahead is the old Oaks Park Camp to the north, identifiable by its main building and a couple of cabins. Oaks Park is listed in the 1927 Mohawk-Hobbs guide as a free camp and in the 1940 Shell guide for its 10 cabins. Shell also listed Sunset View with six cabins .5 mile west of here.

The store and some of the 10 cabins survive at Oaks Park, 3.5 miles east of town.

Lincoln Logs restaurant, 5 miles east of Gettysburg, has sat across from Sunken Gardens for many decades.

Viola Riley and her family had a place here called the Mayfair, which offered food, drinks, and dancing. "It was more like a meeting place," she recalls, "but lots of out of town farmers, salesmen, and tour buses stopped too." They opened it after prohibition ended and sold it in 1968. Mrs. Riley also recalls Oaks Park and the Lorain Lodge restaurant and cabins next to it.

The Lorain Lodge is listed in both the 1940 Shell directory and the 1947 *American Motel Association Motel Guide and Trip Diary.* Run by Miss Helen Barley and Miss Verna Schmauch, the five "electrically heated cottages" were 3 miles east of the city. The lodge was said to serve the "Best Food Obtainable At Popular Prices." A poor postcard of the place shows the cabins next to a two-story house, with a one-story restaurant in front.

In the next 2 miles we pass some antiques stores, then the Homestead Motor Lodge to the north. As soon as we pass over the Route 15 cloverleaf, the Gettysburg sprawl begins. This stretch was relatively

The Globe Hotel, east of the Gettysburg square, was renamed the Lincoln Way Hotel in the teens, then Hoffman's in the early 1920s. Lee Hoffman had a string of hotels in the state—in Bedford and Ligonier on Route 30, and in Cresson on Route 22.

empty until a few years ago, when development became rampant. Some relatively old motels remain, such as the Penn Eagle Motel–Friendship Inn, which has a playground out front, and the Lincoln Way East Motel, now a Superior Inn budget motel. Old postcards show McCoy's Motel, which had a hillbilly on its sign and advertised, "See our jungleland and hear our talking birds FREE." Another, 1 mile east of town, was the Hi-Way Motel, listed in the 1955 *Eastern Motor Court Map* as an "excellent small motel." The Family Fun Center is a newer place with an elaborate miniature golf course and an arcade. Railroad tracks parallel us into town on the north side, and finally we bear right on York Street.

It's only a couple of blocks to Lincoln Square, and just before, at 44 York Street, is the 1787 stone Brafferton Inn, the oldest building downtown. Right on the square is the renovated Best Western Gettysburg Hotel. The original was constructed in 1797 and went through major enlargements over the years. President Eisenhower regularly worked out of the hotel during his term, and today it looks much like it did after its 1925 renovation, except for a recent two-story addition on top. Across from it is the Wills House, where Lincoln finished his Gettysburg Address and stayed the night before giving the speech in November 1863. A small museum offers some history about the man and his speech, and a Lincoln statue stands out front.

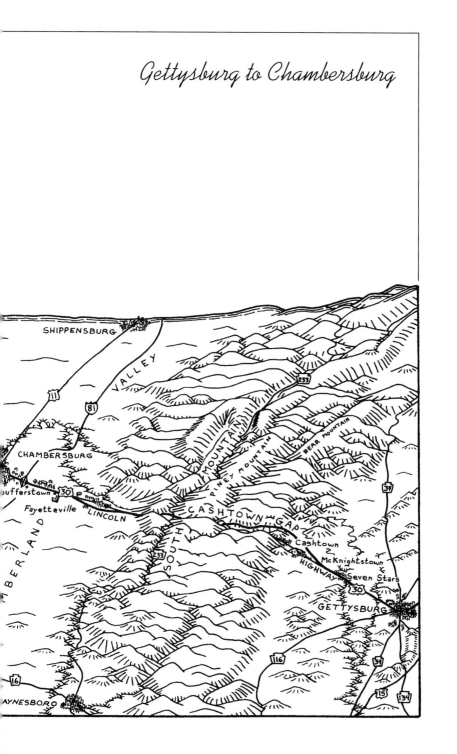

Many roads intersect at Gettysburg. Founded in the 1780s, it was little different from the surrounding towns until the summer of 1863, when it became the focus of a three-day Civil War battle, from July 1 to 3. The convergence of roads drew both armies to the battle. Falling in the middle of the four-year conflict, the Gettysburg battle is often called the "High Tide of the Confederacy," for the war began turning inexorably to the North's favor afterward. Gettysburg National Military Park now surrounds the town, encompassing 3,500 acres and including 1,300 monuments and cannon. Visitation is higher than ever, and the streets are filled with Civil War memorabilia shops and souvenir stands.

The Gettysburg Square was once called a "diamond." It's recently undergone renovation that included new brick sidewalks. A block north of the square, on the side of the Gettysburg Hotel, is the Majestic Theater, with the town's only neon. It was recently restored with funds from Ted Turner so that his *Gettysburg* movie could premiere there. Next to it is the 1858 Western Maryland Railway Station, now a visitors center filled with brochures, and across from that is the Lincoln Diner, a 1950s Silk City-brand diner. The exterior is covered in bland brick, but the inside retains most of its pink highlights and stainless-steel trim.

To get to the Gettysburg National Military Park's visitors center, go south from the square on Baltimore Street, following the Route 15 south signs. You'll enter across from the Lincoln Train Museum and a HoJo Lodge (as some are now called). The center was once a private museum and features exhibits, a large bookstore, and the "electric map," which uses six hundred tiny light bulbs to explain troop movements. The center, which is open from 8 to 5 daily, also has free maps of the battlefield and park.

Across from the center is the National Cemetery, scene of Lincoln's Gettysburg Address. Just south of here is the imposing Pennsylvania Monument, and beyond that is Little Round Top, the scene of dramatic actions on the battle's second day. It's worth a trip to the summit, which overlooks the battlefield—the reason for its battle significance. The clash resulted in more than fifty thousand casualties.

Back at the square, we pass a AAA on the northwest corner as we head west from town on Chambersburg Street. A few doors from the square is the Blue Parrot Bistro, a tearoom for early travelers. A large white building on the southwest corner of Washington Street was built as a theater in 1916 by Frank Eberhart, proprietor of the Eagle Hotel, which

The Blue Parrot, on the left with a parrot atop its sign, was a popular tearoom in the first half of the century and is still in business today. In the middle is the James Gettys Hotel, c. 1930. COURTESY ADAMS COUNTY HISTORICAL SOCIETY

The National Garage, Chambersburg Street, was one of the first to advertise in the 1914 Blue Book *as being on the Lincoln Highway. The garage occupied just a portion of this site then but expanded in 1921, when this picture was taken. Signs on the window show it was a dealer for Chevrolet and REO autos. Also note the "Lincoln Highway Control Station" sign to the right, from which guidebook mileages were measured. It's now the site of an addition for the adjacent bank.* COURTESY GETTYSBURG NATIONAL MILITARY PARK

sat diagonally across the street. Meanwhile, another theater had opened across town, so this never became a theater but rather Eberhart's Garage, later Epley's Garage. It now has antiques on the ground floor and is in need of restoration.

C. W. Epley also ran one of the country's earliest miniature golf courses in Gettysburg. It was a couple of blocks east on the Lincoln Highway in the Moose Building, which stands today. In the twenties and thirties the course was the "finest and most beautiful east of the Rockies," according to its postcard. It was indoors and featured palm trees, lounge chairs, and murals.

At the fork in the road we bear right, following Route 30 signs. We pass the Sunny Ray Family Restaurant and Christopher's Hot Weiners,

Eberhart's Garage was originally built in 1916 as a theater but never served as one. It was soon renamed Epley's Garage and stayed open all night to offer "gas, oil, water, air, rest rooms, towing, supplies, storage, and repairs."
COURTESY GETTYSBURG NATIONAL MILITARY PARK

The next three photos show a panorama of Larson's Motel looking right to left, or east to west. Here are the cottages and the owners' house. Mrs. Larson told Tourist Court Journal *in April 1939 that "the cabins contain everything necessary for the visiting tourist: cabinet, dishes, silver and breakfast sets."* COURTESY ADAMS COUNTY HISTORICAL SOCIETY

which advertises Hershey's ice cream and pressure-cooked chicken. Less than 1 mile from the square we reach the Lutheran Theological Seminary on Seminary Ridge and, across from it, Larson's Motel and the Lee Headquarters Museum. Rumor has it that the museum building, then home of Mary Thompson, served as Lee's headquarters during the first day of fighting; however, although the general may have dined there, he probably worked from his nearby field tent. Today the building is filled with battlefield relics.

Larson's was one of the earliest Quality Inn motels and was once two separate tourist camps: Lee's and Larson's. Lee's seven cabins are listed in the 1928 Mohawk-Hobbs guide as the area's "leading camp." The Larsons erected their cabins in 1936, and took over Lee's in July 1945. All of the cabins were replaced by a motel about 1960, which retains much of its original ambience, including beautifully tiled bathrooms. The adjacent General Lee's restaurant offers country cooking.

As we head out of town, we pass the Buford and Reynolds monuments, plus other markers along the road commemorating the first day's

Larson's Ridge House had apartments, now the location of General Lee's restaurant. To its left is the Lee's Headquarters Museum and behind were the cabins.
COURTESY ADAMS COUNTY HISTORICAL SOCIETY

fighting. To the south is Herr Tavern, an 1815 inn that still offers five rooms and a dining room. Farther ahead is the 30 West Car Wash to the north, then Lincoln Estates mobile home park to the south. The Belmont Inn and Camp was located next to the 30 West Car Wash, across from the airport. The 1940 *Shell Tourist Accommodation Directory* lists another court in this area, Volz Cabins, 2.5 miles west of town, with six units open seasonally.

A couple of miles from town is a turn for the Land of Little Horses, 2 miles to the south, featuring acts and petting opportunities with Fala-

The Lee Museum remains, surrounded by Larson's Motel and General Lee's restaurant, but at this time Lee's Cottages sat behind it. There was originally space for 75 cars. During the Civil War, the house was occupied by widow Mary Thompson. COURTESY GETTYSBURG NATIONAL MILITARY PARK

Shields' Gettysburg Camp Park was a well-known landmark located near the entrance to the Eternal Light Peace Memorial until the National Park Service removed the complex a few years ago. It offered "cabins, gas, oil, refreshments, souvenirs, postcards, guide books, and antique guns."

Ohio tourists in front of the Buford and Reynolds monuments, west of town, 1913. COURTESY ADAMS COUNTY HISTORICAL SOCIETY

Looking west to the Belmont Inn and Camp near Gettysburg. The 1940 Shell Tourist Accommodation Directory *lists eight cabins starting at $1.25, each with its own toilet but community showers. Today it's an empty lot next to the 30 West Car Wash, but the houses in the background remain.* COURTESY GETTYSBURG NATIONAL MILITARY PARK

The Lincoln Way Inn west of Gettysburg. COURTESY ADAMS COUNTY HISTORICAL SOCIETY

bella miniature horses, three feet tall at most. Just past that, in the area known as Seven Stars, a bit of unused road to the north is not the old Lincoln but rather remnants of a detour when the adjacent bridge was rebuilt. A camp listed in the 1928 Mohawk-Hobbs guide near here is Hershey Park, offering camping space for 25 cents, four cabins, and a swimming pool.

A mile later we find a cement Lincoln Highway marker on a front lawn; it lies low near a driveway to the south, just before the original route branches to the south. We make a left to follow the Lincoln Highway through McKnightstown and Cashtown. The road is very straight, and we pass the Grimes beef cattle farm, where each Charolais breeding bull is named after a Civil War general. In McKnightstown, we pass Bennie's fruit market and look for evidence of the Old Oak Park camp, listed in the 1927 Mohawk-Hobbs guide as a nice site with cabins. The 1940 Shell guide also lists the McKnightstown Restaurant and Cabins, with 22 cabins starting at $1.

We pass the post office (formerly Johnson's general store) and find some cabins on the south side .2 mile later. We head to Cashtown, so

At C. W. Johnson's general store in McKnightstown, oil was pumped right from the barrels, including Rexoline, Mobiloil, Atlantic, and Gulf. Here, in May 1932, Mr. Johnson himself sits waiting for customers. The building is now the town's post office. COURTESY ADAMS COUNTY HISTORICAL SOCIETY

named because an early innkeeper demanded all payments in cash. The 1797 Cashtown Inn is known as the site of Confederate general A. P. Hill's headquarters in 1863; he was on his way to Gettysburg with eight thousand Confederate troops. The 1948 Route 30 bypass brought a quick decline to the inn, but it was bought in 1987 and restored by Charles and Carolyn Buckley. Four rooms are still available for travelers, along with a tavern and dining room.

We continue west, past the former Rock Top Inn to the south, and head into a hilly section for a couple of miles. Near the summit, a tollgate was still operating here according to the 1918 *Red Road Book,* though it may have ceased by the book's publication. Out on the bypass are the Mountain View Motel and Restaurant selling groceries and gas, and the 30 West Motel and Apartments across the street to the south (the 16 units were originally called Wayne's but have had this name for decades). There are also a number of peach and apple orchards and some fruit markets. The bypass climbs a big hill, and the new and old roads meet at the top about 7 miles from their split.

Building the Route 30 bypass around Cashtown, May 1948. Approximately twenty thousand trees were removed in clearing the new path. COURTESY PA STATE ARCHIVES, RG-12 DEPT. OF HIGHWAYS

The former Rock Top Inn just west of Cashtown is now a bar. COURTESY
ADAMS COUNTY HISTORICAL SOCIETY

Just before the roads meet, there is a pair of cabins to the south.
Where the old Lincoln joins Route 30, another Lincoln Highway marker
sits just east of their junction in the triangular-shaped rise between the
roads. It was probably moved when the bypass was built. The old road
crosses the new here and heads northwest. Sitting between the old and
new in that section is Mr. Ed's Elephant Museum.

Ed Gotwalt opened this place in 1983, after running Mr. Ed's General Store, just east on Route 30, for 10 years. Mr. Ed's has a small
museum jammed full of every imaginable elephant-related object. Outside are a kiddie playground and Miss Ellie, a big talking elephant. This is
a must stop for souvenirs, all sold by Mr. Ed himself. And don't forget to buy
fresh roasted peanuts, which you can smell from the road. The attraction is open year-round, and signs advertise that Mr. Ed's "loves buses,"
in case you're thinking of taking your friends. Don't ask for anything
with ivory, though. "Only elephants should wear ivory," says Mr. Ed.

We continue downhill, and the old and new roads again rejoin. The
area is part of the 82,000-acre Michaux State Forest (named for a well-

One of the best, if smallest, attractions on the Lincoln Highway is Mr. Ed's Elephant Museum. Just look for Miss Ellie, the talking elephant.

known French botanist) and is thick with pine trees. We pass the Pine Village Shops, which have sold baskets, candles, lamps, and candies since 1948.

The Piney Mountain Inn was formerly located here, and today the Piney Mountain Home Estates are to the north. Across the road is the Herb Cottage, offering handcrafted gifts. The 1927 Mohawk-Hobbs guide lists free camping at Newman Park 12 miles west of Gettysburg, and the Shell directory for 1940 lists nine cottages at Newman's.

About 1 mile later to the south is Colonel's Creek Campground and Cottages, the former Miller's Cabins. The Caledonia Park-In Theater also used to be in this vicinity. This area also has some old segments of road to the north, identifiable as worn cement in front of some houses.

The 1849 Graeffenburg Inn, named for a famous Austrian spa, was a well-known landmark here that offered rooms, meals, and "health springs." Owned by the state since 1902, it was leased through the years, most recently by William Putch and his wife, actress Jean Stapleton. The landmark sat just east of the Michaux State Park Forest District Office but was burned by an arsonist in March 1980. Today it's an empty field.

Miller's Heated Cabins, now Colonel's Creek Campground. COURTESY CY HOSMER

The Graeffenburg Inn, 1924. This nineteenth-century inn, bought by the state in 1902, was burned by arsonists in March 1980. COURTESY UNIVERSITY OF MICHIGAN, SPECIAL COLLECTIONS LIBRARY

On the south side, across from the forest office, is a square stone marker and tablet:

I'm shot—get that man, thus spoke on October 14, 1924 Francis L. Haley, a member of the Pennsylvania State Police force, as he fell at this spot mortally wounded by a bullet fired by the escaping robber of the Abbottstown State Bank, located 27 miles east of here, along the Lincoln Highway. Trooper Haley's motorcycle carried him across the Adams-Franklin county line as death came. He was the 14th state policeman killed in action. The assassin was later arrested and tried, convicted and electrocuted.

We cross from Adams to Franklin County and enter Caledonia State Park, named for the charcoal iron furnace that Thaddeus Stevens erected here in 1837 (burned by Confederate soldiers in 1863). A mile later to the north at Route 233 are the Thaddeus Stevens Blacksmith Shop, also owned by the famous statesman, and a reconstructed furnace. Caledonia Park was once operated by trolley companies, which promoted it as an amusement park. Just south on 233, the Totem Pole Playhouse has

CALEDONIA PARK ON LINCOLN HIGHWAY, NEAR CHAMBERSBURG, PA.

Looking east on the Lincoln in 1919, with the Thaddeus Stevens Blacksmith Shop to the left. It later served as a park office and trolley station before being restored to its original use.

A 1924 Department of Highways guide stated, "One of the 'show roads' of Pennsylvania is the concrete between Gettysburg and Chambersburg." Crowds gathered to watch a parade on October 8, 1921, dedicating the new roadbed. A Lincoln Highway pennant adorns the front car. COURTESY UNIVERSITY OF MICHIGAN, SPECIAL COLLECTIONS LIBRARY

offered summer theater since 1950. Be careful sightseeing on Route 30—cars like to speed through the park area.

The Appalachian Trail, which runs along the backbone of the Appalachian Mountains, crosses the road just west of here. At more than 2,000 miles, it's the longest continuous marked foot trail in the world. To the south, we soon pass a pizza and sub place in the old Park View Restaurant drive-in. There's also a big lighthouse at Greenwood Hills Bible Conference Chapel. To the south is an old stone gas station, closed now, but perhaps it was part of the Jungle Park free camp, listed in the 1927 Mohawk-Hobbs guide as 2.5 miles east of Fayetteville; in the 1940 Shell directory, Jungle Park Inn was listed with 15 log cabins. Another 1.5 miles later, the old Lincoln branches off to the north toward Fayetteville.

Fayetteville is named for the Marquis de Lafayette, a French general who fought with the American colonists against the British in the Revolutionary War. Main Street through town shows little evidence of the early automobile era, such as when the Fayetteville Garage carried a full line of car parts, but it has a number of nineteenth-century homes, notably a white Victorian manor to the north called Lee Way. On the bypass (marked Lincoln Way West) is the Rite Spot Motel and Restaurant to the north, with a very nice neon sign, and 1 mile later is the Ice Cream House, with 32 flavors and miniature golf, in the former office of the White Swan Motel. Also on the bypass is the huge Fayetteville Antique Mall, composed of four large buildings on both sides of the highway and open daily. The roads rejoin after 3 miles, and we pass Lincoln Lanes bowling alley to the north, with a big yellow bowling pin and orange ball. We then pass Hoover's Drive-In Restaurant, a 1960s-style drive-in featuring "Fresh broiled burgers, frozen creme, and thick shakes."

Along Lincoln Way, many businesses use the name, including the Lincoln Way East shopping center. Just past that to the south is the Scottish Inn (the old Keystone Tourist Court); in the 1949 *Ray Walker's Vacation Resort/Motor Court Recommendations,* the motel is described as "tops for miles around." Next door is George and Nick's Chicken and Seafood House, featuring a big chicken with glowing yellow eyes out front, and then come the Snack Shack drive-in restaurant and a cement Lincoln Highway marker sitting so high on a lawn that we can see a mark on the bottom indicating how deep to bury it. An antiques mall lies to the north.

The Five-Points Diner (originally Conrad's and later Burkholder's) to the north has an orange roof and a brick facade, but it was originally a stainless-steel diner. To the south is Eric Von Dar Tattooing; the whole house is painted like a giant tattoo in fantasy themes. Across from it, the Cumberland Valley Visitors Station is a very nice visitors center in a re-created train station. Outside sits a restored 1942 Pennsylvania Railroad caboose. We go under I-81 (to the north is Carlisle, home of giant auto parts swap meets twice a year), past a Howard Johnson motel and restaurant to the north, and past Lincoln Cemetery to the south.

A mile west of I-81, Route 30 splits again into one-way roads bearing east and west. We stay to the right following Lincoln Way, and a few

ANTIQUES.

KITTOCHTINNY INN.
LINCOLN WAY, EAST, CHAMBERSBURG, PA.

ROOMS.

The former Kittochtinny Inn remains a couple of blocks east of the square, now the private Chambersburg Club.

blocks later we come upon a Lincoln Highway marker on the northwest corner of Third Street. In the next block we pass the Chambersburg Club, the former Kittochtinny Inn. Ahead is Chambersburg's Memorial Square, around which westbound traffic snakes on both the north and south sides. Chambersburg borough, with a population of about 16,000, is about the midway point of our journey across Pennsylvania.

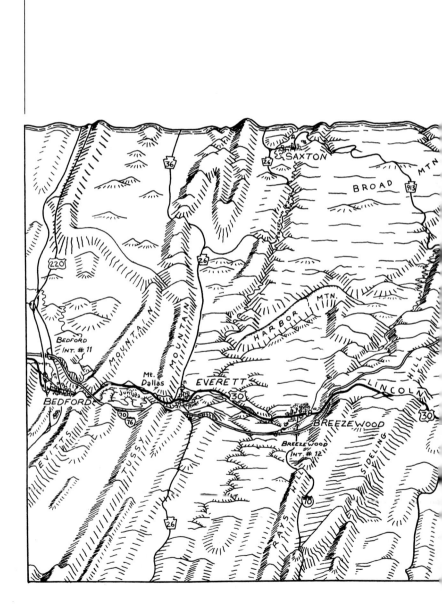

Chambersburg to Bedford

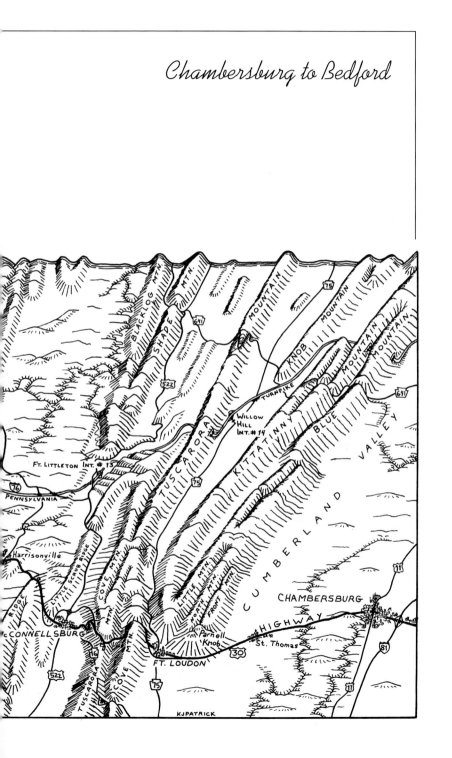

Chambersburg was first settled in 1732 by Benjamin Chambers, one of four Irish brothers who came to America in the 1720s. Forbes Road from Harrisburg to Bedford turned west before reaching Chambersburg, so the town was not on a major east-west route at first. Later turnpikes went right to the square, however, and by the Civil War, the road through town was well established—it was the route of Lee's army in 1863 as the Confederates marched toward Gettysburg.

Chambersburg was burned by Confederate soldiers a year later, when the town refused to pay a ransom. (Confederate vengeance was possibly inflamed because abolitionist John Brown lived here prior to his notorious 1859 attack on Harpers Ferry.) More than five hundred buildings were destroyed by the fire. In the square today, a bronze Civil War soldier stands next to Memorial Fountain, a prize-winning exhibit at the 1876 Centennial Exposition in Philadelphia. The fountain and soldier were dedicated in 1878 and are now listed in the National Register of Historic Places.

South of the square (or "diamond") is the Molly Pitcher Waffle Shop, a "restaurant and soda grill" with a neon sign. Heading west from

The Lincoln Way Arch is dated July 1914, in honor of the 150th anniversary of the town's founding and the 50th anniversary of its burning. It also marks the route Lee took to Gettysburg in 1863. The courthouse to the left is still on the square and in use. COURTESY BERNIE HEISEY

the square, there's a cement Lincoln Highway marker on the northwest corner of Franklin Street. When we reach the end of town, we rejoin the eastbound lanes. The original route was two-way on Lincoln Way, but we can follow the more recent eastbound path going through Chambersburg on Loudon Street. We pass Carson's Motel, which has a sign with a fellow on siesta under a cactus, then pass over Conococheague Creek and stay in the left lane, following the Route 30 east signs around an S curve. We cross South Main Street and pass through a small business section. At just about 1 mile, we arrive at a fork. A sharp left will take us west again; the right lane merges onto the two-way route to the east.

Back at the western end, just before the lanes meet, is a surveying business at 510 Lincoln Way West, the former Mrs. Spahr's Tourist Home. We merge onto the two-way road and immediately pass the Chambersburg Antiques and Flea Market mall to our south. Ahead is the 30 West Family Restaurant, and we pass the junction of Route 995 and soon cross Back Creek (for years a three-arch stone bridge carried traffic over it). We head back into farmland, much of it orchards. Unfortu-

The Hotel Lincoln, 72 Lincoln Way West, had a dining room, taproom, and grill. It was listed in the 1945 AAA directory as having 25 rooms starting at $1.50 a night. It's now restored and serves as apartments just west of the square, next to the stream.

Mrs. S)ahr's Tourist Home
510 Lincoln Way West on
U. S. Route 30, Chambersburg, Pa.
A'' accommodations for a
Comfortable Night away from home.

ROOMS

Mrs. Spahr's Tourist Home at 510 Lincoln Way West now houses a surveying business. Nearby was Mrs. Zentmyer's Tourist Home, in the 1940 Blue Book List *at 651 Lincoln Way West.* COURTESY CY HOSMER

nately, the fruit industry is having hard times, with fruit prices relatively unchanged despite inflation. Many of the orchard owners are starting to give in to the temptation of selling their land for development, and what makes this area unique and scenic is disappearing.

We pass Shatzer's Orchards and Fruit Market to the north. Edison and Martha Shatzer bought and enlarged established orchards here in 1933. Other crops were also grown at the time, but today their 90 acres produce only fruit—cherries, peaches, plums, pears, and apples—as well as pumpkins, gourds, corn, and Indian corn. The Shatzers' daughter Wilma, her husband, Jack, and their son Dwight now operate the business. The market, which sells fruit, gift boxes, and Pennsylvania Dutch cookbooks, is open daily from June to March and offers a free cup of cider to everyone in the fall.

Near here used to be Sycamore Meadows, with its nine cabins. A couple of miles later to the south is the Carlton Motel, advertising rooms with kitchenettes, and ahead is the Oak Forest Restaurant and Grocery. This is a good place to eat, grab supplies, and glance at the cabin camp (now rented weekly) behind it. We pass some residences and reach the main intersection of little St. Thomas where the Hotel St. Thomas once featured chicken and waffle dinners. The 1924 Lincoln Highway Association guidebook warned drivers that the speed limit in St. Thomas was 12 miles per hour, enforced. We're now 7 miles from Chambersburg and 7 from Fort Loudon.

We continue through a dip, where a stone building to the south is the Parnell Tavern, which once advertised itself as the "Lincoln Highway's Most Unusual Hostelry" because it was an 1828 mill remodeled into a "modern country tavern." On the north side, a four-bay stone house overlooks a beautiful lake, and just past that, a stone building to the north was tollhouse number 2 on the Chambersburg and Bedford Turnpike starting in 1818. Tolls were finally dropped the summer of 1913.

The road is three-lane, the middle for turns. We pass a state marker for Fort Waddell, one of a string of minor forts built for refuge from Indian attacks following Braddock's defeat near Pittsburgh in 1755. Now we head uphill through pleasant farms and bountiful orchards, such as Brown's Orchards and fruit stand and then Bingham's Fruit Market, where you can buy cider, jams, baskets, and other gifts. Apples are the main crop of the region, which grows a large share of the state's annual

Sycamore Meadows, 4 miles west of Chambersburg, is listed in the 1940 Shell Tourist Accommodation Directory. *Its 11 cabins offered only cold running water; toilets and showers were shared by all guests.*

Bingham's Fruit Market, in St. Thomas, is famous for its apples. (PHOTO 1993)

production of 13 million bushels. The orchards just east of Bingham's have a sign, though, indicating that a golf course and residences are imminent.

The land has been very flat to the south, with outcroppings of limestone; a mountain ridge has been approaching from the north. The ridge peters out just as we reach it at Parnell's Knob, and we top the small hill. To the south is Apple Ridge Restaurant, a blue and white frame building with a big metal awning out front. Behind it is the Double Decker Motel, formerly Camp Parnell and, later, the New Parnell Motel.

We approach another mountain. In the summer, there are often cows grazing to the south, and sheep to the north. The original road banks off to the north and into Fort Loudon; Route 30 curves to the left. We follow the lumpy old road past fine old homes, a cemetery, and the old tollgate number 3 from the Chambersburg-Bedford turnpike to the north, and cross the Conococheague Creek West Branch on an old, skinny iron-truss bridge. We get into the tiny town, where the houses are up against the street and close together. In front of one is a cement Lincoln Highway marker. The arrow tells us the road bends to the right, and at the town's main intersection we angle right. To the south once sat the Eagle Hotel, in later years serving as the Lincoln Lodge apartments while the lobby and barroom became the town's post office. Today it's the parking lot in front of a new post office.

Camp Parnell, midway between Chambersburg and McConnellsburg, featured barbecues and nine heated cabins with radios. It's now the Apple Ridge Restaurant and Double Decker Motel.

In 1924 a temporary crossing was begun so that the old iron bridge east of Fort Loudon could be replaced. COURTESY UNIVERSITY OF MICHIGAN, SPECIAL COLLECTIONS LIBRARY

In the fork, an old granite marker with a tablet remains to commemorate Fort Loudon, a fort erected in 1756 for defense against Indians and later used as a supply base during the Forbes campaign. The small fort and town were named for the earl of Loudon, who briefly commanded British forces in North America. A reconstructed fort is free to the public just south of Route 30.

We pass the old Orchard White House, now M & M Antiques; its motel rooms across the road are now apartments and a store. The 1940 *Shell Tourist Accommodation Directory* lists 18 cabins at the Orchard and 6 unheated ones at the Fort Loudon Inn. We cross over Route 75; the second building to the north was tollgate number 4 on the Chambersburg-Bedford Turnpike, which was still operating here in the teens according to the *Red Road Book.* Ahead is the old Vance Inn, now just the Inn, which still advertises a gift shop and apartments. A moment later we've met Route 30, and we're on our way into the mountains. The 1940 Shell guide lists 6 cottages at Mayflower Cabins, 1 mile west of town.

Fort Loudon's Orchard White House had cabins across the road and gas pumps on both sides, and it served chicken and waffles for 45 cents. The proprietor for decades was L. C. McLaughlin, who added a pool in the 1950s. The restaurant was later expanded and the building today houses M & M Antiques. COURTESY KEVIN KUTZ

Looking west to the Vance Inn on the old road through Fort Loudon.

We've been heading uphill, and now the first major climb of our ride begins as we ascend Cove Mountain. With few natural mountain gaps, the Lincoln Highway takes on ridge after ridge heading to Ligonier. Even today, the road is often steep and winding and caution should be taken. The land here is part of Buchanan State Forest, named for President James Buchanan, who was born in the area. As we round a curve with a steep falloff to the north, the eastward view behind us is spectacular. Soon the road narrows and becomes winding again, as we ascend Tuscarora Mountain. On the worst curve of all, a garage sits where the Cove Mountain Tea Room once stood to the south, and near the top on the north side is the former Smith Brothers' Tuscarora Inn, built early this century, perhaps on the ruins of the Hotel Summit and using its chimney. We soon reach the top and cross from Franklin into Fulton County.

To the left is the Tuscarora Summit Inn, once better known as Doc Seylar's. Leslie "Doc" Seylar was a pharmacist in McConnellsburg when he erected a simple lunch stand, which grew as more and more tourists took to the road. In a 1924 Department of Highways guide, Doc's is listed for having "all accommodations" and "rabbit, squirrel, turkey, and deer hunting in season." Of course, a place like Doc's had

The name Cove Mountain Tea Room seems a bit delicate for this place, which deteriorated until it was demolished a few years ago. COURTESY CY HOSMER

Looking east from Doc Seylar's tower toward the Tuscarora Summit Inn. The inn was also known as Smith Brothers and offered rooms and meals. The location of the Cove Mountain Tea Room, less than 1 mile away, is also noted in this view.

two things going for it: radiators, hot from the climb, needed water for cooling down, and while customers waited, they could climb to the roof and enjoy the view, with or without Doc's telescope. Behind the hotel is a log house that served as a motel room, as did the string of connected cabins to the left. Lore has it that since the inn straddled the county line, drinks could be had in the Fulton side but not the Franklin County end

Doc Seylar's Rest House, a small place compared with his later building. Doc is barely discernible standing under and to the right of the Coca-Cola signs. A postcard rack sits on the porch between Doc and a fellow in a "PS" shirt. COURTESY CY HOSMER

When compared with earlier views, a lot fewer cars were stopping at Tuscarora Summit Inn in the 1940s, probably because of the new Pennsylvania Turnpike. The Lincoln runs left to right. COURTESY CY HOSMER

because of its temperance laws at the time. Today the mountaintop stop is a bar and restaurant.

We start down the mountain, which is full of winding curves, and the only structure we pass, a private home, was once a roadhouse known as the Eagle's Eyrie or Shamrock Inn. It was still a bar and restaurant until the early 1980s. The road suddenly becomes four-lane, and it's here that the original road angled off to the south; we can't get to it here, but we can from its other end, which we'll meet in a moment. Just ahead is an unmarked exit to the left, and we make this turn toward McConnellsburg, following the Lincoln Highway. The 1960s Route 30 bypass, which we'll meet on the other side of the valley in a few miles, is quick but unremarkable.

Just after our left turn, there's a blocked road to our left, the old "horseshoe curve." This stretch of cement is largely intact all the way up the hill and can be walked. A little past that road are the scars of an even earlier road that wound into the hill.

As we descend into town, we pass a few houses and reach the first major intersection, at which are two gas stations. The Mohawk-Hobbs guide lists Ritchey's Camp here in 1927, at 25 cents overnight. County

Looking east to Eagle's Eyrie, now a private home. A sign on the side points to a "50 mile view."

The "horseshoe curve" east of McConnellsburg being realigned in 1924 to lessen the bend. McConnellsburg is in the distant valley. COURTESY UNIVERSITY OF MICHIGAN, SPECIAL COLLECTIONS LIBRARY

The pavement at the "horseshoe curve" is fading into the landscape. (PHOTO 1992)

commissioner Bob Garlock recalls his father opening Junction Service Station to sell Esso gas at the fork in 1929. During World War II, when stations were only allowed open 8 hours a day, his dad rented two other stations (a Texaco and an Atlantic) at the intersection and rotated their operations to stay open around the clock!

Across from the fork, Johnnie's Motel and Diner has a nice neon sign to compete with the new McDonald's across the street, although owner Dan Robinson isn't worried—he figures that people who would otherwise have passed up the town will now exit on account of McDonald's, then see his place. We pass a sporting-goods store in an old brick garage and, next door, the former Lincoln Lunch, now a chiropractor's office.

On the southeast corner of Third Street is a private home converted to use by a local church; on the southwest corner is the former McDowell Hotel. There are many other old buildings along Lincoln Way, including the Fulton House, a 1793 inn that now houses the Fulton County Historical Society. Here we see a cement Lincoln Highway marker, which was moved from Tuscarora Summit in 1992.

"The Lincoln Way: The Road Without Toll" took the left fork to Tuscarora Summit heading east from McConnellsburg. COURTESY CY HOSMER

JOHNNIE'S NEW MOTEL, DINER & SERVICE STATION - McConnellsburg, Pa.

Johnnie's no longer has a service station, and the diner is greatly remodeled, obscuring its barrel roof.

LINCOLN LUNCH. A good place to eat., McConnellsborg, Penna.

The sign in the window of Lincoln Lunch advertised, "Home Cooked Dinners, 25¢ & 50¢." It was run by Mrs. A. J. Rotz.

The City Hotel advertised "good rooms and table" in the 1914 Blue Book, *with Cline's Repair Shop and Fireproof garage in connection. Shown here in 1926 as the McDowell Hotel, it was also later known as the Glen-Nel. The Lincoln Highway is to the right, South Third Street to the left. The building remains on the southwest corner of the intersection.*

McConnellsburg was settled in the 1760s, shortly after Forbes Road came through. The town square is actually two blocks north, on the north-south alignment of Route 522. On the west end of the village at First Street is the log house of town founder Daniel McConnell, now being restored. A block north is the Market Street Inn, a bed and breakfast in a 1903 home. Then we're out of town, and another mountain looms ahead.

We pass a house near the road to our north at Peach Orchard Road, a former tollhouse that's been moved back from the road, and soon curve to the left and start the next ascent. The Lincoln Highway crosses a bridge over the Route 30 bypass before rejoining Route 30, about a 4-mile sidetrip.

We begin yet another long ascent, this one to Scrub Ridge Summit. There we find the former Long View Lodge, now the Scrub Ridge Inn restaurant and bar, famous for its 84-ounce steaks—if you can eat a whole one in an hour, it's free. Pictures of some winners hang on the wall. For years, a lookout tower sat behind the lodge and a cement Lincoln Highway marker sat in front of it. The inn's rooms still fill during

The small town of McConnellsburg once had many hotels. Here, a caravan lines up in front of the Hotel Harris, which offered "Running water in all rooms. Electric-garage attached."

The card reads "Blue Mountain Summit," but the sign says "Scrub Ridge Summit." The Long View Lodge was later built here and remains as the Scrub Ridge Inn. COURTESY RUSSELL REIN

hunting season. Now we start downhill, and the road is tight and winding. Locals will want you to speed; pull over at the summit if they're tailgating you.

At the bottom, 1 mile later, the road turns back uphill again. This time, though, it's less than 1 mile before we top it and see Pepple's spread out before us. First comes Barnyard Golf, then the Italian Sausage Hut, the Auction Barn, and finally the Kobweb Korner shop, full of lawn balls, ceramic cows, fountains, crafts, and furniture. Next door is the house of Col. Pete and Jean Pepple. Jean says that she's from this hill and Pete's from Everett. They opened the business in 1970. One of the first auctions they held was the estate of "Doc" Scylar, operator of the roadhouse on Tuscarora Summit.

We top another rise and descend into Harrisonville, crossing a 1928 cement bridge. At the intersection of Route 665 is Hollingshead's gas station and general store. Right after the crossroads is a cement Lincoln Highway marker set back in someone's yard, moved from its original location at the crossroads.

We're climbing yet again, but only slightly. At the top, across from a church, is the run-down Green Hill House, an old tollhouse of rubble stone covered with decaying stucco. At the crest is a view of Sideling Hill in the distance. We descend into the valley, passing some cabins to our

A popular view of Sideling Hill, west of Harrisonville, 1925. COURTESY PA STATE ARCHIVES, RG-12 DEPT. OF HIGHWAYS

Decker's Midway Restaurant in Saluvia, with the Mountain Garage adjacent. All three buildings are still there. COURTESY BERNIE HEISEY

south, probably from the White Cottage Inn, listed in the 1940 Shell directory. Rounding a corner at a funeral home, we pass the former Decker's Midway Restaurant to the right in Saluvia, then DeShong's Oil and Gas, which still has a few double cabins intact. Across the road is the Red Bats Nest, a bar named not for the winged mammal, but after an attraction that used to be at Bill's Place, which we'll reach shortly.

The garage and a few cabins can still be found at DeShong's. PRIVATE COLLECTION

We begin climbing Sideling Hill, on another steep and winding road. PennDOT plans on straightening and reconstructing the road here because of numerous truck accidents. To the south is an old Mail Pouch tobacco barn, and as we begin a wide curve, to the north is the Pine Crest restaurant, the former Bur Mar. It was originally Willie's Place, and the 1940 Shell guide lists Willie's cabin camp, but today no cabins are evident. There's a road cut ahead, and we can see that the old road once briefly passed to the cliff side behind a mound of dirt. The road is steep enough for the state to have installed two runaway truck ramps, and ahead the road narrows from three to two lanes.

When we reach Sideling Hill Summit, the elevation is 2,195 feet. This was the location of Budd's Place (also called Sky Top Inn), with cabins, restaurant, and observation tower, replaced in recent years by a garage for the forestry service. As the road starts another downhill slide, there are signs for Sideling Hill State Forest. We pass the junction of Route 915, and then come upon the former Shorty's Place, an old cabin camp with at least three singles and one double remaining. There used to

Willie Davies' Place advertised "Clean Cozy Cabins." The pavilion in the center has ropes around it and a sign reading "Willie Davies Logical Contender for the World's Championship," while a life-size photo of a boxer sits inside the main building. This site later became Bur-Mar Restaurant. To the left is Sideling Hill Garage. COURTESY CY HOSMER

Budd Myers offered everything a traveler needed: gasoline, cabins, food, camping, souvenirs, and beer. It was later called the Sky Top Inn, but it's now gone.

Shorty's Place, on the west side of Sideling Hill, has changed little over the years. COURTESY CY HOSMER

be a playground to the south of the road, with seesaws, swings, and a merry-go-round; it drew huge crowds and lined the road with autos. Today the amusements are promised by signs advertising exotic dancers.

The road from here sticks close to the landscape, and we feel both big and small lumps. This is also still a part of Buchanan State Forest, and the road is tree lined until we suddenly come parallel to the Pennsylvania Turnpike to our north. The Old Mountain House, also known as McIlvaine's, is to our right, and if you stop to see this dilapidated wood structure, note the road trace running behind it toward the Turnpike—it's a remnant of Forbes Road.

Finally we reach the summit of Ray's Hill, once the site of a tollgate, and an old road can be seen branching north, though it's chopped off by a Pennsylvania Turnpike road cut. Up here, above the Turnpike, is where Bill's Place once sat. When the Turnpike was rerouted around the Sideling Hill Tunnel about 1968, Bill's was demolished; all that remains are the road fragments that led to it from the east and west.

William Wakefield started Bill's Place on June 10, 1923, according

Looking east toward the Old Mountain House. Built about 1780 as McIlvaine's, it supposedly served as a chicken house at one point, and today it's just barely standing. The Lincoln goes to the right, and the old Forbes Road forked to the left. A trace of the Forbes can still be found behind the house, but the Turnpike has erased the rest of the path. COURTESY CY HOSMER

BILL'S PLACE, RAYS HILL SUMMIT
11 MILES EAST OF EVERETT, PA.

An early view of Bill's Place shows a house (possibly a tollhouse) that would soon be torn down to expand the business.

to *Pittsburgh Press* writer Gilbert Love, who walked across the state in June 1962. Bill was quite a huckster and seemingly sold just about everything at his place. (He also served as a school director in the 1940s.) He started with a tower across the road but soon moved it adjacent to his place so that travelers could look out over Clear Valley, which Bill named. One attraction proclaimed, "See the Oregon Red Bats"; when the traveler climbed the nine steps, there was a barrel with a couple of bricks in it (a bat, or brickbat, is a brick fragment, often used as a weapon).

Bill always touted his "old back house"—a large outhouse—and he printed postcard views of it with a long backhouse poem by James Whitcomb Riley. He had a single outdoor bowling alley for a while, and advertised his "animal kingdom" of wolves, foxes, and pheasants. And there was always a wide variety of gas pumps, at least 10.

Writer Love described Bill's:

For 10 miles on either side of it, signs tell you that everything's going to be all right because you're approaching Bill's Place. When you get there you find a rambling structure full of souvenirs, chinaware, toys, tricks and what not—and I mean what not. . . . A kitchen and dining room at the east end of the structure [built in 1929] burned last winter and is being rebuilt.

For years Bill's Place boasted that it had the smallest postoffice town in the country, and it doubtless was. Residents were Bill, his wife, his two sons and a hired man. [At one time this was Harvey Eyles, whom we'll meet on the other side of Breezewood.] But Bill's postal contract was canceled during an economy drive in 1954. This bothered Bill more than somewhat, because many tourists used to stop to send cards from the smallest postoffice, and they usually bought more than cards. A big sign now proclaims sadly—"HAD The Smallest Postoffice."

He started his place to earn money to resume his [business administration] studies at Penn State. The Place was started with

Some of the souvenirs offered at Bill's Place. COURTESY CY HOSMER AND THE AUTHOR

$150, of which $110 was spent for the construction of a 10-by-10-foot stand. For a time, Bill lived in a tent behind the Place. The first day's sales amounted to 37 cents.

That stand is seen in early postcards ("excellent camping") with a dog and a chicken standing by, the structure ringed with pennants from across the country, and a sign advertising hot lunches.

"Truck drivers used to take paper bags of money from Bill's Place to the bank in Everett," someone told Love, who added that Bill "has a nice log and stone home across the road" (which postcards call Bill-Mar), but he was "64 and he thinks he would like to lease the Place when the dining room is rebuilt. He wants to go traveling—to see where all those cars have been coming from."

Sure enough, the following June, Bill sold his Place to Paul W. Miller of Greensburg, but it would not outlast the decade.

There's a sign here for the Bedford County line and a blue keystone-shaped Lincoln Highway sign, apparently a state sign from the 1970s. There's also room to pull over near the summit elevation sign and have a look at the old road. Another remnant can be found just west of the summit, before the bridge over the Turnpike; the old road crosses Route 30 heading south, hugging the mountainside. It eventually crossed the Turnpike's path, and the other end will soon be visible on our trip.

As we head west across the bridge, Breezewood can be seen like a mirage a few miles distant. It's especially pretty at night when the "Town of Motels" is fully lit. As we curve to the right, 1 mile from the summit, the old Lincoln merges from our left. Route 30 becomes skinny and hilly, and .5 mile later, to the south, we pass Scenic Acres Cabins, a string of eight cabins that are for sale and look closed. The cabins, all with front porches, used to be Floyd's Place, and they advertised "No Liquor or Beer Sold Here—We Will Honor and Serve the Lord. No Meals on Sunday." At the bottom of the hill, a sharp curve passes a farmhouse and dips under the old Turnpike. The landscape is mostly rural as we reach the next rise, when Breezewood bursts into view.

The businesses go by fast: Breeze Manor Quality Inn, then the Gateway restaurant and motel with its new building and huge neon sign. Breezewood is known as not only the "Town of Motels" but also the "Gateway to the South," hence the Gateway name. Breezewood was just a small town until the Pennsylvania Turnpike opened in October 1940

Looking east through Breezewood to Ray's Hill, site of Bill's Place, c. 1930.
COURTESY PA STATE ARCHIVES, RG-12 DEPT. OF HIGHWAYS

Many postcards portray the Sunset Hill Tourist Court as it grew through the years, but a new Turnpike exit ramp displaced the 57-unit motel in the late 1960s. The earlier ramp can be seen at bottom left.

The Gateway restaurant opened shortly after the Pennsylvania Turnpike put an interchange at Breezewood in October 1940. This building was expanded for more than 50 years, until a new structure replaced it in 1994. It's now called the Gateway/TA Travel Plaza. The original Turnpike ramp can be seen in the foreground.

with an exit at Breezewood. The town became a crossroads where servicemembers transferred or looked for rides during World War II.

Merle Snyder, formerly the manager of Reels Corner Gas Station and Coffee Shop, 40 miles west, opened the Gateway with wife Marion shortly after the Pennsylvania Turnpike opened, as World War II was beginning. Contracts to supply fuel to the military convoys helped the business, and in turn, they often traded a meal or gasoline for a soldier's shoulder patch; this collection of patches is still displayed. The Gateway was taken over in 1956 by their nephew Frank Bittner and his wife, Alice, and today, it's a huge complex open 24 hours to serve every traveler's needs.

Across the street is the Turnpike ramp and Crawford's Museum and Gift Shop. The museum houses an amazing wildlife collection that outgrew the Crawfords' home, then their business in Everett. Sadly, Crawford's Museum is closed, as too many kids were damaging the animals. We hope they can hire a security guard and reopen this neat old attraction; at least they still have the best souvenir shop in town.

*Layton's Inn in Breezewood, c. 1930, offered rooms with a bath for 75 cents,
along with a garage and home-cooked meals.*

The Turnpike Commission counted 6.8 million vehicles through the
Breezewood interchange in 1989. Much of that traffic is heading for I-70,
which heads south to Maryland from a red light here. Across from it are
two giant blinking arrows for the Steak House restaurant and the nice-
looking late-1950s Penn Aire Motel with vintage neon. On the south side
are three more old motels worth a look: the Breezewood, Village, and
Wiltshire.

Within .5 mile, we're climbing out of town. We pass the Breezewood Garage, built in 1937, and head back into farmland. To the south,
the 1815 Maple Lawn Inn advertises a flea market where it served travelers for 150 years. One of its 11 fireplaces can handle nine-foot logs.
Ahead, the road splits; the original route zigzagged around the present
alignment, which cuts through rock, creating big canyons. We come to
the Juniata Crossings Bridge, 1.5 miles from Breezewood, but there are
two old segments worth exploring just before the bridge, both to the
south. The first can be reached from a crossover of the opposing Route
30 lanes. This area, once called the Shades of Death, ends at a wall of
rock formed by the new alignment, but buildings from Floyd's Place,
also known as River Dell Tourist Camp, still stand. It's listed in the 1940

Shell directory as having seven cabins with community toilets. The other segment begins right at the end of the bridge. It's marked "Do Not Enter," which is probably a good idea since it's reduced to almost a footpath, but if you walk back there you'll eventually come to the bridge abutment of the old Juniata Crossings covered bridge. The new bridge was built in the early 1930s while this one was standing, and its graceful arches can be seen from the old abutment.

Both bridges cross the Raystown Branch of the Juniata River. Upstream are wagon ruts worn into the rock at the original crossing. The two-lane covered bridge was built about 1815 as part of the Bedford to Chambersburg Turnpike. When a flood swept away half of the bridge about 1845, the rebuilt part was made only one-lane because traffic on turnpikes was at its lowest. When the automobile and the Lincoln Highway came along, all traffic had to stop at the ends and make sure no one was inside; if you headed in, you didn't want to meet someone in the middle where it went from two lanes to one! Pedestrians also used the bridge, so it's no wonder the replacement was celebrated with a parade. The old bridge lasted two more years, until the St. Patrick's Day Flood

This Floyd's Place was 1 mile west of Breezewood; there was a place by the same name 1 mile east too. The road in the foreground has been destroyed by a bypass. COURTESY CY HOSMER

of 1936. Now the new bridge is considered outmoded by PennDOT and is being considered for replacement.

At the other end of the new bridge stands the 1818 Juniata Crossings Lodge. Today it's again a lodge with nicely restored rooms. The bottom floor houses Godwin's Antiques. The Godwins are the children of Huston and Mary Neptune, who operated the hotel and antiques shop from 1957 to 1979. We continue alongside the Juniata, though the new four-lane road doesn't do justice to the views of the river.

Views of the old road show it curving right up to the water's edge, and it attracted many tourists to stop for the night. One man who took advantage of this was Harvey Eyles, who was 95 in 1991 when he recalled the lunch stand he started along the Juniata about 1920. In addition, he owned a grocery (also on the Lincoln Highway near Everett), worked at Bill's Place, helped build the Pennsylvania Turnpike, managed an A&P and a Clover Farm store, started a chain of four welding schools (though he couldn't weld), worked at American Bridge near Pittsburgh, and hauled steel for Babcock and Wilcox in Zelienople.

> I first started that stand down past Everett, and my wife
> [first wife, Rhoda] and I lived in that tent, to watch our stand.

The original Lincoln passed in front of the Juniata Crossings Hotel to cross the covered bridge, here in 1927. The 1930s bypass cut behind the hotel. COURTESY CY HOSMER

Harvey Eyles had a lunch stand along the Juniata River and lived in a tent behind it. In his arms is Harvey, Jr., born in 1921. COURTESY GOLDIE EYLES

There was a creek in back of our shanty. I made a little money—oh, a good bit we made. My wife and I'd bake 20 pies a day, and we'd cut each pie in four pieces and sell them for 10 cents apiece. We were busy all the time. That's the reason Bill's Place went up there. Bill saw that I was making pretty good money, so he put his place up on the mount right afterward.

Bill was a nice fellow; I liked him. He built that doggone thing up there, and he would put something in a shoe or something down there and charged people a quarter to go up the steps and look down. And he had something saying how nice it would be—a live animal. There was no live animal down there, but see how many suckers there were that'd go up those steps just to look down! He had, oh, "wild boar" or something marked on it, and he charged 25 cents to go up and see it, you look down, and there's nothing down there. When he started he just had a little stand, but he built on and on.

Harvey eventually worked for Bill. "I went down, tore my stand down, down along the river. I hated to tear it down, but Bill was taking all my trade."

I liked Everett. Everett's nice. My brother [Elmer] lived there for maybe 10 years. He had the Chrysler garage, sold Chryslers and Plymouths. It was on the main street but down right at the end of Everett where you started to go to Breezewood. The road between Breezewood and Everett was a dirt road. We oiled a good bit of it, and I had to pay for it!

Harvey remembers selling "loads of sandwiches, hamburgs, and hot dogs, for 10 cents apiece. We had to buy chunks of ice, but that was cheap. We had lots of campers every night. That was free, but they bought a lot of stuff at my stand, like sandwiches or a pie. It looked like a good place to me. There was enough room [and it] didn't cost me anything to be there."

The road today has characters just as colorful, but they're harder to find. Many times you'll meet them at the local lunch counter, like the one inside the Traveler's Rest. It's also a motel, and the restaurant is in the big, yellow pointy-roofed building. An old piece of concrete roadbed can be seen slicing between the restaurant and motel and ending after the Sheepskin Country store. Another piece runs behind the Trading Company sporting-goods store. A longer segment branches off to the south,

This 1935 view of the Traveler's Rest shows that bus service was once available at less centralized locations. COURTESY CY HOSMER

behind a farm and Clark's Motor Lodge (recently closed) and rejoins Route 30 after a road cut. The road then levels for a while, and we pass Olde Store antiques to the south and the tiny Motel 30 to the north. Sue and Jim Caro assure travelers that their motel isn't big or fancy, but it's clean and inexpensive.

Ahead is an exit for Everett, as Route 30 bypasses the town on the Bud Shuster Byway. We turn left and follow the Lincoln Highway into town. Construction of the interchange erased all traces of two tourist camps: Drenning's and River View Park, later called Larry's, Sherm's, and then Gene's.

A golf course sits to the south, and as we reach a hill, to our south is Kelly's Scenic View Restaurant; the original road can be seen running directly behind Kelly's and through the front edge of a cemetery.

Over the crest is Bill & Fred's Ice Cream Emporium, shaped like a scoop of ice cream topped with chocolate syrup and a cherry. As we enter town, some older buildings line the street, most notably the Everett Theater, with a black Carrara glass facade. At one corner are the Carolyn Courts motel and restaurant, with two nice neon signs. Everett was once

River View Park, 1 mile east of Everett, was later known as Larry's, Sherm's, and then Gene's. The pumps and signs note the availability of Sunoco, Atlantic, Gulf, and Mobiloil. COURTESY CY HOSMER

The Everett Theater and Everett Restaurant and Motel have similar neon signs.
(PHOTO 1992)

surrounded by quarries and mines, and today the little town still looks active. Heading out of town, just before a right-hand curve, there's a cement Lincoln Highway marker to the right, in front of a house. The road goes under Route 30 and rejoins it heading west.

An old roadbed can be seen branching up Mount Dallas from the ramp. This old route originally crossed over railroad tracks that themselves had crossed the Juniata River on a bridge with big stone piers. Gulf's c. 1918 Lincoln Highway road map, which is light on descriptive details, nevertheless warns that this was a dangerous crossing. Route 30 was rerouted under the railroad bridge about 1920, and the bridge was torn down a few years ago, though some of the piers can still be seen.

Continuing west, the road goes from four to two lanes. We're still on the newer alignment, but even a bypassed section of the bypass can be found on the right. The old road is still north on the mountain, though at one point it dips down to meet Route 30. It again cuts north, however, until it passes an old stone house and rejoins the current road.

The original road then angles off to the south, and as we go through a small road cut, the old road once again crosses Route 30 to the north side. It's on this northern segment that the house that was once Rusty's Place is found. The bypass, meanwhile, climbs a short but steep hill. Coming down the other side sits a hospital to the north between the old

Looking north across the Juniata River to Mount Dallas, 1921. The bypass (and still current Route 30) dips beneath the railroad bridge. The original Lincoln Highway can be seen to the right, where it crosses the tracks at grade level adjacent to the shack, then follows the telephone poles heading west, briefly meets the new road (seen above the railroad bridge), then snakes north again. COURTESY UNIVERSITY OF MICHIGAN, SPECIAL COLLECTIONS LIBRARY

RUSTY'S PLACE Open All Year Clean Cozy Cabins 3 miles W of Everett, Pa.

Rusty's Place had four gas pumps: Esso, Standard, Gulf, and Sunoco. Cabins can be seen just under the hanging "Standard" sign. Rusty's is now a private home. COURTESY ELEANOR FOREMAN

and new roads. Halfway down, there's a sign for the Moonlite Drive-In Theater. The original Moonlite opened in 1947 north of Bedford, but when Route 220 displaced it, it reopened at this location in 1962. It's open weekends through the summer.

Ahead we can see the "Long Level," though now the landscape is altered by the recent addition of a Wal-Mart and a McDonald's. The old Lincoln rejoins Route 30 at the bottom of the hill, and a little stone building to the south helps us locate the site of Bubbling Springs Camp. Passing the new mall, we curve to the left past the 1787 Defibaugh Tavern to the north; a portion of old road runs through its yard. Next we come upon the Willows Restaurant, with a tall neon sign. Somewhere in this vicinity was Willow Grove Tourist Camp; postcards show a house, gas pumps, and cabins 3 miles east of Bedford.

There appear to be some old road remnants to the north that serve as driveways now. Ahead the road is again flat, and we pass the Mile Level Pizza and Subs to the south, Cross' Diner to the north. As we go under the Pennsylvania Turnpike, we can cross the Narrows Bridge, a concrete arch span built in 1934, or see a short section of original Lincoln by making an immediate right.

This road shortly leads to a stone abutment from the old iron bridge on the left that used to cross the Juniata, and an abutment across the water can also be seen (and can be seen very well from the Turnpike at mile marker 148.5). A tollhouse sat at the western end for years. This area is

Looking west to Bubbling Springs Camp. The tiny stone building behind the gas pumps is all that remains. Other postcards show the cabins. COURTESY CY HOSMER

Lincoln Highway over Raystown Branch of Juniata River at Cliffs, near Bedford, Pa.

This view of the Narrows Bridge looking east shows the original alignment. Nothing remains of the road in the foreground except the bridge abutment. The Pennsylvania Turnpike now travels next to the road across the river. COURTESY CY HOSMER

called the Narrows because of the natural water gap. This gap has been a convenient pass for all modes of transportation; in fact, the Turnpike and Lincoln Highway are so close that plans for working on either road's bridge are turning out to be extremely difficult. The cement Route 30 span across the Narrows is itself narrow with dangerous intersections at its ends, placing it in a perilous preservation position.

Back on Route 30, we cross the Narrows Bridge and the road splits, the bypass to the right taking traffic around Bedford. In early years Smith's Cabins were located out here, in later years the Valley View Motel. We take the original Lincoln into Bedford and see the old Greyhound bus station and Gateway restaurant on the right. The road forks at the Landmark Restaurant, a former Dari-Dell that had carhop service. We stay to the right and follow East Pitt Street. On our right is a bank, the former site of the 1771 Elmwood Inn and New Motor Court; a couple of cabins still sit west of it. Mid-1950s ads also call it the Bedford Village Motel.

Across the street sat the Bedford Motel. A c. 1945 postcard says that proprietor Minick Mellott had 24 units situated five blocks east of

Gateway Restaurant, Greyhound Post House, Lincoln Highway, Bedford, Pa.

The Gateway restaurant and Greyhound bus station have closed, but the building on Bedford's east end is still being used.

"Pride of the Lincoln Highway."
Construction begun 9/15/'15
Will be opened May-1916.
75 Rooms-25 Baths,
C. H. & P.W. Smith
Proprietors

FORT BEDFORD INN,
BEDFORD. PA.

Fort Bedford Inn billed itself as the "Pride of the Lincoln Highway," though it was one block south of the route. Today it serves as a retirement home.

Bedford. *Ray Walker's Vacation Resort/Motor Court Recommendations* from 1949 mentions that it has "35 unusually well maintained 1 to 4 room units" on both sides of the highway. It's possible that the two motels merged, but local resident Paul England remembers when they were in competition. The owners, he says, "would both sit out on evenings and as cars came into town they'd wave them in."

As we enter the downtown area, it's mostly residential with many turn-of-the-century homes. On a corner to our north is the former DeVore's Tourist Home, and at 415 East Pitt was Mrs. Diehl's Mayfair Inn, listed in the 1936 and 1941 Federal Hi-Way Homes guides; the 1957 AAA directory lists two rooms in the house and 11 motel units. Some of those rooms can still be seen behind the house, which now houses a hair-styling salon.

As we approach the traffic light, to the left at 224 East Pitt Street is the Bedford Hotel, once operated by Mr. and Mrs. Ray Stayer. A 1940 postcard of the six-bay brick house calls it the Gephart Inn, with the Stayers as owners. A listing in the 1955 *Eastern Motor Court Map* says it then had nine motel units in back and it too was called the Bedford Motel. Today it's a bar and restaurant.

The original Hoffman's Hotel with the official Lincoln Highway Stutz in front.
COURTESY CY HOSMER

The new Hoffman's, as seen from the road. COURTESY CY HOSMER

The Hoffman's lobby shows a variety of souvenirs and sundries for sale.

Duncan Hines himself congratulated Lee Hoffman on the food at his chain of hotels. Here, they meet at the Hoffman's on the William Penn Highway, Route 22, at Cresson, west of Altoona.

The apartments to our north are where Hoffman's Hotel once sat. Lee Hoffman produced many postcards not only of his hotel, but also of every scene in the area. The hotel went through many changes through the years, including a fire that forced a rebuild (and Hoffman even printed postcards of the charred remains). But it burned again about 1970, never to reopen. Next door, on the corner of Richard Street (Business Route 220) is the Graystone Galleria, full of crafts on one side, antiques on the other. The main structure is the 1768 Graystone Hotel.

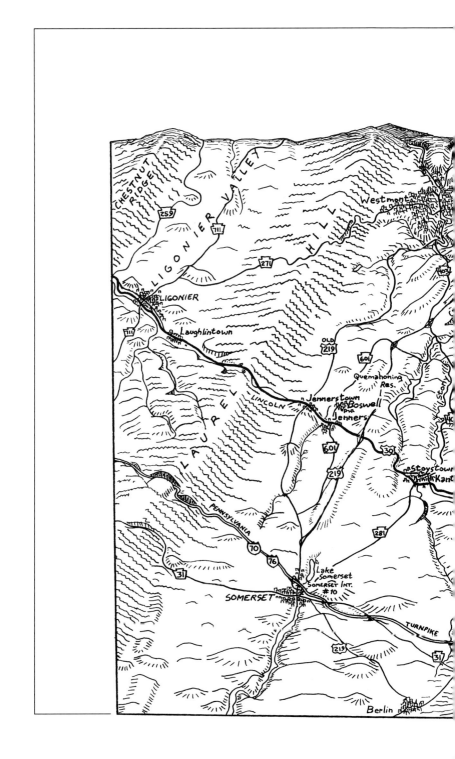

TOWN
219
Beaverdale
8%
Claysburg
160
Blue Knob
MOUNTAIN
Windber
56
DUNNING MOUNTAIN
160
8%
220
ALLEGHENY
OLD
56
220
Central City
96
56
Buckstown
BR
220
Reels Corners
Schellsburg
Wolfsburg
BEDFORD INT.
#11
30
TULL'S
HILL
Grand View Pt.
Shawnee
Lake
Branch
Indian
Lake
Roystown
BEDFORD
160
31
220
70 76
96

K.J.PATRICK

The town that is now Bedford was settled about 1750 and originally named Raystown after an early settler. The town gained prominence when General Forbes constructed Fort Raystown on his expedition toward Pittsburgh in 1758. The fort was later renamed for the duke of Bedford, and the town was renamed after the fort. At the intersection of Forbes Road and the Horseshoe Trail (Business Route 220), Bedford became an important crossroads, continuing into the twentieth century with the arrival of the Lincoln Highway and then the Pennsylvania Turnpike.

A couple of miles north of town on 220 is the Bedford exit of the Pennsylvania Turnpike. The Turnpike was considered quite a threat to Route 30 businesses when it was being built in the late 1930s; monthly meetings were held by a local Lincoln Highway support group, who argued that a limited-access road was contrary to the purpose of a road. In a 1938 *Philadelphia Inquirer* article, the president of the Central Pennsylvania Hotel Association asserted that the new road was "nothing but a political movement," and that "20,000 hotel, garage employees, and other persons who depend on tourists for a living would permanently lose their jobs." Their predictions were partly right, for many businesses on the old roads indeed died, but just as many are now clustered around the Turnpike interchanges. Even after the Turnpike opened, Lincoln Highway booster groups continued their publicity blitz and their campaign for improvements.

On Business 220 south is the Bedford Springs Hotel, a wonderful resort hotel left rotting. After the springs were discovered two centuries ago, the area became a fashionable retreat for the wealthy and notable, hosting presidents and politicians in the nineteenth century. Perhaps Bedford's most prominent resource, the resort has been closed for years, and no one can seem to decide what to do with it.

The Lincoln Highway in Bedford follows Pitt Street, which was the old toll road that ran west to Pittsburgh. Heading west from Richard Street (Business Route 220), the north side of the road has a string of historic buildings. The Anderson House was built in 1814 and now houses the local tourism agency, in case you're looking for brochures. The Espy House is where Washington stayed when he came west to quell the Whiskey Rebellion in 1794. There are also other little candy and ice

A fireproof garage such as King's was a big draw in the 1920s and 1930s. Cars could be stored here for 75 cents.

The Bedford Garage and Hotel Pennsylvania across from King's Garage in Bedford.

cream shops in the area. Bedford once had a Lincoln Highway Garage, and the 1935 *Bedford Echo* high school yearbook has an ad for the Lincoln Highway Shoe Rebuilder at 104 West Pitt Street.

On the south side of the road is the old Hotel Pennsylvania, now apartments, and a block past that is the Bedford House, a bed and breakfast in an 1803 brick home. On the north side at Juliana Street is the Fort Bedford Museum, built in 1958 for the town's bicentennial. This partial re-creation of the original British fort contains exhibits and thousands of artifacts, including a Conestoga wagon and a delivery wagon from the town's old Lincoln Highway Dairy.

At the first bend in the road is Dunkle's Gulf, a beautiful art deco gas station. Jack Dunkle still runs the station that his father, Dick, opened in 1933. He says many people stop just to take pictures of the cream-colored terra cotta building. It was Gulf's showplace between Pittsburgh and Philadelphia on the Lincoln Highway, but Jack says it's hard running the place with just one bay and a pair of pumps. He doesn't recommend

Artist Kevin Kutz has painted many structures along the Lincoln Highway, but none more than Dunkle's Gulf. He's lost track of how many Dunkles he's done, but it's "probably dozens." COURTESY KEVIN KUTZ, PHOTO BY RICHARD STONER

Looking east toward Bedford, past the famous Coffee Pot.

that his son stay in the business, but we get the feeling the family will be here for a long time.

Still on Pitt Street, we pass under Route 220, follow a bend in the road, and there's Lashley's Garage to the north. Just past the station is the famous Coffee Pot. It looks a bit different from the old postcards, when it was covered with metal and everything was perfectly landscaped. The Coffee Pot is no longer sheathed in metal, and the brick underneath is now exposed. Painted red and white, the brick has a few chips in it from overanxious customers. It has served as a lunch stand, a Greyhound station, and most recently, a bar, but it's been closed for years. In a 1986 *Pittsburgh Press* article, former owner Wilson Lashley recalled another owner, Ma, who had a pet monkey. Lashley remembered Ma "in her eighties, sitting up half the night over a gin and Squirt while her monkey climbed over everyone and everything at the bar." The Bedford Fairgrounds are across the street, and they probably accounted for a lot of the Coffee Pot's business in the early days.

We rejoin Route 30 at the end of the 1971 Bedford bypass. Coming downhill, the Lincoln Highway branched off to the south to Wolfsburg, but the route is no longer complete—a covered bridge is long gone, though the abutments are still visible when we cross an adjacent iron bridge on Route 30. We can enter the tiny town of Wolfsburg by turning left at the end of the bridge, onto a road that eventually rejoins 30.

Cabins at the Lincoln Motor Court. (PHOTO 1990)

A painting of Greenland Lodge by artist John Baeder. Note the spelling of "sand-wiches," true to the original. COURTESY JOHN BAEDER, PHOTO BY D. JAMES DEE

On Route 30, we pass a huge cross with "Jesus Saves" on it, and as we pass the road coming out of Wolfsburg, we top another hill. At the bottom is a bend where the Greenland Lodge sat until the spring of 1992, when it was bulldozed in one day. Only the main building remained by that time, but what a sign it had on its roof: a giant neon replica of a tourist cabin. In the early 1970s it also advertised a pool and miniature golf, but today all traces of the business are gone.

Ahead, the scene is beautiful as the road flattens for a while, with a hill in the distance. Route 56 to Johnstown breaks off north before the hill, and the Turnpike is parallel to the north, 100 feet away.

To the south, large mountains have appeared, and we arrive at a fork in the road. A Lincoln Highway marker points right. This is an ancient intersection, originally the fork of two Indian paths: the Raystown path (now Route 30) and the Glades path (now Route 31). A few miles west on 31, at a town called Manns Choice, is Coral Caverns. There you'll see the only known inland coral reef, a result of this area having been under the Appalachian Sea some 400 million years ago.

At the fork is an old stagecoach stop now called the Jean Bonnet Tavern. On the National Register of Historic Places, it's again a bed and breakfast, but there are also a bar and restaurant that are open daily. Built of fieldstone and chestnut beams in 1762, it was purchased by the Frenchman Bonnet in 1780. You'll find Bonnet and his inn (and the road) mentioned in the travel journals of John Heckewelder, the Moravian missionary who crossed the Allegheny Mountains via this path 30 times on his trips to Ohio Indian villages 200 years ago.

The highway passes under the Turnpike (we can see a bit of the Lincoln to the south at Turnpike mile marker 142.7), and on the other side is a long, flat stretch of road. Before we climb the steep hill, a minor road, which looks like a dirtbike path, cuts off to our south. It's the old Lincoln, and it emerges at the top, cutting back southeastward from the intersection. It can be driven, but it's not recommended for the unadventurous.

The summit is known as Tull's Hill, named for an Indian massacre of the Tull family. On the south side is the Lincoln Motor Court, a cute little tourist court, with 11 single cabins arranged in a U shape. Debbie and Bob Altizer have run the place since 1983 and in 1993 changed the name from Country Comfort Motel back to its original. Advertisements from around 1970 tell of an Allegheny Motor Motel and Shawnee Park Motel in this area; perhaps one was this place.

Debbie recalls, "We lived in D.C. for seven years, and then we got totally sick of the rat race. We came up here, fell in love, and bought it, but after the first year and the next couple of years we hated it because

Russ's Place at the top of Tull's Hill, 1929. Mr. and Mrs. Russ Crissey had a dance hall, restaurant, and snack stand, along with a large number of antiques for sale. On August 1, 1932, a passing motorist discovered that it was on fire, and a shortage of water led to its destruction. COURTESY HISTORICAL SOCIETY OF WESTERN PA

we've got 13 bathrooms to take care of, plumbing, the heating kept breaking down. . . . Now we're pulling a tiny little profit after 10 years. We've had to live down some reputations. I don't know which owner it was, but we heard it rumored that he would give you two dollars back if you made your own bed—I don't know if that was with clean sheets or the dirty sheets! We came from the city, where hot tubbing was the big thing in 1983. We tried a hot tub in the corner of one of the rooms, and that just went *phhht.*"

Bob adds, "We put up a sign, 'whirlpool–spa' and I had people stopping by and asking me if I repaired washing machines!" Bob has learned that the motel was built in 1944. "It took a pretty optimistic person at the end of World War II to decide to build a vacation place." In fact, it was built by Thomas Mitchell for a Mr. Crissey, probably Clyde Crissey, then owner of the Hotel Lincoln across the street. Mitchell later bought the motel that he built.

Across the street is Hotel Lincoln Antiques, where we get one of the most bizarre histories of any place along the road. Steve and Darlene Hall purchased it sight unseen at a sheriff's sale in 1988, when they also owned Coral Caverns, not knowing the place had been a pretty wild bar in recent years. There were 40-some bullet holes throughout the place, and the ceiling had been used as a giant X-rated graffiti pad—for $1 per square, visitors could personalize a section of the tin ceiling.

The hotel began as a boardinghouse in 1870. Clyde Crissey bought it in 1926 and tore down everything but the kitchen. He rebuilt it with a large ballroom, a double-deck porch, and nine rooms upstairs. The hotel also offered gas and food. As its reputation slid, it changed names: the Red Bat Cave (there's that Red Bat name again), then Happy Trails Bar and Grill. But according to locals, the wild reputation was nothing new. One recent visitor told Steve and Darlene about a woman who had worked at the hotel in the 1930s, both downstairs at the bar and "upstairs in the rooms." When her husband stopped by one night, he found her in room number one with another man and proceeded to hang his wife and shoot the man. The kicked-in door still rests in the attic. Steve counts 14 deaths at the site: six inside the hotel, two in the parking lot, and six more pulling into traffic.

Besides the stories, which Steve loves to tell, you'll also find lots of antiques, including an old curved porcelain Lincoln Highway marker from the teens. And soon the hotel will again house overnight travelers.

Steve and Darlene Hall outside their Hotel Lincoln Antiques, built by Clyde Crissey as a hotel in 1926. (PHOTO 1990)

After leaving the Hotel Lincoln, we go downhill past the Shawnee Sleepy Hollow campground, on a short piece of bypassed Lincoln to the north. The office and store are housed in the Sleepy Hollow (or Hi-De-Ho) Tavern, built in 1775 along the original Forbes Road. On Route 30, just behind the guardrail, is a c. 1818 marker from the Bedford-Stoystown Turnpike. You can barely make out the lettering: "S24" and "P93" on one side, referring to the distances west to Stoystown and Pittsburgh, and "C59" and "H109" on the other side, the distances east to Chambersburg and Harrisburg. The latter was on the original Pennsylvania Road, and these four towns were terminuses of the five turnpikes, along with Bedford and Greensburg. Another marker is 5 miles west.

Across from the Frosty Bear Drive-In ice cream stand is an entrance to Shawnee State Park. Shawnee covers more than 3,800 acres and is a great place to swim, boat, camp, and hike. It attracts millions of visitors yearly, accounting for some of the roadside businesses in the area.

The road cut is a sure sign that the old road went elsewhere; here it jogged north and then, after the cut, south. After more jogs, the old road can still be seen emerging behind the Shawnee Inn at the bottom of the hill. Old postcards show the lay of the original road, right down to the tiny 1917 state-built bridge that remains on the abandoned stretch. The road now serves as a driveway for a house.

This view, looking east from Schellsburg, shows the sometimes radical straightening and leveling of the route. The original Lincoln can be seen crossing from right to left, in front of the barn. Today the entrance to Shawnee Park is just over the hill. COURTESY UNIVERSITY OF MICHIGAN, SPECIAL COLLECTIONS LIBRARY

LINCOLN HIGHWAY APPROACHING SCHELLSBURG, PA.

Looking west toward Schellsburg. This old route runs behind the Shawnee Inn.

The Shawnee Inn is a great roadside restaurant. Owner Glenn Martin says it was built in 1947 as a plumbing shop and was remodeled into a restaurant three years later. Glenn's family settled near York in 1735. He grew up there, but he crisscrossed the country in the late 1980s looking for a place before buying the Shawnee. He's recently enlarged the restaurant, which is decorated with an American Indian theme.

On the north side, shortly after the family owned and operated Shawnee Motel, is another old turnpike marker: "To S 19, P 88" and "To C 64, H 114." An error can be seen on the western side: after an arrow, the word *TO* was first written *OT* and then corrected. The western-pointing arrow was probably to blame.

We now enter Schellsburg, a beautiful little town. The two blocks of homes and businesses along the street are mostly red brick with little ornamentation, many dating from the 1820s. At least eight businesses are antiques shops, each offering a different slant. John "Buttercup" Smith has dealt in antiques for 35 years; his 1876 building is filled with trinkets and such, nothing too fancy. Across from Smith's is May Brother's Garage with its neon clock.

Perhaps the neatest attraction is Lincoln Highway Packards. It's located in the former Colvin's Garage, which served travelers beginning in 1929. Robert Sweet, Jr., bought the garage in 1989 to do antique auto restorations and added an art gallery up front called the Packard Gallery. Packards were the car of choice for the original Lincoln Highway Association, probably because one-time LHA president Henry Joy was also president of Packard!

Rising out of town, we can turn south on Township Route 443 to the Colvin covered bridge. Built in 1894 across Shawnee Creek, it's about 1 mile south of 30. Continuing on Route 30, the old road banks off south, and it's even called Old Route 30. The new route takes us past Storyland, a kiddie amusement park filled with giant re-creations of nursery rhyme characters, but closed now. Coming out of the road cut, the Lincoln is to the south, running past the 1806 Union Church and through its cemetery. To the north is another turnpike marker, the third one around Schellsburg; it reads, "To S 18, P 87" and "To C 65, H 115."

Ahead is one of the most beautiful vistas on the Lincoln Highway. The road can be seen heading downhill and then into the distant mountains, each green ridge getting progressively paler. A well-kept farm passes to our north—the Lincoln Highway Farm, whose name has been painted right on the red barn since 1918. There's a little fence in front of the barn along the road, and if you stop to take a picture, the cows usually come over to watch what you're doing.

Across the road is the old Shawnee Cabins tourist camp. It operated

Storyland children's park advertised "where fairytales come to life," but the park has been dead quiet since the mid-1980s.

SCHELLSBURG AND CHESTNUT RIDGE UNION CEMETERY AND OLD CHURCH, BUILT 1806, ON LINCOLN HIGHWAY.

LINCOLN HIGHWAY FARM

The original Lincoln Highway cuts through this cemetery and past the 1806 church. Services are still held on special occasions.

The cows will watch your every move at the Lincoln Highway Farm, which has been in the same family for over 150 years. (PHOTO 1993)

until 1985, when it was sold to the adjacent orchard company. Postcards and guidebooks also mention a Lincoln Park in the area, 11 miles from Bedford. Today there are five dark gray cabins and a house in front of an empty gas pump island (which had Boron pumps until recently). Sometimes a bunch of tanned fellows sit, talk, or play cards out front; they're field hands, living in the old cabins while they harvest the orchards.

Lincoln Park, 11 miles west of Bedford, would have been near Shawnee Cabins.
It was listed in the 1940 Shell Tourist Accommodation Directory with seven
cabins starting at $1.25 a night. COURTESY CY HOSMER

At the bottom of the hill is the Route 30 Basket Shop in a little hut. The land levels, and we pass a sign at the road for New Paris that invites all to the Point Pleasant View Mennonite Church. There used to be many covered bridges on the Lincoln Highway, and one sat in this valley. Bedford County once had more than 70 of these old bridges, but only 14 are left.

The mountains start showing themselves again as we climb some small, lapping rises, and we are surrounded by more and more trees. As we top the hill, another mountain ridge lies ahead. Coming down a small rise, we swing past a stone and white-sided house with lots of cars around it, the former Rock Oak Park, which served gasoline and food to travelers. The 1928 Mohawk-Hobbs guide shows that camping space cost 25 cents.

We pass Meyer's, an old Quonset hut garage faced in red-painted wood. Entering the trees again, there are signs for Lada's, "the sweetest spot on the mountain," and another for its "homemade candies, assorted chocolates, assorted fudge." At one of the sharpest bends on any major highway sits Lada's in the old Shot Factory. It's a tall, stone building, and a legend arose that lead was dropped from the second floor to make

Rock Oak Park had nine gas pumps and four major brands: Esso, Gulf, Sinclair, and Texaco.

The road began climbing to Grand View at right after passing the Shot Factory.

cannon shot for the Revolution. The sharp curve in the road was not part of the Forbes Road—the original route climbed straight up the mountain!

As we wind around the bends, arising out of the mist like a ghost ship, silent and still, tattered and worn, is the Ship Hotel, the inspiration of Herbert Paulson, a Dutch immigrant who left Holland in the midteens to work as a tool and die maker at the mills in Pittsburgh. After running

Grand View Park, at the top of the hill, was Paulson's first roadside stand.
COURTESY STEVE LINTNER

Early on, a wall was built at Grand View. The owner of this postcard stopped here on August 3, 1914.

various hotels, he built a stand just above the Grand View lookout in the mid-1920s, calling it Grand View Park. A stand at the lookout itself was operated by someone else, whom Bedford locals recall to have been a Mr. Richelieu, who later owned the Richelieu Theater in town.

Within a year Paulson bought the stand at the lookout. Herbert Paulson's son Walter recalls: "The 13 acres on the hillside cost $3,200. When the mountain was cut to widen the curve, they covered the Lincoln Highway with crushed quarried stone all the way to Bedford." Paulson expanded the stand, calling it Grand View Point Inn. He enlarged it the next year too, using a castle theme and building a matching gas station. "The state was afraid it would slide," says Walter, "but my father told them, 'It's my property—either you let me build it or you buy the property.'"

Three steel I-beams were put under the road and 18 steel piers were sunk to anchor the building, which had four floors, three of them hanging down the hill below road level. The top floor had a dining room, gift shop, and lookout deck; the second and third floors had hotel rooms; the bottom floor was reserved for overnight car storage.

In 1931 Paulson got the itch to enlarge again. He was known as "Captain" Paulson for his love of the sea, and he considered a fish-shaped building. But as Walter recalls, he didn't have enough money for a fantail, and an enlarged castle would have blocked the view, so he finally decided on a ship. Herbert Paulson hired two men who were hunting in the area: Emilio Rossi and Lewis Franci. Work reportedly started in October 1931 and was done by the spring.

GRAND VIEW POINT
ON LINCOLN HIGHWAY ELEVATION 2675

A stand was built at the lower end of the Grand View wall in the mid-1920s. The rock wall to the left was painted with white stripes for safety. COURTESY CY HOSMER

GRANDVIEW POINT ON LINCOLN HIGHWAY, ALTITUDE 2599 FT., WEST OF BEDFORD, PA.

After Captain Paulson bought the Grand View stand, he built a castlelike wall and moved the stand to the central opening.

When he built a full-size hotel and restaurant, Paulson expanded his castle theme.

The Ship was built over the piers of the earlier building. Walter says that the Ship needed 63.5 tons of steel and cost $125,000 borrowed at 16 percent interest. "The contractors from Turtle Creek went broke trying to build the base; they had to go 32 feet down to find rock. They used all the car frames they could buy" to cover the exterior.

Articles in the May 6 and 27, 1932, *Bedford Gazette* announced the grand opening of the S.S. Grand View Hotel (one of the many names the

The lunch board in the Grand View Point Inn dining room proclaims the special: chicken waffle dinner.

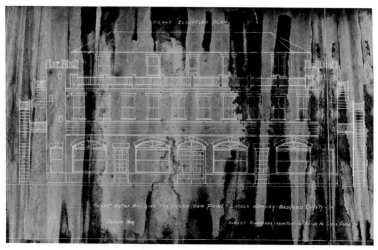

Architect Albert Sinnhuber submitted this rendering for a remodeled Grand View Point resort-hotel that continued the castle theme. COURTESY CARNEGIE MELLON UNIVERSITY ARCHITECTURE ARCHIVES

An aerial view of the S.S. Grand View Point Hotel—the Ship—shows that the final product really did look like a boat out of water.

The area between the two main entrances was originally an open space but was enclosed by the time this shot was taken in the mid-1930s. A captain's wheel and engine throttle were on deck.

The bar and the rest of the Ship continued the nautical theme. The upholstery was salmon colored, but the chairs, unfortunately, have been sold.

Captain Paulson drew this bridge proposal to bypass the dangerous curve at the Shot Factory. Of course, traffic still had to navigate the bad turn in front of the Ship. COURTESY CARNEGIE MELLON UNIVERSITY ARCHITECTURE ARCHIVES

Ship would adopt) at noon on May 29, 1932, offering concerts, tours, and staff inspections. Walter recalls being on stilts for that day. A little German band played, and "a man dropped flowers on the deck from a plane."

The final result was quite authentic, complete with observation decks having a captain's wheel and telescopes, and ringed with life preservers. The wall's stone turrets were covered to look like lighthouses. Inside, a

This is a sampling of the souvenirs that were once sold at Grand View Point.
COURTESY CY HOSMER, RICK KRISS, AND THE AUTHOR

mural around the ceiling portrayed the "captain's" adventures at sea. Herbert's granddaughter Clara Gardner recalls that the upstairs rooms were called "first class," and the budget-priced rooms on lower floors were called "second class" and "third class." The employees living on the bottom floor joked that they lived in the steerage.

The Ship kept a log of visitors, and it was filled with celebrities of the day, among them, Clara Bow, George Burns, Joan Crawford, Henry Ford, Greta Garbo, Lillian Gish, Tom Mix, J. P. Morgan, Buddy Rogers, Rudy Vallee, George Raft, and Mary Pickford. The Ship's ninth log, which ran from September 1936 to June 1938, had more than 102,000 names, including tourists from every state and 72 foreign countries!

The Ship became a famous landmark overnight, but business declined as more drivers switched to the nearby Pennsylvania Turnpike after 1940. The Paulsons sold the Ship in the 1970s, as they were getting older. New owners tried reviving it, calling it Noah's Ark. They covered it with wooden planking and put a zoo over by the gas station, but that failed, and today the Ship sits quiet, waiting for new generations to climb its deck for a grand view of "3 states and 7 counties."

As we top the hill and cross the county line, there's an old stone-faced chimney to the north, all that remains from Harvey's, a restaurant and gas station. Across the road, a new sign warns eastbound drivers of a 5-mile steep grade. Before our next climb is the Route 30 Antiques store, opened in 1993.

We pass a state marker for Fort Dewart, a small fortification built along Forbes Road, and keep climbing to Bald Knob Summit, where it

Topper's was at 2,601 feet according to this 1928 postcard. COURTESY CY HOSMER

Harvey's was apparently at the same place as Topper's. All that remains is the stone chimney. COURTESY JOHN SMITH

flattens out at 2,906 feet. The 1927 Mohawk-Hobbs guide lists free camping space at a lunch stand and blacksmith shop here. At the next bend is a bar, the Buckhorn Inn, supposedly the former location of Shady Park. Wherever Shady Park was, it was later enlarged and renamed Minick's Place. Listings say its cabins had hot and cold running water but community toilets and showers. When Minick's (later called

Minick's Place appears to have begun in a small home. An earlier 1928 postcard called it Shady Park Restaurant and Filling Station. A sign in the foreground implores tourists to "Demand ACE Ginger Beer." COURTESY BERNIE HEISEY

Minick's Place, with an adjacent garage called Sparks, about 1931. COURTESY CY HOSMER

The porches at Minick's Place were later enclosed. Nearby was the similar-looking Bollerhey's Mountain View Park, also with a restaurant and cabins.

Wingard's and Mellott's) burned down, the cabins were reportedly moved down the road to Shawnee Cabins tourist camp.

Ahead is the Seven Mile Stretch, object of many a postcard. The road is beautiful as it fades into the horizon, rising and dipping. This is also the beginning of local strip-mining operations; some mountains are completely cut away, and the grass on others looks like it was planted yesterday. On the north side is another old turnpike marker, barely legible; one part looks like "P 74."

Reels Corners is at the junction of State Route 160. A mid-1960s Gulf station sits abandoned on the northeast corner, and diagonal from it is a giant barn and a big "EAT" sign at a bar and restaurant, also closed. The Reels Corners Coffee Shop was listed in the 1940 *Blue Book List* as having "Good meals. Rooms, Cabins." On the northwest corner is a "Let's Go Bowling" sign for alleys in a Quonset hut, but alas, that too is closed, the alleys reportedly shipped to Israel. Next to it was the Diamond Mine restaurant (the former Black Nugget), which burned in 1994, and tucked in behind that is the Long Vu Motel, with about eight rooms.

Ahead on the south side is an old green garage, which looks to be the old Fern Nook and Bill's Garage. After a few dips, we pass through the village of Buckstown, passing a state historic marker for Forbes Road and Edmund's Swamp. To the south is Duppstadt's Country Store. Jim and Carole Duppstadt have owned the place since 1971, and their store offers a variety of essentials and then some—western boots, oak swings, herbs, moccasins, candy, work shoes, lace curtains, apple cider, hunting and fishing licenses, hickory rockers, and chain saws, as well as maple syrup made right in Somerset County.

Looking west through Reels Corners in 1930, now the intersection with State Route 160. COURTESY CY HOSMER

Bill's Garage and Fern Nook lunchroom. A green-painted garage still stands just west of Reels Corners on the Seven Mile Stretch. COURTESY JOHN SMITH

There are dozens of different postcard views of Seven Mile Stretch, where you can still see seven miles between summits.

To the north is Ednor Place, known locally as Buckstown Mansion. It's a huge summer residence that was built around 1920 in the French eclectic style by Norman Richardson, then owner of the Seventh Avenue Hotel in Pittsburgh. We next come upon Camp Allegheny to the south, and just past it is a Lincoln Highway marker that local roadside artist

Kevin Kutz cleaned up and replaced—it's at the base of a sign to the south, across from Windber Road. At the top of the hill it's another long view, with tree-filled blue mountains in the distance, occasionally dotted by more strip mines and cranes. We've reached the end of the Long View–Seven Mile Stretch.

We head downhill, curve right and then left, and on another right-hand turn, come upon a road that breaks off to the south on a long straightaway; it's the original Lincoln, which cuts away for 3 miles. Unfortunately, the strip-mining operation has overtaken the road and it's closed for now. If we follow the old road, there's a Mail Pouch–painted barn, but the road is blocked after going just .5 mile.

On the new road, Emerald Park straddles both sides of the road. Only a bar and restaurant now, it once had a gift shop, and the 1940 Shell guide lists 10 unheated cabins. Only one cabin remains, though a couple of rooms are still for rent. Emerald Park originally sat on the old Lincoln, but the cabins were moved when the road was changed, though a different reason is indicated above the bar's counter. You'll see an old postcard of "White Star Park, 4 miles east of Stoystown." The caption below it reads, "Emerald Park before it was moved from Stonycreek Twp. to Shade Twp. for the purpose of getting a liquor license."

Just after the Emerald, on the south side, is an American gas station owned by a Russian fellow who might regale you with stories of his heritage if he's in a talkative mood. Hidden on the old road is Blue Bell Auction, former site of the Blue Bell Camp, so named because the "gypsies" who camped here called the morning glory flowers "blue bells." Inside is a sign from the Jenner Pines Auto Camp in Jennerstown.

Also on the old road is a sign for the Stoystown Nut Farm, closed now, although some of the thousands of walnut and chestnut trees remain. There are also a lot of maple syrup signs in the area—Somerset County boasts the state's top maple sugar production. Warnings for trucks begin here too, the first for an 8 percent grade in 1 mile.

Route 30 now crosses over the old Lincoln Highway, which comes from a giant junkyard on the south side and heads northwest toward Kantner and Stoystown, both named for local settlers. You can follow the Lincoln for 1 mile, but the bridge across Stony Creek is gone. To get to the other side, get back on Route 30 and make the next turn, State Route 403 north, to Kantner. Once at Kantner, the little intersection to the right is where the bridge used to end. Early motorists could have stayed at Fort Stonycreek tourist home or gotten gas at Snyder's 24 hours, but today we turn west toward Stoystown. A Lincoln Highway marker sits at the curve into town, where we pass the yellow brick Hite House sitting empty and sad. Out on Route 30, to the south of Stoystown, the bypass becomes two-lane and goes under a 1930s bridge.

On the way out of town on the Lincoln, one of the tollgates remains from the Bedford-Stoystown Turnpike. It looks like any other house, but the white plank exterior and porch cover a one-room log house. (Out on Route 30 is the Kings and Queens hotel and restaurant, an old road-house decorated to look like a castle.) As we go downhill, we see the white and green Mountain View Restaurant between the old and new roads. The roads rejoin, and at the bottom is Lincoln Highway Auto Body in a 1920s garage.

Climbing uphill again, we see Blanset's old garage to the south, built in 1920 and operated until 1979. It's weather-beaten now, the faded yellow paint revealing its last life as an antiques store. A sign at the top of this hill warns of a 9 percent grade ahead. The downhill ride is twisty, and as we curve left, there's an old log home to the north that's been

HITE HOUSE, ON LINCOLN HIGHWAY, STOYESTOWN, PA.

The sign out front says, "Hite House, Auto Head-Quarters." This Stoystown hotel was bricked soon after and remains so. COURTESY RUSSELL REIN

partially sided with Insulbrick. Around the next bend, a roller-coaster hill lies ahead.

At the dip is the Stonebridge farm, where they still make maple syrup, and on the uphill is Lincoln Manor, a trailer park. The top of the hill brings four warning signs for trucks to avoid Route 30 west. Most recommend taking Route 219 south to the Turnpike at Somerset. Johnstown lies 20 miles north on 219.

After the 219 cloverleaf is the Second Time Around shop, which sells used goods but is better known for the giant praying mantis out

This dip west of Stoystown shows how the road could disappear after just a light snow. COURTESY UNIVERSITY OF MICHIGAN, SPECIAL COLLECTIONS LIBRARY

front. The fiberglass creature is decorated for each holiday: In December it's Santa. In October it's a ghost. The big bug was reportedly made about 1970 for Dinosaurland near Front Royal, Virginia.

A strange black, angular, boomerang-shaped sign stood on the south side until 1994. Molded into the plastic was "Modern Golf Ski Swim Inn Room Coffee TV." The 1940 Shell directory tells us this was Mander's Tourist Court, featuring 10 cabins costing between $2 and $5. The 1927 Mohawk-Hobbs guide lists Schrock's Tourist Camp 4.5 miles west of Stoystown, perhaps the same place. Some cabins remain.

Passing through Ferrellton, we see Lincoln Coal and Contracting, and at the junction of State Route 601 is Bob's Atlantic station and mini-imart, covered with new neon. On the right is a building with "GBU" across the top. Originally the German Beneficial Union, a national fraternal union mainly supplying insurance to German immigrants, the name was changed to Greater Beneficial Union in 1941 for fear of anti-German sentiment.

One mile north on 601 is Boswell, a well-preserved coal-mining community. These company towns, or "patches," are common in the bituminous coal region of southwestern Pennsylvania. The company constructed the houses and stores, and even provided company scrip so that you could conveniently spend your wages in only its stores. Though many strip mines remain, the coal industry here is much smaller than at its peak.

West on Route 30, the Jenner name is all around—Jenners, Jennerstown, and Jenners Crossroads. About 1 mile apart, each one is on a different north-south alignment between Somerset and Johnstown. The towns are named for Edward Jenner, originator of the vaccination process for smallpox. Area settler John Dennison had three daughters, and he sent to England for Jenner's vaccine during an outbreak of the disease around 1820. Two of his girls died before the vaccine arrived, but it saved his third daughter. In a show of gratitude, Dennison named his land holdings after Jenner. (The empress of Russia was so impressed by Jenner's discovery that she ordered the first vaccinated Russian child be renamed Vaccinoff and receive a public education and lifetime pension.)

At Jenners Crossroads is Gabo's Hotel and Herb's Old Tavern, both old stagecoach stops. Herb's is now famous for seafood. A mile later we head uphill, past an old church and a tiny antiques shop, into Jenners-

town. The town is home to four brake-testing stations, evidence of the
steep hills on Route 30.

On the south side, a sign proclaims, "Original 2 for 1 Family Diner,
Since 1980." This diner is a nice place, with one of the tiniest counters
anywhere. Across from it is the Tudor-style White Star Residence, built
in 1934 on the site of an earlier White Star that burned. Once a famous
hotel, the stately White Star is now a retirement home. Both businesses
are at Jennerstown's only stoplight, an intersection with State Route 985.
The 1928 Mohawk-Hobbs guide indicates that the town's leading garage
was the Lincoln Highway Garage, which was open evenings and charged
$1 for labor.

A half mile north on 985 is Green Gables restaurant, which won the
nationwide Rockefeller Wayside Stand Contest for its beauty of design in
1928. Since remodeled, the dining room now features four huge oak
trees as support columns, and the adjacent Mountain Playhouse is in a
restored 1805 gristmill moved to the site.

Past the light on Route 30 are a pair of old roadhouses: Turillo's
Steak House (formerly the Highway Café), with a neon sign, to the
north; and the Rocking R (formerly the Penn-Lincoln) to the south. Also
to the south in an old gas station is Babe's antiques shop.

Ye Olde Inn wasn't satisfied with just one porch overhang. COURTESY CY HOSMER

Lunch at the New Penn-Lincoln, on Lincoln Highway, Jennerstown, Pa.

(c) W. B. L.

The sign at the New Penn-Lincoln didn't say restaurant, but rather "EAT."

The Zeppelin Tourist Camp once sat next to Jennerstown Auto Body. John Schmucker, born in 1910, recalls the Zep:

It was built in 1926 by Harry Vincent, who had a garage in Boswell, and when he came here, he was a pretty old guy. There was a counter with stools inside the Zeppelin, and a good meal cost 35 to 50 cents. It had 8 or 10 round cabins in a semi-circle around it, and I think they came as a kit, even the Zeppelin, and had to be put together. There was no liquor, but they had it at Jenner Pines [tourist court].

Without the tourist trade, there was nothing you could have lived on here. Six bus lines all stopped here, and every other person in town kept tourists because the Lincoln Highway was the number one road in the area, and the 219 crossroads was an important New York–to–Maryland road. My brother Robert had Schmucker's Cabins.

I worked at Jenner Pines painting and later went down the Ohio River painting barges. My brother raised chickens for a couple years and delivered eggs, but that went downhill. He had these chickens in coops, and he asked me if I could wash 'em up—clean 'em and fix 'em. So I hosed them out and then we

The Zeppelin Tourist Camp featured a lunch counter inside a big blimp. Few people at this time had ever seen a zeppelin, grounded or flying. COURTESY JOHN BAEDER

boarded up between them and put bathrooms in there, and we stone-cased most of it in. This was about 1934, and that became his motel cabins. He also sold antiques out of one of the cabins, and it was a real payin' thing.

It's surprising how fast business went down when the Turnpike came in; it cut traffic one-third right off the reel. The Zeppelin struggled for a few years, then went vacant. The blimp left in '45, about when everybody wanted to go to a regular motel.

So what ever happened to the Zeppelin? It still lives in Ohio, just south of Edinburg on Ohio Route 14. It was used as a diner for a while but has served as the office to Bob's Motel since 1972.

One last antiques shop sends us on our way—1806 Antiques, which has three floors in an 1806 farmhouse and tavern. The woman behind the counter comes from Tucson for the summers to help her daughter and son-in-law run the former stagecoach stop.

Next door are two stone pillars overlooking the entrance to Jenner Pines Camping Park. It looks unassuming, but it's a very important site.

JENNER PINES CAMP ON LINCOLN HIGHWAY, JENNERSTOWN, PA.

Jenner Pines is an example of a mid-1920s camp that offered camping and, later, cabins. The entrance and office to the left are still there.

Three tourist cabins dot the grounds, as does the old office, but the camping park name reveals that this site is older, dating from the early 1920s, when towns and individuals opened places for roadside campers. It was a short-lived era between when tourists camped by the roadside and when cabin camps were built.

Jenner Pines is listed in the 1928 Mohawk-Hobbs guide as having 13 cabins at $1.50 to $3, or camping for 50 cents. The 1940 Shell directory shows little change—14 cabins, $1.50 to $4, camping space 75 cents—and notes that it was open seasonally. It's hard to tell now, but the cabins were arranged around a U-shaped road.

Just down the highway, hidden under deep foliage, two can still stay overnight for $25 at the Wishing Well Motel in the old Schmucker's Cabins. Across the street is the Laurel Manor Motel. Both hotels still do well because of the Jennerstown Speedway, which lies to the south. The speedway was originally an old fairgrounds, but it's been updated through the years, most recently when the five-eighths-mile track was paved. Now NASCAR Winston racing cars compete on Saturdays from May through September, attracting thousands on warm summer nights.

The Laurel Manor and Wishing Well Motels greet travelers heading west from Jennerstown. (PHOTO 1990)

We pass a drive-in restaurant called Sneakers, formerly Dairy King, where we can stop for a real milkshake. Ahead is a valley where we can take the ribbon straight ahead or veer off to the right on the old Lincoln. Nothing much is on the old road, which has a couple of deceivingly sharp bends. A historic marker on the old road explains a bit about Forbes Road and Clear Fields in the area.

The roads rejoin as they ascend the hill. The old Lincoln actually crosses south, then north again before we pass an old stone house. Now the really big climb begins up Laurel Mountain, the last big climb of our journey across Pennsylvania. Near the top, for eastbound travelers, was an old blue and white state Lincoln Highway sign, recently replaced by a new green one. At the summit are three state parks—Laurel Ridge, Laurel Mountain, and Linn Run—plus the fifty thousand-acre Forbes State Forest.

We pass a bar and restaurant, then the Westward Restaurant & Lodge, advertising, "Truckers Welcome, Barbecue Chicken and Ribs Every Sunday." A barbecue pit is adjacent, so things haven't changed much here at the former Laurel Ridge Bar-B-Que. The 1927 Mohawk-Hobbs guide lists a free tourist camp called Locust Grove Park at a level shady site in the area.

A sign warns of a steep grade for 3.5 miles, and a long descent begins. We immediately pass the Swiss Chalet lodge, shuttered and

Laurel Ridge Bar-B-Que sat at the top of Laurel Ridge, just before the westward descent. COURTESY CY HOSMER

Lincoln Lodge was near the top of Laurel Mountain, probably where the Swiss Chalet now sits closed.

closed. The road gets steeper, and we descend into thick forests. Uphill traffic heading east is usually creeping slowly behind a truck. A sharp bend in the road is so dangerous that it's redesigned every few years, and during 1993 the lanes were finally separated. The old Mountain Inn sat at the bend, a popular respite for travelers with overheated cars. In the early years, it had a trough of water outside for tired horses and cars, but everything is gone, the last of it destroyed with the new roadway in 1993. The 1928 Mohawk-Hobbs guide indicates that there was also water available at a small garage .7 miles west and a spring .9 miles east, showing how badly the old cars overheated.

The hill levels temporarily, with more warning signs for trucks. On the south side is half of the big Lincoln Highway Rock, also called Flag Rock because an American flag often hung from it; nowadays it's usually covered with graffiti. It was blasted in half when the road was widened years ago, and bits of the less fortunate half lay scattered along the road.

These folks stopped to cool their radiators at the Mountain Inn watering trough.
COURTESY UNIVERSITY OF PITTSBURGH HILLMAN LIBRARY, ARCHIVES OF INDUSTRIAL SOCIETY

The curve at the Mountain Inn was broadened in the 1920s. The old road is to the left. COURTESY UNIVERSITY OF MICHIGAN, SPECIAL COLLECTIONS LIBRARY

Looking east to Flag Rock, only half of which survives. The 1927 Mohawk-Hobbs guide lists a small garage .7 mile west of the Mountain Inn, probably the unidentified roadhouse to the left. COURTESY PA STATE ARCHIVES, RG-12 DEPT. OF HIGHWAYS

Coasting downhill again, we pass the Washington Furnace Inn, established in 1931. It's named for an 1809 iron furnace that still stands 1 mile north. There are a number of other local furnaces that remain standing as well. Just down the hill is a runaway-truck ramp, installed recently after a few too many trucks lost their brakes and smashed into Laughlintown at the bottom of the hill. Those with working brakes can stop at the Runaway Lounge, located across the road.

The road finally levels and we're in Laughlintown. Old garages and roadhouses still dot the road; one with a high canopy was Carns' Texaco, which also offered groceries and general hauling. At the intersection is the Ligonier Country Inn, formerly the Laurel Ridge Hotel; the adjacent Laurel Ridge Garage is now the site of a few motel rooms. And don't miss the famous Pie Shop bakery across the street.

Also here is an old stagecoach stop, the Compass Inn Museum. The log half was built in 1799, the stone addition in 1820 to accommodate increased traffic from the newly completed Pittsburgh-Philadelphia Turnpike. The inn has been restored to show what life was like for nineteenth-century travelers, and it features a barn, blacksmith shop, and working kitchen. Showing how few good routes and stops there were at the time,

Washington Furnace Inn before a matching addition was built onto its right side. It still offers a full lunch and dinner menu daily.

LAUREL RIDGE HOTEL
Route 30—3 Miles East of Ligonier
LAUGHLINTOWN, PENNA.

FINE
FOODS

REFRESHING
BEVERAGES

Pleasant Relaxation in the Mountain Air   Fully Equipped for Large Parties
For Reservations Call Ligonier 6701

The Laurel Ridge Hotel, now the Ligonier Country Inn, hasn't changed much from this ad in Laughlintown's 150th-anniversary book, from 1947.

the inn counts among its guests Daniel Webster, Henry Clay, Andrew Jackson, William Henry Harrison, and Zachary Taylor.

Heading out of town, we pass a sign for the Rolling Rock Club, a private club founded by the Mellon family. We travel along on flatlands past cornfields and State Route 381. Immediately to the right, a long stretch of the Lincoln Highway angles away. Between the old and new roads is a string of cabins at Sunset Valley Cottages, which are now rented in the summer.

The old Lincoln undulates over the narrow lane; it's hard to believe this was a transcontinental road. A bit farther, also between the old and new roads, is the Eastwood Inn, with an old neon sign hiding behind its pine trees. Dinner in this beautiful old restaurant is by reservation only.

On the south side of Route 30 is Ligonier Beach, a 400-foot-long swimming pool. It was opened July 4, 1925, by Cono "Nick" Gallo and is still run by his son Tom. Customers originally had to descend an oak staircase from the Lincoln Highway, before present Route 30 was built. Swimsuits could also be rented, and a miniature golf course was soon added. Ten years after opening, the course was replaced by an outdoor

The Eastwood Inn, between the old and new roads, retains its classic menu.

Ligonier Beach once drew huge crowds, before the advent of home swimming pools and water parks. The rerouted Lincoln is at far left. COURTESY LAKE COUNTY MUSEUM, CURT TEICH POSTCARD ARCHIVES, WAUCONDA, IL

band shell ringed by booths and a wooden dance floor (that had to be squeegeed after rains). The dancing is gone now too, but the stone band shell and course ticket booth remain, surrounded by vegetation. A white frame bathhouse still has its varnished ticket booth, and another building houses a snack bar (with a 1950s popcorn popper) and a bar with knotty pine paneling. The buildings used to be ringed by double tubes of neon— it must have been quite a sight!—but these had to be turned off for fear of fire. A 1951 Ford engine, fueled by natural gas, still powers a huge fountain in the pool.

Nearing Ligonier on Route 30, we pass Ruthie's Diner (formerly Burnsey's) and the rustic-looking ABC Motel, with 10 rooms available. Route 30 becomes four-lane, but we turn right to join the old Lincoln into town. We go uphill and start down tree-shaded Main Street. At the town's square, or "diamond," is a Lincoln Highway marker on the northeast corner. This corner was once the site of the Brenizer Hotel.

Ligonier is a prosperous little town. It has always been an escape for Pittsburghers for summer camping or for winter skiing on the nearby ridges. The town is filled with specialty shops offering books, gifts, and lots of antiques. The diamond has a gazebo and landscaped gardens in the center. It was restored with help from the Mellon family in the late 1960s. You'll hear all sorts of thoughts on it in town: most people like it, though some resent the "Disneylike" feel to things. There's no denying it's one of the most beautiful town squares anywhere.

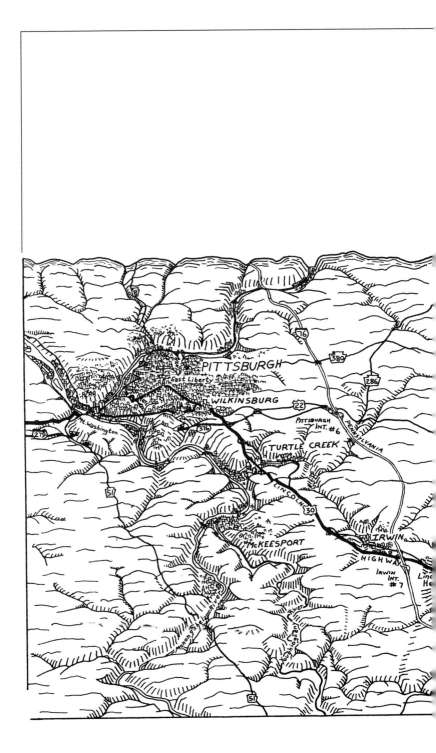

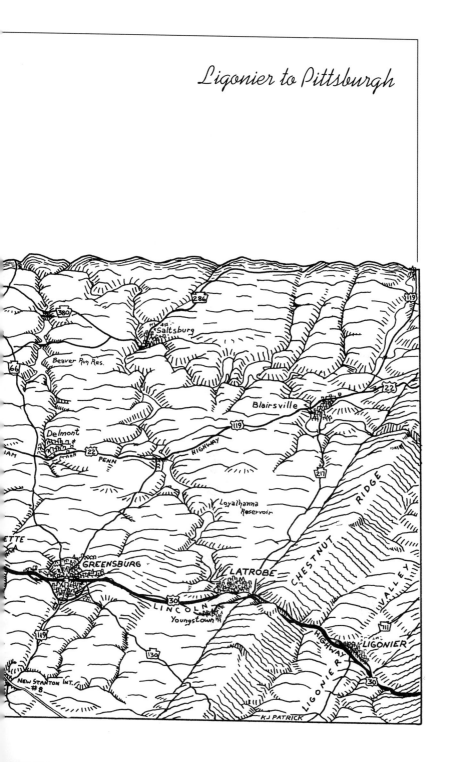

The original Fort Ligonier was built in 1758 as Forbes's troops marched from Bedford to capture French Fort Duquesne, present-day Pittsburgh. The fort was named by Forbes for the commander in chief of the British Army, Field Marshall Lord John Ligonier. The town was laid out in 1817, along with the new Pittsburgh-Philadelphia Turnpike, and was named after the fort.

Completed in 1969, Fort Ligonier is one of the most detailed fort re-creations in the world, and a visit to the museum is essential to understanding the forces that settled this area and built the first road. A three-day celebration known as Fort Ligonier Days, held every October, features a living-history encampment of troops, frontiersmen, women, and Indians, with drills, crafts, and music.

The town square has always been called a diamond, a term that seems peculiar to Pennsylvania squares. The word is apparently of Scotch-Irish origin, and once was used widely—Pittsburgh Diamond Market at Market Square is proof. The squares weren't always so picturesque, though. Drovers transporting livestock would keep their animals and hitch their horses at the town squares. Ligonier's diamond evolved into a public park and has been restored and beautified.

SECTION I. LIGONIER TO ADAMSBURG

Route 30 heads west from the State Route 711 intersection, where we see the Fort Ligonier Motor Lodge, with its big neon-arrowed sign. The original Lincoln Highway runs parallel to Route 30 two blocks to the north, heading west on Main Street from Ligonier's diamond. Some historic homes and antiques shops line the street. The Ligonier Tavern is the former Lincoln Café, and to the south is Big Pap's, a café full of fifties memorabilia and known for its big ice cream cones.

Next door is the former station of the Ligonier Valley Railroad, with a terra cotta facade; it now houses game commission offices. Beginning in 1877, the railroad ran from Ligonier west to Pittsburgh, but it was losing money by 1950. When the railroad discontinued operations in August 1952, its roadbed through the Loyalhanna Gorge between Kingston and Long Bridge became the westbound lanes of Route 30. Between the gorge and Ligonier the roadbed is now the eastbound lanes.

Just before Main Street merges with Route 30 is a street marked Old Lincoln Highway, and we bear right to follow it. There are three generations of roads west of town. First is the original Lincoln, the northern-

BLUE RIDGE SERVICE STATION
¼ Mile West of Ligonier, U. S. Route 30

Blue Ridge Service Station had 24-hour service and a ladies restroom inside.

most of the three. Then, in 1928, the road was moved south to what now serves as the westbound lanes (originally two-way). Finally, there's the railroad's roadbed, now Route 30's eastbound lanes.

The old Lincoln winds behind the remaining tourist cabins from Shirey's Lake View Motel. The cabins were closed in 1988 and sold off one by one, and the adjacent motel with about six rooms closed in 1994. It was run by Dean and Barbara Shirey, who own the adjacent farm. Dean's parents bought the farmland in 1916. He says his parents were glad when the Lincoln was rerouted because they were afraid their children would get hit by a car: "After they moved the highway, they put a sign down at the road, 'Rooms for Rent,' in 1932. And there were people from New York who saw the sign, and they came and rented a room that night and mother gave them breakfast, she served them lunch and dinner. And that family had a little baby, and they kept coming back for their vacations from New York until the children were grown up and went to college."

In 1938 the Shireys erected a string of 10 cabins, which they designed and built themselves. "When we first opened the cabins, we didn't have an office. My dad would sit on the front porch of the house, and when a car would come up the lane for a room, he had a sign on the front of his garage, 'Blow Your Horn.' He would get out on the running

*If you look west on Route 30, the lake seen from Shirey's Lake View Motel lies
south of the highway. Colonial Cabins can be seen to the right in the distance.
The railroad tracks running between the road and the lake later became the eastbound lanes of Route 30.* COURTESY CY HOSMER

*The Shirey family built its tourist cabins across the road from the lake. "There
are 30 acres across there," says Barbara Shirey, "and the Consolidated Ice Company in Pittsburgh used to cut the ice in the winter. The Ligonier Valley Railroad
would haul the ice to Latrobe and Pittsburgh."*

board of the car and tell them which cabin to go to. He would get off, open the door, and get them to register and pay for the room, and then he would walk back to the house." Business was so good, they built another 10 cabins the following year. "At first we called them Shirey's Cabins," recalls Dean. "Then when they started building motels, we wanted it to sound a little better, so we called it Shirey's Lake View Motor Court. People used to really like to rent these cabins. Before the Turnpike, the cabins would all be rented every night of the week with out-of-state cars."

Barbara agrees. "People liked to sit out under the pine trees. It's an interesting business," she continues. "You meet all kinds of people, and you make lots of friends. But it's pretty much a livelihood that depends on the highway."

Next to Shirey's on the old road was Sunnybrook Park, with a gas station, café, and eleven acres of free camp space. The site later became the Colonial Inn, with a coffee shop and cabins. The cabins, which

The Colonial Coffee Shop was a regular stop for buses, an important mode of transportation mostly forgotten today. The café sat just west of Shirey's Motel on the rerouted Lincoln Highway; the Colonial Inn and Colonial Cabins sat behind it on the original alignment. A sign for Piel's beer hangs over the right door, while "Women" hangs over the left. The Great Eastern System bus has New York and Washington listed as its destinations, while "Pittsburgh" is painted on its open door. The building now houses the Country Cottage gift shop. COURTESY ABRAHAM YALOM

looked nearly identical to Shirey's, closed after a 1954 flood. Today, only a couple remain adjacent to the Colonial Inn, which is still a restaurant. Another of the cabins, painted yellow, sits in a yard west of the inn. Out on Route 30, the Country Cottage sells collectibles, gifts, dinnerware, herbs, and tea in the former Colonial Coffee Shop.

We're forced to turn left and then turn right onto 30, but the original Lincoln kept going uphill; you can still make out the road, which is used for driveways. From Route 30, the old road can be seen coming down the west side of the mountain, where it crossed a stream and ran behind

You can still buy a pop from the cooler at Donato's Sunoco. (PHOTO 1990)

Donato's Sunoco before rejoining Route 30. Charles Donato's parents built the station in 1930 after the road was rerouted to its present course, and today the small station is full of neat stuff. Behind it was his parents' house with "the two cottages they built to rent to tourists." On the original path is a bar called Tree Tops, the former Ridgeway Inn. The 1927 Mohawk-Hobbs guide lists camping on grass here for 25 cents.

Peg Brindza remembers taking trips over Laurel Hill in the late 1920s and stopping at the Ridgeway:

My grandmother liked to travel. She and my grandfather in their earlier days would travel a lot. On these old cars they had running boards, and my grandmother loved weekends to take the family on a road trip, more or less, because it would take a weekend to go 50, a hundred miles in those days. On one trip we had packed up food in the car because she always took her good cooking with her, and she had made these apple pies, and in putting the food in the car and getting ready to go, somebody set the pies on the running board and forgot to put them in the car. So we were out on the highway and going up a mountain, had to stop halfway up to put some water in and let the car cool off, and there were the pies, still on the running board!

We sometimes made trips out to Chester, Pennsylvania, and then to the seashore, and we traveled by car. There were no turn-

Young Peg Brindza at the Ridgeway Inn, about 1929 or 1930. COURTESY PEG BRINDZA

pikes, nothing like that, but traffic wasn't as heavy, you didn't have all the truck traffic, and you had lots of time to do it in. People didn't rush in those days. If somebody somewhere along the roads broke down, help always came. In those days, there was always a kind hand out there, sometimes a horse and buggy.

We had our spots that we stopped at that we were familiar with. Now there was a place called Bill's Place, and that was a familiar place with us. It was a rest stop. You didn't have as many rest stops along the road then as you have now. You'd get something to drink, and you would meet people.

[Visiting the Ship] would be a weekend trip, because you'd go up and spend a night there, and it would take—I can't tell you how many hours it would take to get there then, but it was a long ride on a Saturday. . . . Everybody of course had to join in. There would be five, six cars; we called it the caravan. I remember one night one couple, whether they didn't want to pay the fare or what, they climbed in the window up at the Ship to get into a room, and we thought that was terrible!

[Sometimes we'd play] penny ante. Somebody'd carve a little wooden top, and everybody knew to take their pennies—they'd save up pennies, take their pennies—and then they would play a few hours of spinning the top, and go to bed in one of the rooms that they would rent for the night.

I thought it was fantastic. The Ship was very fancy, and there was a little shop there that sold souvenirs. Not too many years ago, Bill [Peg's husband] and I were up that way. We went to see about the Ship, and it was closed. Then we stopped at a place that had some of the old souvenir plates, but I didn't get one. I've always felt bad about that, because I would have liked to have had a reminder of it, but the reminder's all in my mind.

We didn't stay in the fancy hotels. [We'd stay at] the Ship or something like that, but otherwise it would be a cabin somewhere, and on most of the trips that's where you'd spend your nights, and they were adequate for the times; people weren't spoiled back then.

After Donato's, we pass the Driftwood Inn, with a late-1950s sign, then crest a hill to see the twin ribbons of highway before us. To the south, across the eastbound lanes, is Idlewild Park—especially noticeable is Fairyland Forest, a kiddie land of fairytales come to life. Idlewild was established in 1878 by the Mellon family of Pittsburgh as a picnic grounds to entice customers for their Ligonier Valley Railroad. The railroad brought many Pittsburghers out for a day's picnic, and in 1931, new managers began turning the spot into a modern amusement park. They bought the Mellon interests in 1952, and Kennywood Corporation (of Kennywood amusement park in Pittsburgh, across from the Westinghouse Bridge) took over in 1983. The park offers all the modern attractions of a medium-size amusement park but still retains much of its verdant charm.

We pass the former entrance, crest another hill, and head down toward the Loyalhanna Gorge, one of the prettiest stretches of the Lincoln anywhere. We pass the Road Toad restaurant to the south, and then the opposing lanes of traffic take opposite sides of the stream. Heading west, we stay on the north side, along the old LVRR roadbed, which becomes obvious as we pass a concrete tipple, used to load railroad cars. The westbound lanes are much more level than the eastbound. Loyal-

The original entrance to Idlewild offered gasoline, a "Trading Post," and "Ligonier Valley Farm Products." The fortlike structure to the right of the overhead sign remains. COURTESY CY HOSMER

The new Long Bridge across the Loyalhanna hovers over the old bridge as a car crosses it. The great Long Bridge has since been replaced. COURTESY UNIVERSITY OF MICHIGAN, SPECIAL COLLECTIONS LIBRARY

hanna Creek keeps peeking through the trees, and it's often shallow enough that we can see rocks and plant life.

We can see Sleepy Hollow Inn across the water to the left, and there's a crossover just past it. We reach a red light at the intersection of State Route 217 at the Kingston Dam, where people often take a dip in the summer. We pass a BP gas; the gorge has ended, and both lanes of Route 30 rejoin.

To the south, a huge Ideal Mobile Homes sign shows the time and temperature; across the road, Mayflower Glass Company now sells antiques. We pass under State Route 982 and go uphill past a 1960s Gulf station with a big neon sign to the north. To the south is the Hi Way Drive-In Theater. Marie Zimmerman, manager since 1978, says that the theater is mostly patronized by families nowadays. Across from it is Lincoln Lanes bowl.

We enter a growing strip of franchises. At the intersection of State Route 981 is the Mission Motor Inn, some of whose rooms have been rebuilt to house small businesses. On the southwest corner sits the Westmoreland County Airport. The original Lincoln Highway cut through what is now the airport and headed east into Youngstown, until the airport was begun in 1936. We turn south on Route 981 to follow that route.

We take Route 981 .25 mile south to the street sign that says Old Route 30. Across from it we see a road into the airport closed by a gate; that's the old Lincoln. We turn left and head east into Youngstown. The road here rises and dips with the land. We head downhill, past an apartment complex, and to the south we see a cement Lincoln Highway marker resting behind high bushes in someone's yard along Club Manor Road.

We arrive in Youngstown, first settled in about 1797 as a turnpike stop. It's remained a small town, with a population of about 500. At the intersection of Main and Latrobe Streets is the former Youngstown Hotel, a three-story, turn-of-the-century brick building now housing the Tin Lizzie tavern. The town had many inns and taverns in its early years, and a number survive, including the Washington Inn, identifiable by its oval ground-floor windows. Continuing east, we take the left fork to follow Main Street, which bears north to meet Route 30 at the entrance to the Loyalhanna Gorge. Two tourist camps are listed in the 1940 *Shell Tourist Accommodation Directory* in this vicinity: Pop Inn and White City.

Now on the eastbound lanes through the gorge, the route follows the contour of the land. The road briefly merges into one lane at the State

The original Lincoln stayed on the south side of Loyalhanna Creek, past Kingston Dam. These lanes were made one-way when the westbound lanes opened across the water on the roadbed of the Ligonier Valley Railroad, October 12, 1954.

Route 217 intersection; to the south is the stone Kingston House, built in 1815. Motorists often drive fast through the wooded area ahead, so be careful. Heading down the first big dip, we see a monument to Arthur St. Clair to the south. St. Clair settled in the Ligonier Valley and commanded Fort Ligonier before serving as president of the Continental Congress in 1787. He later became first governor of the Northwest Territory. A change in fortunes brought him back to Ligonier destitute and ill, but he opened a small inn along the old Forbes Road south of this spot on Chestnut Ridge.

After the bend at the bottom, you'll pass the Sleepy Hollow Inn, which was preceded by a gas station and sandwich stand in the 1920s. It was bought in 1931 by Charles, Joe, and Bernard "Bus" Neiman, and it earned a reputation for its hot dogs. Kelley's Hollow, as this area of the gorge is called, was renamed Sleepy Hollow after Joe's habit of dozing in his rocking chair. Sleepy Hollow Tavern was started in September 1939, and it opened as a roadhouse on May 17, 1940, with 12 rooms to rent upstairs. The exterior resembled a giant log cabin. When the westbound lanes of Route 30 were moved to the roadbed of the Ligonier Valley Railroad, Sleepy Hollow lost half of its drive-by customers. After

Sleepy Hollow, built in 1939, is a well-known landmark along the Lincoln Highway in the Loyalhanna Gorge.

much political wrangling, a small concrete causeway was built on the west side of the restaurant to connect the east and westbound lanes of Route 30. It's still used today, but it's often flooded in the winter and spring. New owners remodeled the restaurant in 1981, adding a locally quarried stone facade, and in 1985 a large solarium was expanded toward the water. The restaurant was closed in the early 1990s, but Bob and Kathy Jones reopened it in 1995, with son Robby as chef, and plan to turn the upstairs motel rooms into a bed and breakfast.

Ahead, Long Bridge station was originally built in the 1930s as an Esso station and lunch stand. A left turn just before it is Long Bridge Road, the original Lincoln Highway, which led to an iron bridge. It runs behind the station, passing a few houses, and rejoins Route 30 on the far side of the station. To the left as we merge is an abutment from the old bridge. Route 30 continues across the new Long Bridge. At its end, across from the Road Toad restaurant, we turn left to head west again.

We follow the same route west that we originally took from this point to the airport. Then, heading west from the airport on Route 30, we encounter St. Vincent's College to the north. Founded in 1846, the St. Vincent Archabbey was the first of the Benedictine institutions in the country. As we climb uphill, the original route can be seen angling in

An outdoor band shell, dance floor, and tables at the Mission Inn.

from the south through fields west of the airport. The best place to see it
is halfway up the hill at a small opening where farmers often sell produce. The old Lincoln meets Route 30 at the top of the hill near the
entrance to the now-closed St. Xavier's Academy, once the oldest institu-
tion of the Sisters of Mercy.

Heading back downhill, we pass Tim's Recycling to the north. Its
entrance road is the old Lincoln, which crossed over from the south side
at St. Xavier's. The pavement is overgrown with brush or missing alto-
gether and passes right under the billboard at Tim's and out the other side
into a cornfield. In the middle of the corn is a house, which sits along the
old Lincoln, the broken cement still used as part of a driveway.

We continue downhill on four-lane Route 30. At the bottom to the
north is the Glass Mart Food Store, where the old road—now a private
driveway—comes down from the hill. At the traffic light, the road would
have been just to the north, cutting through the trailer sales business, crossing a ravine, and hooking up with an extant section of the old Lincoln.

We turn north and then west to get on that old section of the Lincoln.
We immediately pass an old roadhouse to the north, and then the Frye

*Owner A. J. Thomas proclaimed that his Buvett Inn was a "place of fair and
courteous treatment." It was reportedly replaced by a small sewage plant, and
today it's a gravel lot.*

The original wings of the Mountain View Hotel can still be discerned from the current structure.

farm, with a wonderfully decorative barn, to the south. Farther ahead is a dental office, once Willow Terrace restaurant. Then we pass Statler's miniature golf and driving range, established in 1950; a go-cart track was recently added. The road returns to a rural setting, and the next .5 mile is a photogenic stretch. (As you head uphill, you may want to stop at the Monsour School to take a photo pointing east.)

A gravel clearing on the south side was the site of the Buvett Inn. At the top of the hill is the Mountain View Inn, lying between the old and new roads. The Mountain View, built in 1924, was long famous for its huge pool. Vance Booher, Sr., bought the hotel in 1940, and after World War II, his sons Vance, Jr., and Ned ran the hotel until the 1980s. The third-generation Vance is the current owner, along with his wife, Vicki, whom he met in nursery school in the 1950s and married in 1972. They've operated the hotel since the 1980s and have expanded it and built a new pool. Inside is a wall full of early hotel photographs.

Ned Booher retired in 1984. He recalls that many tourist camps were in the area before the Mountain View was built, but "they catered to a different clientele. As for the Buvett Inn, it was strictly a bar, and its main attraction was the square dances they put on Saturday nights. There was also the Beatty Inn about two miles east of Mountain View, which may have been some competition at one time."

Fergusons'—4 mi. East of Greensburg, Pa., Rt. 30
L. L. and J. B. Lancaster, Prop's.

One of many different postcard views of Ferguson's. The cabins are gone but the house remains. COURTESY NED BOOHER

We can head west from the Mountain View on either road, but we'll continue on the old Lincoln, on the north side of the hotel. At a fork in the road, the Lincoln Highway originally followed the north branch, then was switched to the south. Where the branches rejoin sits an old house with a large building attached behind it; this was Ferguson's. The house is located on the south branch, but the 10 cabins across from it lay on the north branch. Also near here was Bickel's Tourist Court, with seven cabins, and the 1927 Mohawk-Hobbs guide lists Huckleberry Hill Tourist Camp at 1.2 miles west of the Mountain View, though the next year's guide corrects that, listing the Huckleberry Inn at just .2 mile west.

About .5 mile from the Mountain View, the Lincoln rejoins Route 30. As we head downhill, a section of old concrete still lies to the south with some businesses along it. Near the bottom of the hill is the Italian Oven restaurant. Ned Booher recalls that the Lincoln Highway originally cut north behind the restaurant, then made a sharp turn back south. "It was somewhat of a landmark because of the number of accidents at the spot. It was called 'dead man's curve' or 'Head's curve.' Judge Head's home was on the hill above this curve and is now a medical complex."

At Peaches and Cream dairy stand, the old road can be followed by turning south. This meets another road at Generations, a children's clothing store on our right. It was also once known as Ulshafer's Tourist

Home and the King's Inn. To the left, old pavement extends about one hundred feet before dead-ending and may have been an old alignment. We turn right and continue west; the road has little of note other than a bland strip mall called Old 30 Plaza, until we arrive at Burger King, next to the Westmoreland Mall.

Route 30 could also get us there through a strip of franchise businesss. Of note are Cozumel, an authentic Mexican restaurant, and the half-century-old Lincoln Inn, which still sports a neon sign and a giant Kentucky Fried Chicken bucket.

After the Burger King, the road levels at a fork, where to the north is McFadden's Select Used Cars, with a nice neon sign, and a couple of motels. The Route 30 Greensburg bypass goes left, but we stay right to take the old Lincoln Highway through town.

Greensburg is named for Revolutionary War general Nathanael Greene, said to be second only to Washington as a strategist. The town was founded in 1785, and evidence of its early role can be found on the route through town. Immediately to the south are the Toll Gate Apartments, a reference to the first turnpike tollgate, which sat east of town. As we head downhill, across from the modern Family Diner behind a tall

The main building remains from Ulshafer's, which offered rooms and a restaurant. The small building to the left has "Gulf Lube" out front, and there appears to be a dollhouse between the two buildings. Autos could apparently pull into the main opening. COURTESY D. B. GRUBBS

condominium are two brick buildings, remnants of the Duchess Motel, which had 12 colonial-style units. At the bottom of the hill, the road splits, and our westbound lanes follow Otterman Street as we go uphill. The 1906 domed courthouse can be seen at the top.

After crossing Main Street at the hilltop, the restored 1926 Manos Theater (now called the Palace) is one block west on the right. The road meanders out of town and rejoins the eastbound lanes underneath a bridge for Route 30. Both lanes continue west, but we can double back and take the eastbound lanes (on Pittsburgh Street) through town. There are a number of historic buildings, including three 1920s-era gas stations to the north, and after Main Street, to the south is a former car dealership, with a spoked wheel in relief at the top of the facade. Greensburg also once had a Lincoln Highway Drug Store.

As we head west on the old Lincoln, the road climbs Mount Odin; at the top is a state historical marker for a former tollhouse from the Greensburg-Pittsburgh Turnpike. The road then goes downhill and rejoins Route 30 from the south. On the northeast corner is Greensburg Plaza, the site of the former Mount Odin Drive-In Theater.

Crown Fuel station on West Pittsburgh Street at Bell Way, Greensburg. Today the garage is painted yellow with brown shingles. COURTESY WESTMORELAND COUNTY HISTORICAL SOCIETY

Heading uphill we find Greengate Mall to the north, perhaps the location of the Hillcrest Camp, listed in the 1928 Mohawk-Hobbs guide as "a fine shady site" costing 50 cents to camp overnight. Ahead lies "Roller-coaster Hill," famous in the early years for its steep descents. Today Ferrante's Lakeview Inn sits near the bottom. We cross what is marked Pennsylvania Turnpike Route 66, a toll road. To the north is Castine's Italian restaurant, with a neon sign, then we pass Monsour Hospital, which started as a six-bed clinic in the 1783 stagecoach stop in front.

At the next intersection is an Eat n' Park restaurant to the northwest, one of a chain of dozens, but the last one to have its original 1950s building and sign. This area is known as Lincoln Heights; Jeannette, to the north, was once an important glass-making town. Also just north is Bushy Run Battlefield, scene of a 1763 battle as the Indians tried one last time to reclaim frontier lands from the British.

Ruth Drengwitz Joyce, born in 1914, remembers a slower-paced Lincoln Highway here: "Our town was renamed in the 1920s from Old Grapeville to Lincoln Heights by my mother and another neighbor. Lincoln Highway was a two-lane highway until 1937. In those days there were no motels, and travelers seeking overnight lodging found it here. Many of the homes took in overnight guests; signs on the lawns invited the travelers. Lincoln Highway through Lincoln Heights was called 'Petunia Hill.' All the neighbors grew petunias in their yards, one trying to outdo the other. It was a beautiful sight."

After the light, to the north, is the little Lickety Split ice cream stand. The road through here was redone in the early 1990s, and a Jersey barrier was put down the middle. A short stretch of original road to the north was also blocked off at the next traffic light. The 1928 Mohawk-Hobbs guide lists the Tea Cup Inn Camp, .8 mile east of Lincoln Heights, as offering supplies, camping space, and 10 furnished cabins.

The road continues past a Chevrolet dealer, which eradicated a portion of old road to the south. You can see where the western part of it rejoins Route 30. Ahead, the Lincoln Highway and Route 30 diverge for a few miles.

SECTION II. ADAMSBURG TO CIRCLEVILLE

The Lincoln angles off to the right past the Village Inn, through Adamsburg and Irwin, to the top of Jacktown hill. The bypass was constructed in the late 1930s to accommodate traffic from the Pennsylvania

Turnpike. When the Turnpike opened in 1940, Irwin was its western terminus.

Another Route 30 bypass was considered from here west to Route 48 in the late 1960s and early '70s. After study, the state planned the new road to diverge south here, crossing over at Circleville (with an interchange at the Maple Drive-in Theater) and continuing on the north side until reaching Route 48. Residents successfully mounted opposition to the plan that would have destroyed 85 homes, but officials seemed to indicate it would always be considered.

1915–1938. The Village Inn is an old-fashioned dinner spot where they still serve waffles with every meal. Former owner Jack Kessler recalls that Ann Pierce remodeled it into its current form about 1945, and the Kesslers had it from around 1970 to 1995.

The road heads down into Adamsburg, then over a few hills and through residential areas, until it winds its way into Irwin. The business district runs north-south, between the Lincoln Highway and railroad tracks about five blocks north. Irwin's Main Street has an old theater, a jewelry store, and a good restaurant called the Colonial Grille. There is also an Isaly's, a regional dairy chain with an attractive Carrara glass front.

Back on the Lincoln, we pass the John Irwin house to the north, now selling antiques, and head uphill past the closed Stern's Auto Museum to the south. At a small intersection with a gas station, the Lincoln goes

Lincoln Towers in Adamsburg, now Rocco's Village Inn. COURTESY JACK KESSLER

*A matchbook
from the Jacktown Hotel.*

straight, running beside Route 30, where we find Electra Lighting in the former John Serro's car dealership. An alternative is to turn right at the gas station on Old Trail Road, part of the Greensburg-Pittsburgh Turnpike, or Greensburg Pike. At the hilltop on Old Trail Road is a gathering of old buildings known as Jacktown, including the 1798 Fullerton Inn, which was so successful that an addition was added in 1805. It was also known for a while as the Jacktown Inn, and at the base of a historical marker is an old mileage marker for the Pittsburgh-Philadelphia Turnpike. The marker once indicated 21 miles to Pittsburgh and 274 to Philadelphia.

Old Trail soon meets the Lincoln at the township building, site of the original Jacktown Hotel, a stagecoach inn that burned in 1966 and was rebuilt on Route 30. We pass the Jacktown Ride and Hunt Club to the north at the top of Jacktown hill, where the old road crosses over Route 30 and makes an immediate right to head west. When we meet the Clay Pike at the 1790 Larimer House in Circleville, the old Lincoln continues down a short hill to merge with Route 30, but it's one way heading east, so we must turn left and double back.

1938–Present. On the four-lane Route 30 bypass, the road travels through a dip and again heads downhill past Motel 3 (originally Thompson's Terrace Motel). Passing under the Turnpike, to its west is Teddy's restaurant in an old Howard Johnson's. To the north, the Norwin Chamber of Commerce offers brochures. At the next light, the Ames Plaza was the site of the Super 30 Drive-In Theater, one of five drive-ins between here and Turtle Creek Valley.

Most of this area was farmland until the 1850s, when coal became the leading industry. Today that's hardly evident, looking at the Irwin strip. After the Turnpike opened in 1940, the road filled with motels; most have disappeared, with the exception of Conley's, a local chain, and

The Super 30 Drive-In opened September 19, 1947. Today it's the site of Bob Evans and Ames in Irwin. COURTESY KEVIN KUTZ

the Penn-Irwin. The Penn-Irwin rooms have knotty pine walls and tile bathrooms, and a large neon sign above the office. Built in 1946, the Penn-Irwin has been run by Deborah and Gary Salada since 1985. Gary recalls that until recently, most of the old motels were still here, and that the Penn-Irwin was one of three hotels run by a Mr. McCauley. "That's why the room numbers here run from 39 to 54. The Royal Plaza had 1 to 38, and the Penn State had the higher numbers. The Penn State eventu-

The Penn-Irwin Motel still greets travelers with a neon-lit entryway. (PHOTO 1992)

The Pine Motel survived into the 1980s, its brick cottages joined under one roof in later years.

Quality mattresses mattered to travelers choosing between unfamiliar motels, and Conley's had Serta Perfect Sleepers. Conley's has changed a great deal but is still built around this original structure.

ally burned, as did the Royal Plaza. Another motel, the Pine, had 21 rooms but is now a Kentucky Fried Chicken." The motels were replaced mostly with franchise restaurants. A Kocolene gas station, the only one in the state, closed in 1994.

After passing Conley's (with a big neon sign on its western wall) and going up through a cut, we cross a bridge and pass the gas station to

PANORAMIC VIEW OF IRWIN, SHOWING CONSTRUCTION WORK ON THE NEW FOUR-LANE LINCOLN HIGHWAY IN THE FOREGROUND

Looking northeast as work progresses on the bypass around Irwin, c. 1938. The original road can be seen parallel, a block to the north. COURTESY CY HOSMER

the north, where we found Old Trail Road on the Lincoln. To the south is the Norwin Diner, the third factory-built diner at this location. The first diner arrived in 1938, when Louis Serro, Sr., decided to leave his truck transport business. The diner was brought in by rail from the O'Mahony plant in New Jersey. Lou Serro, Jr., recalls, "He knew what the truckers wanted to eat." Lou Sr.'s brother, Joe, joined him as a cook.

After two successful decades, the Serros decided to expand and upgrade to a new stainless-steel diner. Lou, Jr., says: "In the fall of 1957, we went up to the Mountain View factory, Delores [Lou's wife] and the kids and I, and toured the plant as they were making our diner. While we were there, we saw another diner being built. We didn't know it at the time, but that would also become our diner when we sold the Irwin diner and moved to Greensburg." That Serro's Diner was on Otterman Street in Greensburg, just east of Main Street, but it was relocated when the adjacent bank expanded its parking lot in the mid-1980s. It sat empty along the Pennsylvania Turnpike until it was moved to Seaford, Delaware, in the early 1990s and restored.

The 1938 Serro's Diner was moved south of Greensburg, where it served as the Willow Diner until 1992. It was then bought by the Historical Society of Western Pennsylvania for inclusion in its new history center. The Serros operated the 1957 diner until the late 1960s, then new operators ran it until 1976, when it was moved north to Butler. It was replaced by the current Norwin Diner, also a factory-built diner made by Kullman, one of the few big diner companies still in business. Next door is a beer distributor in an old gas station once owned by a third Serro brother, Martin. Today Lou Serro, Jr., still has a small catering business.

We pass Jacktown Manor residences to the north, opened in 1989 in the newer Jacktown Motel. At the hilltop is the former Klanchar's Esso, then Exxon, to the south. Anthony and Emil Klanchar began working at John Serro's service station at the bottom of Jacktown hill in 1932. (John was the fourth Serro brother.) When construction began on the Route 30 bypass in 1938, the station was knocked down, and John built Irwin Motor Sales; Anthony became manager, and Emil built his own station across from today's Norwin Diner. In 1945 Anthony bought his brother's station, and in 1949 he built the station at the hilltop. His son Donald and daughter-in-law Rita took over in 1965 and ran it until retiring

John Serro's One Stop Service was at the bottom of Jacktown Hill, near the present-day car wash. This 1933 photo shows workers Tony Klanchar (left) and his brother Emil (right). COURTESY DONALD KLANCHAR

Jacktown Hill is in the distance looking west past Serro's Diner. A Serro Brothers Transfer truck is in front, owned by brothers Lou and Joe. COURTESY HISTORICAL SOCIETY OF WESTERN PA

Klanchar's Esso, about 1950. Today an auto accessories business retains the station's look.

GEBERT'S *Hotel*

LINCOLN HIGHWAY WEST
IRWIN, PENNA. *Phone* IRWIN

CLOSE COVER BEFORE STR

FOOD AT ITS B
FOR RESERVATIONS PHONE

GEBERT'S
3½ MILES WEST OF TURNPIKE
ON ROUTE 30

PITTSBURGH
WILKINSBURG
E. McKEESPORT
IRWIN
PA. TURNPIKE
GREENSBURG

SHRIMP PLATTERS
LOBSTER TAIL
SHRIMP
STEAK DINNERS
CHOPS
CHICKEN DINNERS
TURKEY DINNERS
CHICKEN SALAD
TENDERLOIN
VIRGINIA HAM STEAKS
GEBERT'S *Special*
Served at GEBERT'S Daily

FOOD AT ITS BEST
FOR RESERVATIONS PHONE IRWIN 161

*These large matchbooks
from Gebert's show the
old and new roads, along
with Lincoln Way, a non–
Lincoln Highway route.*

in 1992; it's now Back East, a car accessories dealer, and the owner has
done a masterful job of restoring the original look of the station, including
the rooftop neon clock.

At the top of the hill, the old Lincoln merges from the northeast and
crosses over to the southwest into Circleville. Just past the intersection is
Lenhart's, a large auto repair shop. The station was established in 1930
by Joseph Lenhart on the old Lincoln, near the Jacktown Ride and Hunt
Club. At the next light, to the south we see the Georgetown Inn hotel,
formerly Gebert's Hotel and Adrilee Motor Hotel.

SECTION III. CIRCLEVILLE TO EAST
MCKEESPORT

At the traffic light, a road called Lincoln Way heads into Mc-
Keesport. It was never the Lincoln Highway but was likely named to
lure early motorists through McKeesport. McKeesporters were relent-

THE EL DORADO, LOCATED 13 MILES EAST OF PITTSBURGH, ON LINCOLN HIGHWAY NEAR IRWIN, PA.

The El Dorado, later the Ben Gross and now Chesterfield's, but without the cabins. The signs advertise beer, dinners, and dancing to an orchestra.

less in trying to bring Lincoln Highway traffic through their town. In 1924, McKeesport's auto club sponsored a plan to connect the Lincoln Highway and National Road (Route 40) by placing markers through town. In 1927, the city directory reported that "the Chamber of Commerce is popularizing the short route between Irwin and Pittsburgh through the scenic Monongahela Valley over the White Oak Level [now Lincoln Way] and Long Run Roads via McKeesport, thence through Dravosburg and Hays . . . saving six miles, avoiding traffic congestion, fifteen mile speed limit signs, and dangerous grades." As late as 1939, the McKeesport Travel Club was campaigning for a Lincoln Highway bypass through the city.

To the north at the light is Kirk Haight Auto, with a revolving Vega on a pole to advertise its used-car business. West of the light is Chesterfield's, the former El Dorado but perhaps better remembered as the Ben Gross restaurant. We pass through another traffic light; a couple of sign poles to the north are all that remain of the Maple Drive-In Theater. We pass the big wrecking yard of Spitz Auto Parts; to the north is a little string of abandoned motel rooms. This area is known as Stewartsville, and ahead is Lincoln Coach Lines to the north, once the site of the big

Byerly Crest swimming pool. Charles Shirley recalls working there as a concession stand worker, life guard, and bathroom attendant. He also worked at the dance pavilion as a waiter.

The Byerly Crest Pool was 402 feet long and 125 feet wide, with variable depths. To swim it cost 25 cents, with privilege to use the bathroom. To spectate inside the fence cost 10 cents, and you had to bring your own chairs. There were food stands where you could buy pop, hot dogs, candy, waffle dogs, and tobacco. In front of the fence there was a roadhouse that was used as a dining room–dance floor combo, with an orchestra stage and a large kitchen for cooking meals. Attached to the dining room was an outdoor dance floor among the trees.

A hot day in the 1920s at the huge Byerly Crest Swimming Pool, now the site of Lincoln Coach Lines. COURTESY CHARLES L. SHIRLEY

STEWARTSVILLE SCHOOL HOUSE. *1883-1929*

The Stewartsville schoolhouse, now gone, is a reminder that the Lincoln Highway was not just for tourists, but also functioned as a local-access road for each municipality it passed through. COURTESY CHARLES L. SHIRLEY

Charles Shirley also recalls going to school in the one-room Stewartsville School on the Lincoln Highway, located west of the gasoline storage tanks after leaving the village of Stewartsville. "I attended from 1918 to 1926. We walked to school; there weren't any buses. During 1918 World War I was on, and convoys of U.S. Army trucks loaded with uniformed soldiers rumbled by. We were permitted to stand on the bank and wave miniature flags to show our loyalty."

We pass Colonial Manor Drive, then to the north the old Lincoln branches off behind Lincoln Mobile Home Sales. The road is called Crown Road, but it looks like there's an even older section called Mack Road. Both make their way back to Route 30 after perhaps a quarter mile.

Heading west, we pass Doug's Motel to the south; just ahead is Park's Motel, with a neon sign. When Russell and Estella Park bought the place in 1954, it was Frank Gasnik's Uncle Frank's Cabins, with outdoor toilets and a hot dog stand. In 1963 they added a string of 20 motel units in the valley behind, and they've remodeled the 10 cabins. The motel was featured in the movie *Passed Away* a few years ago.

Next door is another old motel, the Hiland Terrace, also with some cabins but best known for its theme rooms, such as the Jungle Room. Russ Park recalls that another court once lay between these two—Lutzenhizer's Cabins, of which one cabin remains as a storage shed. He says that because of the turnpike, a lot of other motels opened along here, including Lincoln Cabins at the entrance to the Penn Lincoln Cemetery, Bogg's Motel in Stewartsville, Buck's Cabins where Mason TV is now, the Staging Post Inn cabins next to that, Green Gables Motel where Doug's is now, Blue Moon Cabins at Route 48, Orchard Trailer Park just east of Park's, and the Village Motel.

Across the road stands the screen to the former Blue Dell Drive-In Theater, now the site of Vangura Laminated Products. This company has adapted the 1960s "Sputnik" marquee for its own use. The Blue Dell Drive-In was originally so popular that a second drive-in was opened behind this one. Called the Bel-Air, it included a "balcony," where cars sat on an inclined level.

Next to the theater was the Blue Dell Diner. Later known as the Delta and Jerry's, it eventually moved west on the Lincoln Highway to Pittsburgh's West End and was renamed Laverne's. Behind that was the

The original marquee at the Blue Dell Theater. COURTESY CY HOSMER

Blue Dell Pool, built in 1927. It's still there but closed in the late 1980s and since vandalized. The pool had a brick bottom, was 100 yards long, and held 1.5 million gallons.

Next to the pool is Penn Lincoln Memorial Park, and at the State Route 48 intersection, there were a number of earlier businesses, including Preston's Grille (later Preston's Island) and Paul Bondy's Blue Moon, both of which featured dining and dancing. A little past that on the south side, the old road appears to run in front of some houses below street level. Farther west, locals recall a giant windmill atop the long-gone Gypsy Tea Room at McKee Road on the south side. As we approach a traffic light at Broad Street, we see to the south Bishop's Pizza. Next to that is an abandoned building (reportedly Barber's Motel), and then Matt's Furniture at the corner across from Grandview Cemetery.

This intersection was the site of the famous Lighthouse, run by Robert "Red" Crystol. There was a floor show every night, along with the Crazy Crystols Orchestra, and Red offered free spaghetti and chicken every Thursday night. Red began with a place called the Grandview Inn, and later he had the Lighthouse Market produce stand adjacent. The lighthouse itself is gone, but there's still a Lighthouse Bar just down Broad

LIGHTHOUSE HAPPY HOUR

Route 30, East McKeesport, Pa.   Valley 5228 - 9978

ROBERT CRYSTOL & SONS, PROPRS.

For food and dancing, East McKeesport offered the Lighthouse at Broad Street, with "No Intoxicants Served."

SYCAMORE COURT TOURIST CABINS 5 Mi. West of Turnpike Lincoln Hy. Route 30

This postcard says that someone stayed at the Sycamore Court on August 15, 1948. Today no one can remember the place.

Street. Crystol's son Robert, Jr., says that his dad moved the dining room to the present location not long after a car hit the building in 1957. Photos from the period show signs for 65-cent lunches and "Southern Fried Chicken in the Rough" in the "Air Cooled Dining Room." Crystol, who still owns the business, says it's now for sale.

Ahead there are a number of small old motels, including the Siesta, the Castle Loma (in an old pink house), and Taylor's Motel, now mostly apartments. The 1940 *Blue Book List* reported "Excellent accommodations and free garage" at the Henderson Tourist Home, 482 Lincoln Highway in East McKeesport. As we pass through East McKeesport, we cross State Route 148. Just past this intersection once sat the Hotel Victory, which was torn down in the 1960s and replaced by the Inn Motor Lodge and a small shopping plaza. The road makes a sharp turn left, then right, as it goes uphill, then the old and new roads split again for a short distance through Turtle Creek Valley.

SECTION IV. EAST MCKEESPORT TO EAST PITTSBURGH

The Lincoln Highway originally descended into Turtle Creek Valley past the Westinghouse Electric Manufacturing plants. The town stayed

*Heading west from East McKeesport, the road splits, the old road going right to
Turtle Creek, the new heading left to the Westinghouse Bridge, January 1932.*
COURTESY PA STATE ARCHIVES, RG-12 DEPT. OF HIGHWAYS

busy around the clock, creating a traffic nightmare for those passing
through. In 1932 the Westinghouse Bridge was opened to span the valley
and bypass one of the worst congested sections on the whole cross-country Lincoln Highway.

1915–1932. We can take the Lincoln Highway into Turtle Creek
by following Greensburg Pike Section 1 to the north. (Section 2 to the
south is the original route and now crosses over Route 30 eastbound.) The
Lincoln Highway runs behind the Greater Pittsburgh Drive-In Theater.
The road tops a rise, passes a driving range (with a good view of the valley), and heads down a steep hill toward Turtle Creek borough. The winding Turtle Creek Hill was paved in brick until recent years, and at the
bottom a sharp curve originally led onto a narrow bridge. Many accidents
occurred on the hill or at the bottom turn. In December 1925 a new bridge
was dedicated that eliminated the curves at both ends, but it was still inad-
equate for the cross-country traffic load.

We cross the 1925 iron bridge and at its end bear left onto Penn
Avenue, following it as it curves left onto Braddock Avenue. Braddock

TURTLE CREEK HILL, LINCOLN HIGHWAY; DEAD MAN'S CURVE, TURTLE CREEK, PA.

Dead Man's Curve, which slides down into Turtle Creek from the east, is just one reason why this route was bypassed.

One of three signs erected and illuminated by the Duquesne Light company. This one stood in front of the Westinghouse plant in East Pittsburgh at the bottom of Electric Avenue, an important intersection with Braddock Avenue. COURTESY UNIVERSITY OF MICHIGAN, SPECIAL COLLECTIONS LIBRARY

runs past the former Westinghouse Electric Company manufacturing plants in East Pittsburgh; now that they're closed and most of the surrounding businesses are gone, it's hard to imagine this place congested. The plants are now occupied by Keystone Commons, an industrial mall, and a postal encoding center.

The Lincoln originally turned right onto Electric Avenue, but Braddock now dead-ends, so we must turn around and get on the short four-lane Tri-Boro Expressway. Turning left onto it, we proceed parallel to Braddock until we come to Electric Avenue. We turn right and climb uphill to merge with Route 30, which is elevated above us. Actually, the lanes that come off 30 going east are the original route of the Lincoln, which we see to our left.

1932–Present. Modern Route 30 continues straight and passes the Super 30 Motel and Greater Pittsburgh Drive-In Theater. The drive-in opened in 1954 and is still run by the Warren family. Joseph Warren and his sons owned both deep and strip coal mines, but demand for coal was waning by the 1950s. If you had lots of idle land and earth-moving equipment back then, building a drive-in was a natural progression, perhaps the reason why the once coal-rich Pittsburgh became known as "the city of drive-ins."

Low spots are filled on the Turtle Creek bypass, August 1930. To the east of the Greater Pittsburgh Drive-In Theater entrance, the road is now lined with businesses.

The Candy Cane Playground at the Greater Pittsburgh Drive-In Theater sat between its first two screens. It included a ferris wheel, a merry-go-round, and a "little theater" to show cartoons before the show.

The Warrens eventually owned seven drive-ins, including the Super 30 in Irwin and the Blue Dell near East McKeesport, both on the Lincoln. The Greater Pitt opened with stereo in-car speakers and a wide screen, and it proved so popular that it was twinned the next year. It now has five screens and a miniature golf course. The Warrens' other drive-ins have closed through the years, following the broader trend—of the region's 40-some drive-ins, only a half dozen remain open.

Joseph's son Marty helped expand their business, and now Marty's son Joe keeps it running. Joe says that better movies have helped in recent years, but it's more than that: "You get two movies for the price of one, and you can enjoy the outdoors." Marty always said, "We'll be here as long as people will have us" but he passed away in 1995 and the drive-in may be sold to a Kmart, much to Joe's dismay.

As we approach the Westinghouse Bridge, we pass a retirement hotel that was once the location of the Sunrise Inn, a tiny restaurant remembered for its backroom gambling. We cross the bridge, a monumental five-arch cement span, the largest in the country at the time. At its dedication, the director of public works, Norman Brown, stated that the

On September 10, 1932, the Westinghouse Bridge dedication included a line of
five hundred Boy Scouts holding a rope to separate traffic. A ribbon was cut in
the center by the brother of George Westinghouse, inventor and industrialist for
whom the bridge was named. The bridge straddles Turtle Creek Valley, eliminating one of the worst bottlenecks on the original Lincoln. When built, the Westinghouse Bridge's center span was the largest concrete arch in the United States.
It was also a boon to the local economy during the Depression. This photo is one
of many in the dedication booklet.

bridge "eliminated 3.4 miles of old roadway and shortens the distance three-fourths of a mile through East Pittsburgh and Turtle Creek boroughs, and saves the motorist approximately thirty minutes." The time estimate seems unbelievable now, but it shows how congested the valley route was.

The old Westinghouse Electric and Manufacturing Company shops can still be seen in the valley beneath the bridge today. The company employed more than fifteen thousand at its peak, but it has since moved out. Looking southwest, we can see the USX Edgar Thomson steel mills in Braddock and, beyond, the roller coasters of Kennywood Amusement Park on the hill above the Monongahela River. Route 30 crosses the bridge and meets the old Lincoln near North Braddock.

SECTION V. EAST PITTSBURGH TO HOMEWOOD

Electric Avenue merges onto Route 30 at Ardmore Boulevard. Continuing west on Ardmore, we enter Forest Hills; the road looks like an

Work begins on the Turtle Creek bypass, August 1930. To the east, toward East Pittsburgh, the original roadbed heads downhill. Here, preparations are made for arches over the road to carry traffic to the new Westinghouse Bridge a half mile beyond. COURTESY PA STATE ARCHIVES, RG-12 DEPT. OF HIGHWAYS

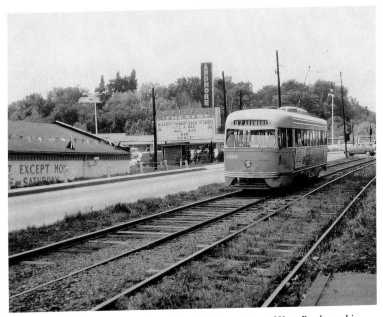

Looking west on Ardmore Boulevard to the intersection of Yost Boulevard in Forest Hills. The 87 Ardmore trolley was still running down the middle of the Lincoln Highway in August 1964. The roller rink to the left was built as a streetcar barn, but is now the site of a tall bank. PHOTO COURTESY JIM SMITH

early parkway, with a grass strip in the middle of four lanes, but that was the location of the Ardmore Trolley line. At Yost Boulevard there's a cement Lincoln Highway marker to the south, and it's the last one we'll see until Chester, West Virginia. There's also a marker here commemorating Braddock's defeat, which occurred just south of here in 1755 at the hands of the French and Indians.

We go through a small business district, and at 2104 Ardmore, we pass Kliment Brothers, an authorized Studebaker sales and service dealer, even though Studebakers have not been manufactured since 1966. Now most of the business consists of restoring old cars. The road becomes three-lane in each direction as we approach the Penn-Lincoln Parkway (U.S. Routes 22 and 30 and I-376). *Note:* Do not follow Route 30 unless you want to skip the original route through Wilkinsburg and Pittsburgh.

We continue straight, the original Lincoln Highway now following State Route 8 north. We stay in the right lane, passing the Lincoln Garage (founded in 1925) to the right, and remain in the right lane against the wall until the traffic light. Here we join the old cross-state William Penn Highway; to the right, on the triangle of land, formerly stood a statue of

Looking west, July 1948, to the new Penn-Lincoln Parkway bridges, which now take Route 30 around Pittsburgh. COURTESY PA STATE ARCHIVES, RG-12 DEPT. OF HIGHWAYS

The Lincoln statue that overlooked the intersection of the William Penn and Lincoln Highways was funded by pennies donated by Wilkinsburg school children. (PHOTO 1990)

The Penn Lincoln Hotel, built in 1927, was named for the Lincoln and William Penn Highways, which run past its door at the lower left.

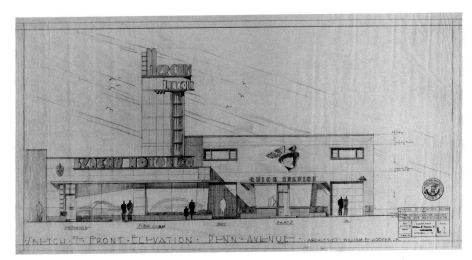

Architect's rendering of an auto dealership, now an American Jeep-Eagle dealer just west of Wilkinsburg. COURTESY CARNEGIE MELLON UNIVERSITY ARCHITECTURE ARCHIVES

Scotty's Diner, now Charlie's, on an early June morning. (PHOTO 1990)

Abraham Lincoln, financed by children who donated their pennies in 1916. Today it rests in the Wilkinsburg Borough Building waiting to be replaced. Twice in recent years it's been cut off at the feet. In 1981 it took 10 months for the couple who stole it to confess that they'd buried the copper and bronze statue in Harrison City. Its face was crushed, a hand severed, and limbs flattened, but the thieves paid $10,000 to repair it in exchange for the charges being dropped. In September 1992 a passerby found Lincoln beside his base; this time high winds may have torn the statue off. There are plans to restore and replace it again, but for now it sits inside.

We go straight at the light and are now on Penn Avenue, which cuts through the heart of the Wilkinsburg business district. The Penn Lincoln Hotel is on the northwest corner at Center Street. We pass under railroad tracks, and on the other side we see an American Jeep-Eagle dealership with a glass-block tower. Also to the north we come upon Charlie's Diner, formerly Scotty's, a shiny stainless-steel National-brand diner built about 1940. (There are few such diners, as National became Fodero after only a few years.) Manager Chuck Huwalt purchased it a couple of years ago and is doing a great job of restoring and revitalizing the historic diner, which is open 24 hours.

We cross North Braddock Avenue and head into an area that was "Millionaires' Row" a century ago. To the south is Clayton, the restored home of Henry Clay Frick. An iron fence west of North Lang Avenue once fronted the Heinz estate, Greenlawn, but all that remains is the carriage house, itself now a residence.

We're soon presented with two Lincoln Highway routes through Pittsburgh: the original route following Penn Avenue to Baum Boulevard and then Bigelow Boulevard; and a later route via Dallas Avenue, Forbes Avenue, and the Boulevard of the Allies. We'll trace both routes here.

SECTION VI. HOMEWOOD TO PITTSBURGH'S POINT

1915–1920. We pass Dallas Avenue, and immediately to the north we see on a tree stump an 80-year-old plaque commemorating the 1758 Forbes Road. We arrive at a major intersection and cross over Fifth Avenue, no longer following Route 8.

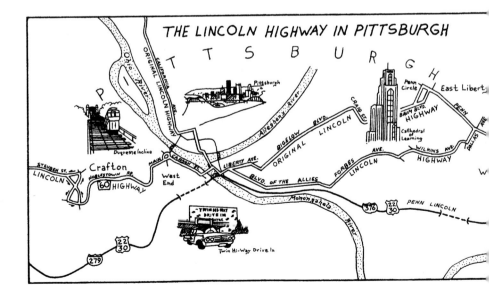

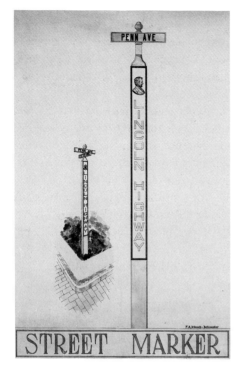

STREET MARKER

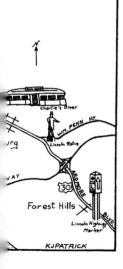

This intersection was the location of an experimental marker for the Lincoln Highway route through Pittsburgh. Records in Carnegie Mellon's Architecture Archives document the marker and a resulting competition: According to a February 25, 1915, *Pittsburgh Press* article, Department of Public Works Director Robert Swan "announced that 25 of the markers will be placed at intervals along the route. . . . Each marker will extend nine feet above the ground. It will be made of a concrete composed of granite chips and cement." The city's Art Commission soon protested that a better design could be found, but Pittsburgh's Special Committee on Good Roads replied that its design had been submitted to the Lincoln Highway Association, which considered it "the most attractive on the route between New York and San Francisco." Nonetheless, a competition was held, and nine entries were anonymously submitted by local architects (including one by the renowned Frederick Scheibler). Meanwhile, the Lincoln Highway caravan was to pass through town at the end of May, so the city's original design was erected at Penn and Fifth Avenues.

In June, Raymond Marlier received $50 for his winning marker design, but there is no known record of his effort and it is not known if any such markers were produced (though the lone surviving drawing with a script *L* on a shield hanging from a pole is possibly his design).

Crossing Fifth Avenue, we pass a Nabisco plant to the north and arrive at Penn Circle. We enter the business district and turn left on Highland Avenue, then right onto Baum Boulevard. We pass Motor Square Garden to the south, now home to AAA. It was built in 1898 as the Liberty Market House but was renamed when the Pittsburgh Automobile Association bought it in 1915 to use for auto shows. It was later

Looking east on Baum Boulevard, November 1937. The AAA office on the left was founded in 1903, moved across the street diagonally in 1947, and left the intersection completely in 1972. The AAA office returned in 1992, when it moved into Motor Square Garden, a former market house. COURTESY UNIVERSITY OF PITTSBURGH HILLMAN LIBRARY, ARCHIVES OF INDUSTRIAL SOCIETY

The world's first architect-designed drive-in gas station opened with 13 pumps on Pittsburgh's Baum Boulevard at St. Clair Street on December 1, 1913. Most gasoline at the time was dispensed from curbside pumps or tanks. Attendants were required to crank-start customers' cars after serving them. COURTESY CHEVRON CORPORATE ARCHIVES

a boxing ring, a Cadillac dealership, and most recently, an upscale indoor mall.

As we head down Baum Boulevard, we first pass St. Clair Street, the site of the world's first architect-designed drive-in gas station, opened by Gulf in 1913. This location made sense because Baum was once Pittsburgh's "automobile row," and many dealerships remain. Gulf's Pittsburgh to Gettysburg map, c. 1918, has a photo of this style of station and brags "No Tips—Drive In." The station offered free air, water, and the country's first free commercial road maps. At Negley is a car dealership with a round corner tower. This building was designed by Albert Kahn.

We cross Liberty Avenue and spot Ritter's Diner to the north, a mid-1970s Fodero-brand diner, much less interesting than the Ritter's that used to sit across the street. (That 1951 DeRaffele-brand diner now sits across from downtown Pittsburgh at Station Square, a complex that includes two nineteenth-century railroad-car shops.) The current Ritter's Diner sells T-shirts with a drawing of the original. At the southeast corner of Morewood Avenue is an old brick building housing an electrical supply company; "Ford Motor Company" in script can still be seen along the top edge of the building. According to a 1915 *Gazette Times* article, it opened that March as one of 24 assembly plants to help with production and distribution for Ford. Unassembled parts were shipped to these plants, where the cars were assembled and distributed regionally. The Pittsburgh plant had 300 employees and turned out 40 Model T's a day.

West on Baum Boulevard is San Remy's Lebanese restaurant, with an interesting neon sign. At the end of Baum, we turn right onto North Craig Street and go uphill for a block, then merge onto Bigelow Boulevard. In the teens this was known as Grant Boulevard, an extension of Grant Street in Pittsburgh, and the area as we approach the Bloomfield Bridge was filled with stores and auto-related businesses, most of which have since been destroyed to make way for a replacement bridge and modern alignments.

Bigelow curves to the left as we head west into town. There are some nice views of the Allegheny River valley to our north, and Bigelow becomes like a parkway, but as it descends into town, the original alignment has been rerouted. We stay in the right lane and follow signs for the Civic Arena and Sixth Avenue. We pass the grand Pennsylvania Station to our right, and we merge right onto Sixth Avenue at the base of the USX tower.

We cross Grant Street and continue four blocks on Sixth, then make a left on Liberty Avenue and arrive at Stanwix Street looking at Gateway Center, a complex of high-rises built during Pittsburgh's first renaissance in the 1950s. The Lincoln went to Pittsburgh's Point and crossed the Manchester Bridge (which replaced the Union Bridge about 1913) to the North Side. The Point was also redone during the 1950s, eliminating the Manchester Bridge and creating a park with partial reconstructions of Fort Duquesne and Fort Pitt.

1920–1953. From Penn Avenue, we head south on Dallas Avenue, passing some large homes. There's no indication that the Lincoln ever cut through this suburban area. After a few blocks, we see Homewood Cemetery to our left as we bear right on Wilkins Avenue, following it west over Beechwood Boulevard and Shady Avenue. At a fork, we take the left lane and follow Beeler for a few blocks until it meets Forbes Avenue.

The Schenley Park Tourist Camp, in Pittsburgh's Oakland section, shown here in August 1926, was about as close as you could camp to a big city. The 1927 Mohawk-Hobbs guide calls it "a fine free camp" with "free kitchen and free gas." There were accommodations for 40 cars, 120 people. COURTESY UNIVERSITY OF PITTSBURGH HILLMAN LIBRARY, ARCHIVES OF INDUSTRIAL SOCIETY

Going west on Forbes, we pass Carnegie Mellon University. The University of Pittsburgh's Cathedral of Learning is straight ahead, a 42-story building that resembles a Gothic cathedral. We cross Panther Hollow and Craig Street; two storefronts to the north is the Caliban Book Shop, a good source for used regional history books.

Forbes goes straight but becomes one-way, so we turn right in front of The Carnegie (famous for its dinosaur collections) on South Bellefield Avenue. The Cathedral of Learning (which offers tours of its 23 "nationality classrooms") and Heinz Chapel are to our left, and a block later we turn left on Fifth Avenue. Crossing Bigelow Boulevard, we see the Hotel Schenley, now Pitt's Student Union, on the southwest corner and the

Looking east near the Forbes Avenue entrance to Schenley Park, a crew in two Ardmore-made Autocar trucks posts a porcelain Lincoln Highway marker in front of Pittsburgh's Carnegie Library, September 1920. COURTESY UNIVERSITY OF MICHIGAN, SPECIAL COLLECTIONS LIBRARY

large Soldiers and Sailors Memorial Hall on the northwest corner. On the original route on Forbes, the streetscape is commercial, and some buildings, such as the Iroquois, are being restored.

After a few blocks on Fifth, we get in the middle lane to turn left onto Craft Avenue. We stay in the right lane on Craft, which immediately turns right onto Forbes and becomes the ramp to the Boulevard of the Allies. This four-lane undivided road runs along a bluff overlooking the Monongahela River and the city's South Side.

The Boulevard of the Allies goes straight into town, but it becomes one-way eastbound, so we get in the right lane, curve right onto Crosstown Boulevard, then immediately take the left lane, the Seventh Avenue exit. Seventh crosses Grant Street, and three blocks later we turn left on Liberty Avenue, taking it to Stanwix at Gateway Center.

(*Note:* To bypass downtown Pittsburgh, take the first exit off the Boulevard of the Allies following I-376 (also U.S. Routes 22 and 30). This right-hand exit is just after you get on the Boulevard, and it takes you to the Penn-Lincoln Parkway. Stay on the parkway until you reach a long underpass section. Here you can follow either of the Lincoln Highway routes west of town: For the 1915–1927 Route, stay right and follow the signs for Three Rivers Stadium. For the 1927–1953 Route or present Route 30, stay left and follow the signs for the airport and I-279 South, crossing the Fort Pitt Bridge.)

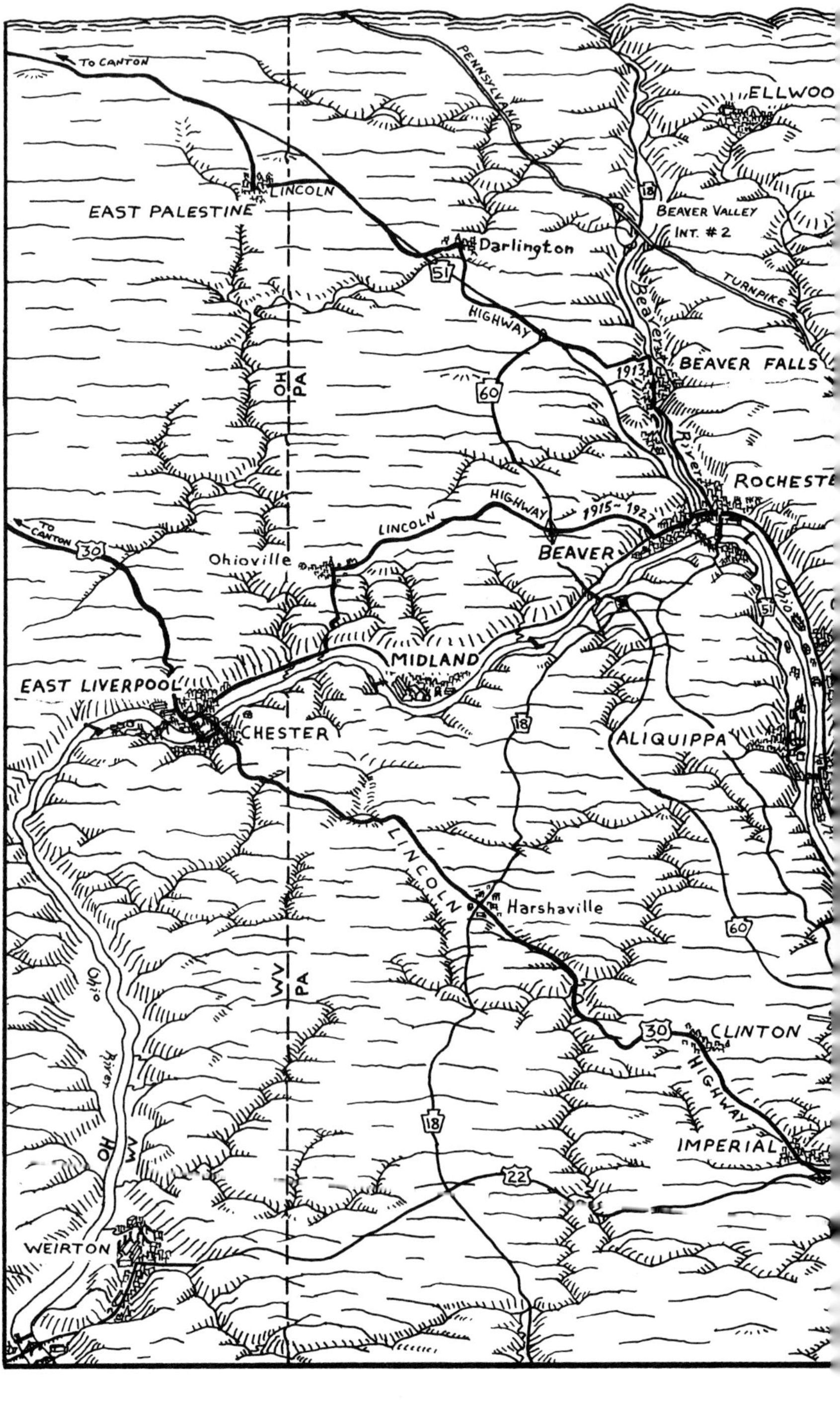

TO CANTON
ELLWOO
PENNSYLVANIA
LINCOLN
EAST PALESTINE
18
BEAVER VALLEY
INT. #2
Darlington
51
TURNPIKE
Beaver
HIGHWAY
BEAVER FALLS
1913
60
OH
PA
River
ROCHESTE
HIGHWAY
1915–1927
LINCOLN
TO CANTON
30
Ohioville
BEAVER
Ohio
51
MIDLAND
EAST LIVERPOOL
CHESTER
18
ALIQUIPPA
LINCOLN
Harshaville
60
WV
PA
Ohio
River
30
CLINTON
HIGHWAY
18
IMPERIAL
OH
WV
22
WEIRTON

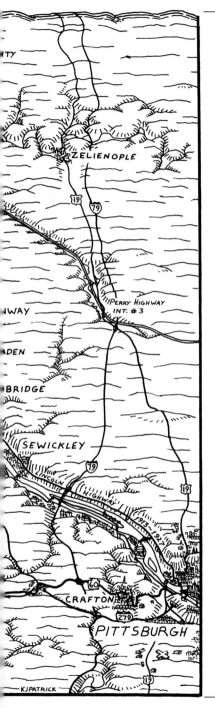

Pittsburgh to East Liverpool, Ohio

At one time, the occupants of what is now Pittsburgh spoke French. The junction where the Monongahela and Allegheny Rivers join to form the Ohio was recognized in the eighteenth century for its importance by both France and England, which were battling for supremacy on the continent. France built a string of forts along the frontier from Quebec to New Orleans. In 1753, 21-year-old George Washington brought a letter here to inform the French of the English claim; they didn't leave. But General Forbes's expedition in 1758 ended with the capture of the forks of the Ohio, and a new English fort was named to honor British statesman William Pitt. Fort Pitt soon fell into disuse (the original blockhouse remains at the Point), but it gave the growing town its name. Coal supplies and the rivers led to Pittsburgh's dominance as an iron and steel producer, but today most of the mills that lined the rivers are shuttered or gone.

The Lincoln Highway followed two different official routes west to Ohio during the lifespan of the Lincoln Highway Association. The original route down the Ohio River followed an old Indian trail known as the Great Path. It later became the primary corridor for wagon traffic heading west. This route through Beaver to East Liverpool, Ohio, had three disadvantages: It was very congested, because it took travelers through a series of long-established small towns. Also, the road was not a state highway route, so it was constantly in disrepair. Finally, the road east of Beaver was often foggy, while west of Beaver the road was of dirt. This section is regularly mentioned in road reports issued biweekly by the Lincoln Highway Association in the early 1920s. Reports from 1922 and 1923 said that the Ohio River route was dirt and "in bad shape," as was the alternative through Clinton. A detour was recommended from Beaver through East Palestine, Ohio, and to Canton, which was "much longer but paved." Reports from 1924 and 1925 additionally recommended traveling the south side of the Ohio River through McKees Rocks and Aliquippa to Rochester before following the "well-marked" detour to Canton.

Work began in the mid-1920s on improving the southerly route through Crafton, Imperial, and Clinton that sliced through a few miles of West Virginia. Photos of this route were taken by the Lincoln Highway Association as early as 1926, and the 1927 Mohawk-Hobbs guide announced that the route would be complete by late 1927. The Lincoln Highway Association board of directors officially changed the route on December 2, 1927, cutting 13 miles from the drive.

Pittsburgh's Point, 1927. The Manchester Bridge over the Allegheny River is to the lower left, and Bigelow Boulevard can be seen along the bluff to the upper left. The Point Bridge over the Monongahela River is to the right, and this river's dirtier water is obvious where it meets the Allegheny to form the Ohio River.
COURTESY HISTORICAL SOCIETY OF WESTERN PA

When the Lincoln was marked for the final time in 1928 with signs and cement posts, the southerly route was designated. None of those markers remain in Pennsylvania, but the little town of Chester, West Virginia, has three.

1915–1927 ROUTE

We turn right from Liberty Avenue onto Stanwix Street in downtown Pittsburgh, and then get in the left lane to turn left onto Fort Duquesne Boulevard. We follow the signs for I-279 north and Fort Duquesne Bridge. Once on the bridge, we get in the left lane for Three Rivers Stadium and follow the ramp down. The original route crossed the Union Bridge, replaced in the teens by the Manchester Bridge, and

Looking northwest from the end of the Manchester Bridge, February 1935. Pat's Diner can be seen at the corner of Shore Avenue. COURTESY UNIVERSITY OF PITTSBURGH HILLMAN LIBRARY, ARCHIVES OF INDUSTRIAL SOCIETY

headed north on Galveston Avenue; an old bridge abutment can be seen by the Allegheny River's edge to the left. When our ramp ends, though, we turn right on Allegheny Avenue.

We stay in the left lane on Allegheny (the right loops back onto Fort Duquesne Bridge) but make a right turn onto Ridge Avenue, then a left on Galveston Avenue to get us back on the route. Two blocks later, we turn left on Western Avenue at the Modern Café, which has tall glass-block windows with a blue and black Carrara glass corner. Follow Western across Allegheny Avenue, then turn right onto Chateau Street.

Chateau has changed greatly since the teens and 1920s; first, brick walls appear to both sides now, then everything to the west side is now gone, the victim of urban renewal and the construction of Ohio River Boulevard, a road that we sometimes jump onto during this leg of the journey. We soon take a left ramp and follow signs for Route 19 north. Once on the freeway, we stay in the right lane, and we soon exit for California Avenue. This exit loops around, and at the traffic light we go straight. We now rejoin the original route, which was lost beneath the ramps and overpasses, for good.

We head uphill past brick homes and a church, and continue to follow California through a five-way intersection and a fork. After Windhurst Street, we cross a bridge over the Pittsburgh city line into Bellevue. The bridge has decorative ends with eagles and lions, and a plaque dedicating it to the men and women of World War I.

We follow an S curve into the Bellevue business district, and we're now on Lincoln Avenue. We pass the CJ Diner to our south and Classic Chevrolet to our north. In town, there's a Sweet William Restaurant and Deli and a Lincoln Bakery. When we cross into Avalon, the road becomes California Avenue again, which eventually winds down to Ben Avon about 2 miles west. We turn left on Cliff and right on Ohio River Boulevard.

The original route soon angles to the north on Brighton Road, which becomes Beaver Avenue when it crosses into Emsworth. It rejoins Ohio River Boulevard (State Route 65) at a Yamaha dealership in an old garage to the north. Big cement pylons on each side of the road mark Ohio River Boulevard, and murals on their backs tell of earlier local transportation marvels: the Portage Railroad near Altoona and the Pitts-

Parker Chevrolet, 616 Lincoln Avenue, proudly advertised its floral display in the 1940s and '50s. The address is now occupied by a discount hearing aid establishment.

The Lincoln Highway followed Beaver Road through Osborne, Sewickley, Edgeworth, and Leetsdale from 1913 to 1928. The Edgeworth area pictured remains sylvan.

These monuments along Ohio River Boulevard honor earlier forms of transportation, including the Portage Railroad, which dragged canal boats across the Allegheny Mountains, and the New Orleans, *the first Ohio River steamboat.*
(PHOTO 1994)

burgh-built *New Orleans* steamboat, the first on the Ohio River. An art deco building to the north here now houses a janitorial business.

Heading west, we pass Horne Camp Road and soon pass under the I-79 bridge. About 5 miles after passing the pylons, we enter Haysville. We see a sign for the borough of Osborne and take a ramp to the right at the next traffic light onto Beaver Road. Passing numerous Victorian homes, we enter Sewickley, once an important river town, and head into its gentrified business district. We cross Broad Street and pass more stately old homes, and 1 mile after entering Sewickley, we cross into Edgeworth and, at the fork, we stay to the north on Beaver.

Local history buff (and Edgeworth mayor) William Kelly has collected some interesting facts about the Lincoln Highway in this area. A January 1916 ordinance by Sewickley Borough Council changed Beaver Road's name to Lincoln Highway; nearby Osborne, Edgeworth, and Leetsdale boroughs soon followed suit. Also, Deadman Island in the Ohio River was dredged in the 1920s and used for creating a new riverfront, allowing relocation of the railroad nearer the river, which then allowed the construction of Route 65, bypassing Beaver Road. The Lincoln's coincidental move from Beaver Road to the Clinton route left the original Lincoln relatively unchanged from its 1920s state.

The *Sewickley Herald* reported the Transcontinental Army Truck Convoy leaving Washington on July 7, 1919, and arriving in Sewickley between 3 o'clock and dusk on July 11. They were served coffee, sandwiches, and Coke by the local Red Cross. The road was closed overnight in Edgeworth so the trucks could park, and the men camped in Way Park. The Lincoln Highway in Edgeworth was also closed January 20 and 21, 1922, from 7 to 10 o'clock—for sled riding! Riders coming down Chestnut Hill had to cross the highway, so traffic guards with red lanterns stopped traffic upon the approach of a sled.

After leaving Edgeworth we eventually cross into Leetsdale, and 1.5 miles later, at a sharp S curve, we start climbing a brick-paved hill; ahead we see a pair of Greek Orthodox church domes. The end of the brick pavement marks our entry into the borough of Ambridge, and we're on Merchant Street. Ambridge is named after Andrew Carnegie's American Bridge Company, once the world's largest steel fabricating plant but now closed. Today the business district is active but quiet. Ambridge is also the site of Old Economy, a religious community founded in 1805 by

George Rapp as the third and last home of the utopian Harmony Society. Costumed interpreters give tours of some of the seventeen buildings, and there's a gift shop. The Harmonists adopted celibacy in 1807 and eventually had no members left, hence the site is now state run.

Heading through Ambridge on Merchant Street, we pass Café Frappé, which sells ice cream and pastries, on the southeast corner of Fifth Street. We also pass the Ambridge Theater with a neon sign and chase lights. At 14th Street we turn right, and a couple of blocks later we turn left on Duss Avenue (also State Route 989 west). As we proceed northwest on Duss, the area begins as mostly residential, with a few old gas stations, and then a steel mill to the left. The stretch of Duss from Ambridge to Baden is listed in the 1914 *Blue Book* as a "very poor dirt road." We do not follow Route 989 when it turns right, but stay on Duss.

We pass through an industrial area; to the south is a bronze marker in a large rock for Logstown, one of the largest Indian settlements on the Ohio River in the early eighteenth century. At Legionville, early motorists would have found a free campsite, according to a 1924 Department of Highways guide. Today there are four markers commemorating the camp of Gen. Anthony Wayne on his expedition against Northwest Indians, which resulted in the Treaty of Greenville. About 2,500 men in 500 structures waited out the winter of 1792–93, and 17 are buried here. There's a billboard with a site plan for a future park and historic re-creation of the camp, but according to a recent *Pittsburgh Press* article, a local developer who wants to put a mall here called the mall protesters "a bunch of sick people—jerks—who want something for nothing, and care more about a bunch of dried-up bones than living people who want to make a living."

At Baden the road becomes State Street, and we see a little red building across from Ehman Street that looks like a castle. We soon merge back onto Ohio River Boulevard, but then we angle off to the north on Beaver Road, just after a Tastee-Freez ice cream stand. We enter Economy. The big field to the right was the site of the ABC Drive-In Theater from the late 1940s to the early 1980s. Just past that is Northern Lights Shopping Center, then we cross into Conway. At an old Arby's sign we rejoin Ohio River Boulevard. To the southwest spreads Conrail's Conway Yard; opened in 1880, it's still the country's largest push-button railroad yard.

We take the Freedom exit, past the beautiful c. 1830 cut stone Vicary house, built by sea captain William Vicary when the view to the river was not obstructed by concrete and rails. We head into Freedom on 3rd Avenue then merge back onto Ohio River Boulevard; the original road jogged southwest, crossing a bridge over the railroad tracks, and "turning right in center of bridge," according to the 1914 *Blue Book*. The route then headed north on today's Railroad Street (called Sycamore Street in the *Blue Book*). It progressed between the railroad and the river through East Rochester to the Rochester borough line, just over 1 mile.

The Lincoln Highway then turned right on New York Avenue—at the Speyer Hotel, according to a 1918 Goodrich tour book (Speyerer in the 1915 LHA guidebook), across from the Pennsylvania Depot—and crossed the railroad tracks. The crossing can still be seen by the Beaver Valley Bowl, which perhaps is the former hotel. The Lincoln then beared left on Brighton Avenue. (A couple of blocks east of Brighton Avenue is a street named Lincoln Way, though there is no apparent connection.)

Back in Freedom on Ohio River Boulevard, follow the Rochester exit and take State Route 68 onto Brighton Avenue, which goes uphill through the business district. To the left, facing a side street, is the once opulent Oriental Theater; to the right, in the triangle formed by intersecting roads, is the Beaver Hotel. At Rochester's town square, where a number of roads converge (including Adams Street, location of a AAA office at 300 Adams), we leave Route 68 and continue straight on Brighton for two more blocks, until it joins Madison. There we turn left and head west over the Beaver River on the Bridgewater-Rochester Bridge.

We head into Bridgewater and follow the signs for State Route 68 west. Bridge Street used to head into Beaver, but now State Route 51 cuts the road off. We enter the Beaver business district on Third Street and pass a marker for Fort Macintosh, the first U.S. military post north of the Ohio River, built in 1778. Another marker tells us that Beaver is named for King Beaver, a Delaware Indian chief. Beaver has also made it to the big screen—it served as the town in the 1980s film *Gung Ho*.

We pass the courthouse, and across the street is a park with a bandstand. Three blocks later, we turn right, or north, on Buffalo Street. After two blocks, we follow a short brick wall left around a cemetery to Tuscarawas Road, which we'll follow for about 10 miles through a thinly populated area. Tuscarawas Road was part of the Great Path Indian trail

The Greek Catholic Union's Saint Nicholas Chapel is based on data the designers gathered from 120 wooden churches in the Carpathian Mountain region of Eastern Europe. The lower level houses a museum. (PHOTO 1994)

and derives its name from the path's routing through the Indian town of Tuscarawas, now Bolivar, Ohio. The Lincoln leaves the trail just west of Dawson, Pennsylvania. We cross over Route 60, the Beaver Valley Expressway, and pass through some suburbia; at the top of a long climb we see Tusca Plaza with an old sign for a Walgreen Agency in the drugstore. Six miles after turning onto Tuscarawas, we pass the Tusca Drive-In Theater to the north, now for sale, advertising "10 acres prime commercial." A number of ceramic lawn ornaments still dot the grounds. Just past it is the Greek Catholic Union's Seven Oaks resort, which includes a re-creation of a wooden church from the Carpathian Mountain region of Europe. Free tours are offered on weekdays.

We're on a high ridge, and the view is sometimes grand. We pass through the town of Fairview, then an area that Lincoln Highway Association guidebooks called Esther. We go by a snack stand and driving range, and then the Ohioville Borough Building. A sign warns of horse and buggy crossings. We pass State Route 168 and finally arrive at Smith's Ferry Road; here we turn left, or south, and follow this road down to the town of Smith's Ferry, crossing a stone bridge over Upper

Dry Run along the way. We turn right, heading west, on State Route 68, about 15 miles from Beaver.

We soon arrive at the Pennsylvania-Ohio border. Three markers at the state line commemorate the "Point of Beginning" of the survey of the Western Lands as required under the Land Ordinance of 1785. A marker dividing Pennsylvania from what was then Virginia was planted on August 20, 1785, and the actual survey began with the driving of a stake on September 30, 1785.

Once in Ohio, the road becomes Ohio Route 39, and we enter the village of East End. Here, 39 follows Harvey Street, which eventually dead-ends, making us turn north past a boarded up 1905 schoolhouse. Two blocks later, we head west again on Pennsylvania Avenue. There are some old garages along this route, which is overlooked by a mountain ridge to the north. When we reach a traffic light, we bear left to stay on 39 and Pennsylvania Avenue. After one more light, the road becomes a freeway, which we follow toward East Liverpool.

On Broadway at Fifth is the Museum of Ceramics, celebrating the region's ceramics heritage; the building, in an old post office, has a cement Lincoln Highway marker in front and a plate inside commemorating the Lincoln Highway Tour, which came through town in the teens. There's a AAA office one block up on Broadway.

We can also take the Route 30 bridge south into West Virginia. The first exit will land us in Chester, where we can visit the Teapot just east of the cloverleaf.

1927–1953 ROUTE

From the intersection of Liberty Avenue and Stanwix Street in downtown Pittsburgh, we continue straight on Liberty through Gateway Center and follow the signs for Routes 22 and 30 and I-279 South. As we go up the ramp to the Fort Pitt Bridge, we see Point State Park spread out to our right, the Ohio River in the distance.

We merge onto the Fort Pitt Bridge, which is four lanes wide, and get into the far right lane. We get off the bridge at exit 7 for Route 51 West End. (*Note:* Do not follow Route 30/I-279 toward the airport, unless you want to skip the original route through the West End and Crafton.) From the ramp, we merge onto Carson Street, passing the Duquesne Incline to the left. We take the left lane to the traffic light of the West End Circle. Staying far left, we go halfway around the traffic circle

Looking south on Main Street through the West End, November 1938. Launie's (or Lester's) Diner is now the site of Laverne's Diner. Laverne Yorkgitis began running this diner in 1973, then replaced it five years later with the Blue Dell Diner, which she still owns. COURTESY UNIVERSITY OF PITTSBURGH HILLMAN LIBRARY, ARCHIVES OF INDUSTRIAL SOCIETY

and follow the signs for State Route 60 north, Crafton, which puts us in the right lane as we break from the circle. We turn right from the circle onto Main Street, as we dip under an overpass.

We pass Laverne's Diner, the former Blue Dell Diner, open from 6 A.M. to 3 P.M. It's a 1955 Silk City that has retained most of its original look, though a fire the day before it opened here in 1978 forced some interior changes. We continue through the West End, formerly Temperanceville. At the third light at Wabash Street, it's worth a side trip to Pip's Diner. To get there, go left on Wabash, then left on Woodville Avenue, only a few blocks away. It's Pittsburgh oldest diner, a 1920s Tierney, though it's mostly remodeled; the attraction is not the diner, however, but the food and service. Peg and Keith Pippi serve some of the best-tasting meals in one of the friendliest diners anywhere.

We continue straight on Main Street past Wabash but make the next left on Noblestown Road, following the signs for State Route 60. Martin's Auto Service is in an old church to our left as we begin a long uphill climb. At the top, we enter Crafton on Crafton Boulevard. Local resident Walt McGervey recalls that on a bus trip across the Lincoln Highway in 1947, talk turned to slow driving when the bus was in the Rocky Mountains and the bus driver said, "This is no worse than being stuck behind a trailer truck crawling up Crafton Boulevard!"

Now we follow the signs for Route 60, which takes us downhill. We turn right on Dinsmore Avenue and pass through a residential area. At a five-way intersection, we bear right on Noble. (Note the Campbell Land company building with portico and red tile roof to the left.) From Noble we turn left on East Steuben Street and continue downhill past West Crafton Avenue.

(*Note:* The Lincoln Highway through Crafton is one-way, with a different eastbound routing. To take Route 60 eastbound through town, turn left on Crafton Avenue, which becomes Crennell Avenue, pass under railroad tracks, and turn right at the traffic circle onto White Avenue. Turn left onto Bradford Avenue over Noble. Finally, turn left from Bradford onto Crafton Boulevard, which heads to the West End.)

Choice Pharmacy, at 40 East Crafton Avenue, is worth a visit. Dan Sakmar opened the business in 1994 to re-create the feeling of an old apothecary. He's collected remnants of other old businesses, from the wooden exterior to the tin ceiling, to create an authentic feel. Inside, a soda fountain sits behind a marble counter.

We continue west on Steuben Street. The 1947 *American Motel Association Motel Guide and Trip Diary* lists M. & M. Guest Home at

A Gulf station at Crennell Avenue and Linwood Street in Crafton, October 1934.
COURTESY CHEVRON CORPORATE ARCHIVES

231 West Steuben Street, run by Mrs. Martin, with rooms starting at $1.25 a night. Carr's Tourist Home was at 237 West Steuben.

At the traffic light at Ingram Avenue, we stay in the right lane to cross the bridge over Chartiers Creek. We see the Pittsburgh Motel, built in the '50s, on our right and head uphill, passing under an I-79 interchange. To our right, we see some houses on Old Steubenville Pike, which soon merges onto Steubenville Pike (Route 60); its eastern end was erased by I-79.

In this area was the Blue Bird Inn, a bar and restaurant in a house. As the road levels, we come around a bend to see the Del-Kid Family Restaurant to the north, open 24 hours except Sunday. The name derives from its owners, the DelGrossos, and their grandmother's last name, Kidonis. They bought the place in 1968, and all four DelGrosso children work there. Stop by for a six-egg omelet! Just past it is the Twin Hi Way Drive-In Theater, named for the years when Routes 22 and 30 used this alignment. Michael Cardone has been operating it since the mid-1980s and says that business is excellent. We pass an old general store for sale to our south, and we soon pass over I-279, which is the Penn-Lincoln Parkway. Routes 22 and 30 now join the Lincoln and head west on Steubenville Pike.

This handyman drove up to the Twin Hi Way Drive-In Theater in his 1960 Chevy. The road here was once called Lincolnway. (PHOTO 1991)

Looking east past the Summit Hotel. The signs advertise "Eddie Peyton's Summit Club, Dine—Dance." Today it's the Moon Run Volunteer Firemen's Club, and the Twin Hi Way Drive-In Theater sits just beyond it.

We cross over the parkway and get in the right lane to exit for Old Steubenville Pike. (To the south is the Tonidale Motel.) At the exit's stop sign, the road in front of us is the old Lincoln Highway; to the right the road eventually dead-ends in a hotel parking lot overlooking the parkway interchange. We turn left and cross over Routes 22 and 30, then we bear right and cross them again.

There's little along this stretch other than a tiny string of motel rooms to the south just after the bridge. A couple of miles later, we come to the Fort Pitt Motel, which now offers "Pocono Touch Rooms" featuring heart-shaped Jacuzzis. Erma Dodd and her husband, Chuck, have been here since October 1969, but she says, "The market's changed. New motels in the area took some of our business, so we came up with the Pocono Touch Rooms as a means of survival. We're always busy on weekends, and we get a lot of couples back for anniversaries." The old rooms in the front part don't all have heart-shaped tubs, but many have original bathrooms from the 1950s with pink ceramic tilework. Next to the motel is the Fort Pitt Inn, a bar built to resemble the 1764 British fort. After World War II, Fred Werner took over the restaurant from his parents. He had served as executive chef in both North Africa and France before returning to the family business with his wife, Ethel Hankey Werner.

Phone IMPERIAL 300. On U. S. 30 and 22. 11 Miles West of Pittsburgh, Pa. R. D. No. 1 Oakdale, Pa.

Paul Werner, proprietor of the Fort Pitt Inn, advertised "Old style German Rathskeller and Beer Garden" plus dancing. There's still a bar in the hexagonal-shaped part.

Fred Hood ran Hood's Tavern and Tourist Court in Oakdale, 11 miles west of Pittsburgh.

Just west of here, a little segment breaks off to the south, rejoining at the next hilltop near the Scio China building, now a gift shop. As we curve downhill, we pass the former Rest-A-While Motel, recently renamed Starlake Motel to capitalize on (and attract customers from) the new Starlake Amphitheater. At the bottom of the dip, Don's Pizza is in an old gas station, and at the next rise are the Hilltop Motel and the remains of the Super 30 West Drive-In Theater. It was originally the Penn Lincoln Drive-In, named for the two highways that passed by; now only the screen and marquee are left. Across the street is a VFW post with a jet fighter out front.

At the Sunset Inn, we reach a stop sign, then bear right toward Imperial, rejoining Route 30. Soon afterward, an access road to a church parking lot is part of an old route through Imperial, though not necessarily the old Lincoln. It can be reached at the next right turn as it heads through trees to a raised railroad alignment, where it becomes only a footpath under the tracks. On the other side, the tiny underpass emerges onto Railroad Street, which rises to Main Street, eventually rejoining Route 30.

We pass the Hotel Imperial bar and grill and go under the railroad, whose bridge was probably constructed when the Lincoln Highway was rerouted around Pittsburgh in 1927. Beyond it, we skirt the little town of Imperial. As we head west, we see to our south an old motel with at least one cabin that now houses a lawn-care business; perhaps it was Neely's Motor Court, which an old postcard shows as being 20 miles from Pittsburgh. To the north is a canopy gas station, though the pumps were recently removed. The area along the road west of here is rather sparse,

Looking east to the Route 22–30 split, February 1930. Route 22 is in the foreground; Route 30 branches off to the left, heading northwest to Imperial and thence to West Virginia. COURTESY PA STATE ARCHIVES, RG-12 DEPT. OF HIGHWAYS

some coal mines and small farms dotting the landscape. A few miles later, we pass through Clinton, and at the next fork we stay left; in the fork's triangle is Persin's lounge and restaurant, and behind it is an aluminum-sided tourist cabin, the lone survivor of Green Castle Barbecue.

We pass Marada Golf Course and the Clinton Motel, listed in the 1957 AAA directory as having seven "well-kept rooms," five of them with coin-operated radios. The 1960 directory lists "most rooms with TV." We pass through farmland, and at one point we start downhill to the right; the road that goes straight ahead is not the old Lincoln. At the bottom of the hill we reach Raccoon Creek State Park; just past it is the Little Traverse Inn, advertising a bar, grill, sandwiches, frosted mugs, beer, and liquor. It was originally Saunders Cabins, and 14 cottages sat across the road.

We pass a state gameland to the north and RJT's soft-serve ice cream to the south. Just beyond, at a stand of pines, is what remains of the Red Gables Inn: a tourist cabin in a backyard and an old gas station next door. The road remains rural, and we pass through the intersection of State Route 18; to the left is the former Willmawr Motel on a hill overlooking the road. A postcard from about 1950 for Bishop's Modern

W. C. Shand, owner of Green Castle Barbecue in Clinton, assured "clean, neatly furnished, electrically lighted cabins with running water. Free tourist kitchen and service station building housing modern rest rooms and other conveniences."
COURTESY CY HOSMER

Saunder's Modern Cabins. John H. Saunders, Prop.

RED GABLES INN - 30 MI. W. of PITTSBURG, PA. - ROUTE US 30

Saunders was later renamed Little Traverse. Today the cabins are gone, but the main building survives 25 miles west of Pittsburgh near Raccoon Creek State Park.

"Dear Mother, We got here about 6:00; cooked our supper; and walked to the top of the big hill back of the cabins," postmarked August 1951. Only one cabin remains from the Red Gables. COURTESY RUSSELL REIN

Cabins says that they were 6 miles east of West Virginia and 30 miles west of Pittsburgh, placing them in this area. The cabins were said to be "well-furnished and heated" and "in a quiet, scenic location."

We head uphill, past Reed's Ice Cream and Deli, and a couple of miles later pass Lincoln Estates, advertising "12 acre+ lots." Soon we pass the junction of State Route 168, with a Getty station and an Amoco

New pavement west of Clinton, September 1929. COURTESY PA STATE
ARCHIVES, RG-12 DEPT. OF HIGHWAYS

This overhead "Welcome to Pennsylvania" sign was taken down about 1990.
COURTESY KEVIN J. PATRICK

Rock Springs Park sat astride the Lincoln in Chester, West Virginia.

connected to Laughlin's Restaurant. A c. 1940 aerial postcard of the restaurant when it was John Deck Fine Foods calls the location Georgetown.

Ahead on the right, there's a lake with decorative steps down to the water, and some outbuildings; it's the former Beavers Lakes, which once offered fishing and swimming and even had a bathhouse to change in. Today it's privately owned. Two miles later, we top a hill, and then a dip takes us past a Billy Oil gas station.

We now enter West Virginia, and we pass the remains of an old motel to the north. Going uphill, we pass the site of the Cactus Restaurant, across from Cricksters self-serve restaurant. Going down Stewart Hill, we see a printing company with a gift shop attached that sells "World's Largest Teapot" shirts. We cross West Virginia Route 8, and at the next hilltop is Sunset Plaza, a former motel, now a video store. We pass a sign for the Homer Laughlin Factory Outlet, maker of Fiesta Ware; the outlet is just off our route in Newell, West Virginia.

Finally, we head down into Chester, where a third truck lane was being added in late 1994. When the road divides into one-way lanes, we turn right, following a sign for Johnsonville Road, on the old Lincoln Highway. We curve around to the left and spot an old motel hidden back to the left; ahead we can see the Ohio River valley. At the stop sign at the

Route 30 exit ramp we see the big teapot, now repainted for display. Chaney's Sunoco across the street sells Chester Teapot postcards.

Turning left on Carolina Avenue, we pass under Route 30. To the right, in front of a house, is a "Cabins" sign. There's also a historical marker for Rock Springs Park, a well-known amusement park that stood at the site from 1897 until the new bridge came through in the 1970s.

Susan Boulden moved to Chester when she was a teenager. She remembers what it was like to grow up there.

I came with my parents and older brother to Chester from Hull, England, in 1957. From England to the northern panhandle of West Virginia was extreme culture shock! When I think about Route 30, the first thing that strikes me is how little it was actually used by Chester residents. For me and my family, that road was our escape route from what was, for us, the backwoods of Chester and West Virginia to the civilization of Pittsburgh and Pennsylvania.

I recall that the last section of Route 30 came down the very long, steep, winding hill into Chester. About three-quarters of the way down, it took a sharp turn to the left. That corner was the scene of many bad accidents. My uncle lived at that corner, and it seemed he was constantly calling the police and taking care of injured motorists.

There were two clubs on opposite sides of Route 30. One was Club 30, and both clubs supposedly had illegal gambling in those days, and it was widely rumored that under the highway there was a tunnel connecting the two clubs so that when the local constabulary raided one club, its patrons could scramble through the tunnel and continue gambling at the other. Certainly there was gambling, especially with all the people who came down Route 30 heading to Waterford Park for the races.

Chester is now bypassed by Route 30, but it looks to be a lively little town. As we head down Carolina Avenue, we turn right at Third Street and cross over a small bridge. At the corner of Third Street and Virginia Avenue is a cement Lincoln Highway marker; we follow its arrow and turn left on Virginia. There's another Lincoln Highway marker at Second Street. (A third cement Lincoln Highway marker can be found in a yard east of First Street beneath a green "Pughtown" sign.) At First

Street we turn right. The highway followed this route through town until 1938, when a bridge connected First Street to the Carolina Avenue route. First Street ends abruptly because the Chester Bridge, which it once crossed, was removed in the 1970s. The bridge's approach is now an Ohio River overlook. Cracks in the pavement mark the location of the bridge's tollbooth.

Back in Chester, the C&P Telephone building just east of the First and Carolina Avenue intersection was the original site of the famous teapot. The East Liverpool and Chester areas were once renowned for their pottery, and many such products are still made here. The teapot was originally built as a Hires root beer barrel advertisement. It was brought here and converted to a teapot in 1938 by Wilford "Babe" Devon to attract customers from the newly rerouted Route 30. Ice cream and other refreshments were served from the red and white teapot, and behind it, Devon sold art ware, pottery, and souvenirs. It was sold in 1947 and changed hands a few times afterward, slowly slipping into disrepair. In 1984 the phone company bought the property and gave the teapot to the city. Just before it was moved, the teapot was painted blue and white and had cheap letters stuck on it. It read as follows: "Welcome to the Tea Pot.

The "World's Largest Teapot" was homeless for a while but is now displayed at the Route 30 cloverleaf in Chester, West Virginia.

The East Liverpool-Chester Bridge

Chester, W. Va.   Lincoln Highway. U. S. 30   East Liverpool, Ohio

The East Liverpool–Chester Bridge across the Ohio River was built in 1897 and remained a private enterprise until 1938, when the state aquired it with the intent of making it tollfree. It was closed about 1970 and dismantled; taxes paid for a new bridge, which finally opened in 1977, but it took four more years to finish all the ramps.

Wind Chimes, Cannisters, Cookie Jars, Mugs, Flower Pots, Dinner Ware, Novelites, Music Boxes, Baskets, Bird Baths, Figuriens, Lamps, Banks, Baking Dishes, Crocks, Teapots."

An effort to restore and display the teapot gained momentum, and plans were to display it at the Route 30 cloverleaf. Highway officials worried that accidents would be caused by rubbernecking motorists, but the town's enthusiasm prevailed, and today the teapot sits next to Route 30 and the Lincoln Highway, the result of many hours of hard work by Chester residents.

From Chester we can cross the Ohio River on Route 30 and follow the old Lincoln Highway back into Pennsylvania. Or we can continue west on the Lincoln . . . visit the Museum of Ceramics in East Liverpool . . . eat at two great diners in Lisbon . . . and continue beyond through Ohio, where the Lincoln beckons with interesting sounding names: Minerva, Wooster, Bucyrus, Gomer, Van Wert . . .

Appendix A

1928 LINCOLN HIGHWAY MARKERS IN PENNSYLVANIA

There are twenty-three 1928 Lincoln Highway markers in Pennsylvania. All remain close to their original locations. Please honor private property, and please use this list and the next one as aids to documenting and preserving the markers, not to removing them.

Nearby Town	Side	Landmark
Malvern	S	East of General Warren Inn, near former underpass
Leaman Place	S	Behind guardrail at Amtrak overpass
Hellam	S	Across from Wise Owl and municipal building
York	N	East of Lincoln Highway Garage
York	N	At firehall
Thomasville	S	In hedges across from Martin's Chips
New Oxford	—	Town square
New Oxford	S	East of Black Star Antiques at golf carts
Gettysburg	S	West of town
Caledonia Park	S	Just east of Mr. Ed's
Stoufferstown	S	Across from Dice's Tire Shop
Chambersburg	N	Third Street, east of town, westbound
Chambersburg	N	One block east of Federal Street, westbound
Fort Loudon	N	At curve in town
McConnellsburg	N	At Fulton House
Harrisonville	N	In front yard west of crossroads
Everett	N	Across from Amoco
Bedford	N	East of Routes 30–31 intersection and Bonnett Tavern
Buckstown	S	Behind post across from Windber Road
Stoystown	S	At curve to Kanter
Ligonier	N	On northeast lawn at square
Youngstown	S	West of town, across from apartments
Forest Hills	S	At Yost Boulevard

Markers are also displayed at the State Museum in Harrisburg and the Gettysburg Historical Society. At least five others are known to exist away from the route in private yards.

Appendix B

TURNPIKE MARKERS IN PENNSYLVANIA

The remaining turnpike markers vary in design and era, but most date from about 1800. Because they are small and easy to miss, others probably exist. Markings here are abbreviated and are occasionally incomplete. Please honor private property.

Markings	Nearby Town	Side	Location
P5	Wynnewood	N	In front of St. Charles Seminary
P6	Wynnewood	N	Clover Hill Road
P7	Lower Merion	N	Township building parking lot
P8	Lower Merion	N	Llanalew Road
P12	Ardmore	N	Near Villanova University
P14	Ardmore	S	Reproduction, at Sugartown Road
P15	Devon	N	In wall on old Lancaster Road
P16	Berwyn	N	Behind guardrail west of station
P25	Exton	--	Inside Ship Inn
P34	Thorndale	S	Across from Barley Station
P48	Sadsburyville	N	Front yard, stone house
P47, L15	Gap	N	Front yard, farm
P51, L11	Paradise	N	Front yard, suburban house
Unsure	Lancaster	N	.25 mile east of Willows covered bridge
P65	Mountville	N	.5 mile east of Tinson Hill housing development
P71, L8, C2	Columbia	N	West of Prospect Diner
P89, Y43, L25	York	N	Route 462 before light at Route 30 junction
P97, Y11	Abbottstown	N	East of town, just west of string of cabins
P99, Y13	Abbottstown	N	Just west of Lincoln View Motel
G14	Abbottstown	N	.25 mile east of square
P102, Y16, G12	Abbottstown	N	West of auction barn
S, P, C, H	Schellsburg	N	Hi-De-Ho or Sleepy Hollow Tavern
S, P, C, H	Schellsburg	N	Near Shawnee Motel
S, P, C, H	Schellsburg	N	Near cemetery
P74	Reels Corner	N	On ridge
P12, Ph274	Jacktown	N	Old Trail Road

Bibliography

BOOKS

Ardmore Centennial Corporation. *1873–1973 Centennial.* Ardmore, PA: Ardmore Centennial Corporation, 1973.

Automobile Club of Pittsburgh. *Runs and Tours, 1906.* Pittsburgh: Automobile Club of Pittsburgh, 1906.

Baeder, John. *Gas, Food, and Lodging.* New York: Abbeville Press, 1982.

Belasco, Warren. *Americans on the Road: From Autocamp to Motel, 1910–1945.* Cambridge, MA: MIT Press, 1979.

Best, James R. W. *A History of the Chambersburg and Bedford Turnpike Road Company.* Master's thesis, Shippensburg State College, 1962.

Beyer, George R. *Guide to the State Historical Markers of Pennsylvania.* Harrisburg, PA: Pennsylvania Historical and Museum Commission, 1991.

Brandt, Francis Burke, and Henry Volkmar Gummere. *Byways and Boulevards in and about Historic Philadelphia.* Philadelphia: Coin Exchange National Bank, 1925.

Bruce, Robert. *The Lincoln Highway in Pennsylvania.* 1920.

Carstens, A. H. *Pennsylvania's Best.* Clearfield, PA: Kurtz Bros., 1960.

Chambersburg Bicentennial Committee. *"From This Valley": Crossroads of Destiny, Chambersburg, Pennsylvania.* Chambersburg, PA: Chambersburg Bicentennial Committee, 1964.

Commonwealth of Pennsylvania. *Report of the State Highway Department of Pennsylvania, 1906.* Harrisburg, PA: Harrisburg Publishing Co., 1907.

Duncan Hines Institute, Inc. *Adventures in Good Eating*. Ithaca, NY: Duncan Hines Institute, 1947 and 1957.

———. *Lodging for a Night*. Ithaca, NY: Duncan Hines Institute, 1947 and 1957.

East McKeesport Anniversary Committee. *Golden Memories: East McKeesport Fiftieth Anniversary, 1895–1945*. East McKeesport, PA. 1945.

East McKeesport Diamond Jubilee Committee. *Diamond Jubilee Reflections*. East McKeesport, PA: Diamond Jubilee Committee, 1970.

Evans, Benjamin D., and June R. Evans. *Pennsylvania's Covered Bridges: A Complete Guide*. Pittsburgh: University of Pittsburgh Press, 1993.

Fleming, George T. *Pittsburgh: How to See It*. Pittsburgh: William Johnston Co., 1916.

Fox, Elise Scharf. *Hotel Gettysburg: A Landmark in Our Nation's Past*. Gettysburg, PA: Downtown Gettysburg Inc., 1988.

Frassanito, William A. *The Gettysburg Bicentennial Album*. Gettysburg, PA: Gettysburg Bicentennial Committee, 1987.

Gille, Frank H., ed. *Encyclopedia of Pennsylvania*. New York: Somerset Publishers, 1983.

Gutman, Richard J. S. *American Diner: Then and Now*. New York: HarperPerennial, 1993.

Henry, William M. *The Greater Greensburg Profile*. Greensburg, PA: Chas. M. Henry Printing Co., 1962.

Hokanson, Drake. *The Lincoln Highway: Main Street across America*. Iowa City, IA: University of Iowa Press, 1988.

Jakle, John A., and Keith A. Sculle. *The Gas Station in America*. Baltimore: Johns Hopkins University Press, 1994.

Jennerstown Fall Festival Association. *History of Jennerstown, Pa. 1772–1986*. Jennerstown, PA: Jennerstown Fall Festival Association, 1986.

Jordan, Philip. *The National Road*. Indianapolis: Bobbs-Merrill Co., 1948.

Kimes, Beverly Rae, and Henry Austin Clarke, Jr. *Standard Catalog of American Cars, 1805–1942*. Iola, WI: Krause Publications, 1985.

Klein, Philip Shriver. *A History of Pennsylvania*. University Park, PA: Penn State University Press, 1980.

Langdon, Philip. *Orange Roofs, Golden Arches: The Architecture of American Chain Restaurants.* New York: Alfred A. Knopf, 1986.

Laughlintown Anniversary Committee. *Laughlintown, Penna., Commemorating Its 150th Anniversary.* 1947.

Liebs, Chester. *Main Street to Miracle Mile: American Roadside Architecture.* Boston: Little, Brown, and Co., 1985.

Ligonier Valley Observance American Bicentennial. *The Stoystown and Greensburgh Turnpike Road Company.* Laughlintown, PA: Southwest Pa. Genealogical Services, 1976.

Lincoln Highway Association. *The Complete Official Road Guide of the Lincoln Highway.* Editions 1–5. Detroit: Lincoln Highway Association, 1915, 1916, 1918, 1921, 1924.

———. *The Lincoln Highway: The Story of a Crusade That Made Transportation History.* New York: Dodd, Mead & Co., 1935.

———. *Lincoln Highway Road Report.* October 1921, May 1922, May 1923, April 1924, May 1925, and September 1925. Part of Seiberling Papers. Ohio Historical Library, Columbus, OH.

———. *A Picture of Progress on the Lincoln Highway.* Detroit, 1920.

Maier, Phyllis C., and Mary Mendenhall Wood. *Lower Merion—A History.* Ardmore, PA: Lower Merion Historical Society, 1992.

Margolies, John. *Pump and Circumstance: Glory Days of the Gas Station.* New York: Bulfinch Press, 1993.

Miller, Denis N. *The Illustrated Encyclopedia of Trucks and Buses.* New York: Mayflower Books, 1982.

Miller, Frederick, Morris J. Vogel, and Allen F. Davis. *Philadelphia Stories: A Photographic History, 1920–1960.* Philadelphia: Temple University Press, 1988.

———. *Still Philadelphia: A Photographic History, 1890–1940.* Philadelphia: Temple University Press, 1983.

Myers, James Madison. *The Ligonier Valley Railroad and Its Communities.* Ph.D. diss., University of Pittsburgh, 1955.

Nelson, John H. *Down the Pike: A History of the Chambersburg-Bedford Turnpike Company.* McConnellsburg, PA: Fulton County Historical Society, 1989.

Patton, Phil. *Open Road.* New York: Simon and Schuster, 1986.

Pennsylvania Department of Highways. *Facts Motorists Should Know.* Harrisburg, PA: Department of Highways, 1924, 1926.

Pennsylvania Dutch Tourist Bureau. *Pennsylvania Dutch Guide-Book.* Lancaster, PA: Pennsylvania Dutch Tourist Bureau, 1966.

Pennsylvania State Police. *Rodeo, Troop A, Thursday, August 25, Greensburg, PA.* 1932.

Pennsylvania Writers' Project. *Pennsylvania: A Guide to the Keystone State.* New York: Oxford University Press, 1940.

Plummer, Wilbur C. *The Road Policy of Pennsylvania.* Philadelphia, 1925.

Polk, R. L. *Polk's McKeesport City Directory, 1927.* R. L. Polk and Co., 1927.

Ritter, Lawrence S. *Lost Ballparks.* New York: Viking Studio Books, 1992.

Rowe, James W. *An Historical Guide of the Lincoln Highway.* Scottdale, PA: Mennonite Publishing House, 1935.

Sachse, Julius Friedrich. *The Wayside Inns on the Lancaster Roadside between Philadelphia and Lancaster.* Lancaster, PA: Pennsylvania-German Society, 1912.

Smith, Helene, and George Swetnam. *A Guidebook to Historic Western Pennsylvania.* Pittsburgh: University of Pittsburgh Press, 1991.

Stetler, Polly, and David A. Walsh. *Pfaltzgraff: America's Potter.* York, PA: Historical Society of York County, 1989.

Stotz, Charles Morse. *Outposts of the War for Empire.* Pittsburgh: Historical Society of Western Pennsylvania, 1985.

Twaddell, Meg Daly. *Inns, Tales, and Taverns of Chester County.* N.C.: Country Publications Inc., 1984.

U.S. Bureau of Public Roads. *Report of a Survey of Transportation of the State Highways of Pennsylvania.* 1928.

Wallace, Paul A. W. *Indian Paths of Pennsylvania.* Harrisburg, PA: Pennsylvania Historical and Museum Commission, 1987.

————., ed. *The Travels of John Heckewelder in Frontier America.* Pittsburgh: University of Pittsburgh Press, 1985.

Webster, Richard. *Philadelphia Preserved.* Philadelphia: Temple University Press, 1981.

West, J. Martin, ed. *War for Empire in Western Pennsylvania.* Ligonier, PA: Fort Ligonier Association, 1993.

Williams, Edward G. *Bouquet's March to the Ohio: The Forbes Road.* Pittsburgh: Historical Society of Western Pennsylvania, 1975.

Witzel, Michael Karl. *The American Gas Station*. Osceola, WI: Motorbooks International, 1992.

Zilka, Daniel. *American Diner Directory*. Self-published, 1993. (Copies available from American Diner Project, P.O. Box 852, Burlington, VT 05402.)

Zook, Jacob, and Jane Zook. *Hexology: The History and Meanings of Hex Signs*. Paradise, PA: Jacob Zook, 1990.

ARTICLES

"Auto Club Has Been in Existence Over Quarter of Century." [McKeesport] *Daily News* (June 30, 1934).

"Auto Pioneers Recall When Lincoln Highway Trip Was Adventure." [McKeesport] *Daily News* (March 1, 1955).

Binzen, Peter. "After 73 Years, This Auto Dealership Is Still in a High Gear." *Philadelphia Inquirer* (July 25, 1994).

Bogaert, Pauline Pinard. "Lancaster Avenue's History Is a Bumpy One." *Philadelphia Inquirer* (September 23, 1990).

Butko, Brian. "Still a Grand View: The Ship Hotel and the Lincoln Highway." *Pittsburgh History* (Fall 1991). pp. 140–148.

"Bypass Bonanza." [West Chester] *Daily Local News* (February 10, 1993).

"Club Seeks Route Shift." [McKeesport] *Daily News* (June 17, 1939).

Conard, Wes. "Downingtown Mall Avoids the Upscale." *Philadelphia Inquirer* (May 15, 1994).

"Cyclers Provided First Impetus for Building Lincoln Highway." [McKeesport] *Daily News* (March 2, 1955).

Daquila, Phillip. "Apothecary 'Choice' Throwback to Yesterday." *Pittsburgh Tribune-Review* (May 1, 1994).

Davidson, Jim. "Just Another Roadside Attraction." *Pittsburgh Press* (June 29, 1986).

"Eastern Section of Lincoln Highway Proves a Delightful Drive." *The Lincoln Highway* (July 5, 1916).

"[Ford] Establishes Assembly Plants." [Pittsburgh] *Gazette Times* (April 25, 1915).

"Freeing the Last Toll Road on the Lincoln Highway." *The American City* XX, no. 2 (c. 1918). pp. 123–124.

Goshorn, Bob. "When the Fireworks Factory in Devon Blew Up." *Tredyffrin Easttown History Club Quarterly* (Fall 1978). pp. 57–63.

Herrick, Michael J. "The Conestoga Wagon of Pennsylvania." *Western Pennsylvania Historical Magazine* (April 1968).

Hicks, Joseph B. "York County Remembers Its War Dead." [Lancaster] *Sunday News,* York edition (May 31, 1953).

"Highways of County Improved by Good Roads Day Workers." [Pittsburgh] *Gazette Times* (May 27, 1915).

"Historic Amish Farmers Market Not Quite What It Used to Be." [McKeesport] *Daily News* (January 25, 1994).

"Hotel Men Assail 'Dream' Highway." *Philadelphia Inquirer* (July 10, 1938).

Kane, Paul. "Bridge Work Takes Toll on Diner." [West Chester] *Daily Local News* (December 13, 1993).

Kimball, W. A. "An Ideal Vacation for Teachers." *Motor Camper & Tourist* (June 1926). pp. 918–919, 939.

"Lincoln Highway Meeting Draws Many to Bedford." *Bedford Gazette* (May 3, 1940).

Long, John D. "The Lincoln Highway." *Motor Camper & Tourist* (June 1924). pp. 24, 56.

Love, Gilbert. "Bill's Place." *Pittsburgh Press* (June 28, 1962).

Lowry, Patricia. "Ligonier's Diamond Sparkles among Town Squares." *Pittsburgh Post-Gazette* (June 20, 1993).

Matthews, James G. "Reminiscing about the Matthews Ford Agency." *Tredyffrin Easttown History Club Quarterly* (April 1993). pp. 65–70.

McClure, James. "Going Nowhere Slowly: Route 30 in York County Is a Nightmare." *Pittsburgh Post-Gazette* (March 28, 1993).

"Memorial Day in York Will Be the Greatest in History of the City." [York] *Gazette* (May 30, 1922).

Metz, Gretchen. "It's Back to the Future at Downingtown Diner." [West Chester] *Sunday Local News* (March 10, 1991).

"New Highway Will Connect York with Caledonia State Forest Vacation Land." *York Dispatch* (July 17, 1948).

"Norwin Rt. 30 Bypass Still Anybody's Guess." [McKeesport] *Daily News* (May 8, 1974).

"Old Inn and Barn to Rise Again in Cemetery 'Village.' " [York] *Gazette and Daily* (November 29, 1962).

Pascal, Leo. "History of the Automobile Industry in Pennsylvania 1805–1941." *Antique Automobile* (January 1962). pp. 12–13.

"The Passing of the Toll Roads of Eastern Pennsylvania." *Pittsburgh Bulletin* (July 22, 1916).

Patrick, Kevin J. "The Lincoln Highway: Lost and Found in Philadelphia." *The Lincoln Highway Forum* 1, no. 4 (Summer 1994). pp. 4–15.

Paul, Barbara. "The Blob Comes to Downingtown—Again." *Village News* (April 20, 1994).

Randall, Laura. "Mexican Pickers Dominate Pa. Mushroom Business." [McKeesport] *Daily News* (March 24, 1993).

"Remember When? Lincoln Diner—A Rich Part of C'ville History." [Coatesville] *Daily Record* (May 22, 1993).

Richley, J. W. "The York-Philadelphia Sweepstakes." *Keystone Motorist* (March 1932). pp. 8–10, 29.

"Route 30 Bypass Opposition Mounts." [McKeesport] *Daily News* (September 22, 1969).

Salpukas, Agis. "Born as Place to Rest, Town [Breezewood] Doesn't." *New York Times* (October 1, 1990).

Schreffler, Rebekah Scott. "The Battle of Legion Ville." *Pittsburgh Post-Gazette* (May 10, 1994).

"Sell Gasoline from Greek Temple." *National Petroleum News* 10 (April 17, 1918). pp. 18–20.

Skoch, George F. "On the Road to Gettysburg: Cashtown Inn." *Blue and Gray Magazine* (April 1991). p. 39.

" 'S.S. Grand View Hotel' to Embark on Maiden Voyage Next Sunday, May 29th." *Bedford Gazette* (May 27, 1932).

" 'S.S. Grandview' to Open on May 20th." *Bedford Gazette* (May 6, 1932).

"State Said 'Settled' on Rt. 30 Path." [McKeesport] *Daily News* (August 16, 1969).

"Teapot Commemorative Issue." [Chester, W.Va.] *Evening Review,* Weekly Echo supplement (October 3, 1990).

"Twaddell's Diner." *Diner Drive-In* (December 1958). pp. 28–31.

"Vandals Set Lincoln Free—Again." [Pittsburgh] *Allegheny Bulletin* (September 18, 1992).

Wiegand, Virginia S. "She Saved an Old Attraction's Soul." *Philadelphia Inquirer* (July 30, 1995).

Wylie, Nancy. "Old [McIlvaine] Hotel Recalls Early County History." *Bedford Gazette* (c. 1985).

"Yorker's Lincoln Highway Records to Be Added to University Exhibit." *York Dispatch* (July 31, 1951).

"Zinn's New Diner." *Diner Drive-In* (March 1957). pp. 22–29.

GUIDEBOOKS, BOOKLETS, AND MAPS

AAA Service Station Directory, Pennsylvania, 1932.

AAA Tour Books: Mideastern, 1928, 1929, 1930, 1936, 1938, 1940, 1942, 1955, 1957, 1960, 1967; *Accommodations Directory,* 1945, 1957.

American Motel Association Motel Guide and Trip Diary, 1941, 1947.

Blue Book List: Approved Travel Homes, 1940.

Dedication of the George Westinghouse Bridge, 1932.

Eastern Motor Court Map, 1953, 1955.

Federal Hi-Way Homes Motorist Guide to America's Better Tourist Homes and Eating Places, 1941.

Federal Hi-Way Homes Motorists' Handbook, 1936, 1939.

General History of Pennsylvania Roads, Pennsylvania Department of Highways, c. 1968.

Goodrich Tour Book of Pennsylvania West, 1918.

Gulf road maps, including the Lincoln Highway, Pittsburgh to Gettysburg, and Blazed Trails in Pennsylvania, c. 1920.

Mohawk-Hobbs Grade and Surface Guide: Lincoln Highway (East), 1927, 1928.

National Motorists Association Eastern Tours, 1925.

Official Automobile Blue Book, vol. 3, 1914.

Official Pennsylvania Dutch Guide Map, 1965.

Pennsylvania Motel Association Directory to Motels, c. 1968.

Ray Walker's Cabin Trails, 1937.

Ray Walker's Vacation Resort/Motor Court Recommendations, 1949.

Red Road Book for the New England States, Middle Atlantic States, and Southern Seaboard States, 1918.

Shell Tourist Accommodation Directory and Trailer Space, 1940.

Tail-Gate, vol. 27, no. 7 (July 1950).

Trailer Tour Map of the United States, c. 1945.

United Motor Courts Inc. Guide, 1946 Special Edition.

United Motor Courts Inc. National Motor Travel Guide, 1948.

U.S. 30/Exton Bypass, 1993.

ORGANIZATIONS

Curt Teich Postcard Archives

Teich Archives, at the Lake County Museum, is the nation's largest publicly held repository of postcards and related materials, with more than 360,000 cataloged images. The core of the collection is from the Curt Teich Company, which produced postcards from 1898 to 1978. (Many postcards in this book were originally printed by the Teich company. Their use here is courtesy of the Teich Archives.) Services include publications, topical research, souvenirs, and special programs. Individual and family memberships available. Curt Teich Postcard Archives, Lake County Museum, 27277 Forest Preserve Drive, Lakewood Forest Preserve, Wauconda, IL 60084.

Lincoln Highway Association

The Lincoln Highway Association helps preserve and document the history, routings, and roadside businesses of the Lincoln Highway through publications and an annual conference. Efforts are made to prevent further deterioration or demolition of extant remains of the highway. Individual and family memberships available. Lincoln Highway Association, c/o Bob and Joyce Ausberger, 987 P Avenue, Jefferson, IA 50129.

Lincoln Highway Heritage Corridor

Pennsylvania's Lincoln Highway Heritage Corridor is a state-sponsored project created to help preserve and interpret resources across five west-central counties, from Caledonia State Park to Irwin. The corridor project encourages and fosters economic development, intergovernmental cooperation, cultural conservation, recreation, and education. Lincoln Highway Heritage Corridor, P.O. Box 166, Bedford, PA 15522.

Society for Commercial Archeology

Established in 1977, the Society for Commercial Archeology is the oldest national organization devoted to the commercial-built environment. Through publications, conferences, and tours, the society helps preserve and document twentieth-century structures and architecture, including diners, gas stations, drive-in theaters, tourist courts, highways, and neon signs. Individual and family memberships available. Society for Commercial Archeology, c/o Room 5010, National Museum of American History, Washington, DC 20560.

About the Author

B rian Butko is a board member of the Society for Commercial Archeology and a founding board member of the Lincoln Highway Association. He earned an M.A. in history at Duquesne University in Pittsburgh and served as associate producer of the award-winning WQED-13 documentaries "Pennsylvania Diners and Other Roadside Restaurants" and "Stuff That's Gone." A member of the editorial department of the Historical Society of Western Pennsylvania, Butko is at work on a history of the Isaly Dairy/Klondike companies and a novel set along the Lincoln Highway.

Abridged Index